Freezer to Microwave Cookery

Freezer to Microwave Cookery

Cecilia Norman

Illustrations by Philip Kerrey

Pitman for Hitachi Sales (UK) Limited

Hitachi Sales (UK) Limited
Hitachi House, Station Road, Hayes, Middlesex UB3 4DR

This is the Hitachi owner's edition of FREEZER TO MICROWAVE COOKERY,
© Cecilia Norman 1978,
Reprinted 1981 (twice), 1982
published in a trade paperback edition (ISBN 0 273 01044 1) by
Pitman Books Limited,
128 Long Acre, London WC2E 9AN

Text set in 10/12 pt Palatino, printed and bound
in Great Britain at The Pitman Press, Bath

Contents

Introduction

I have tried to write this book in the same way as any conventional book, as the few microwave books now available are mostly issued by the manufacturers and make use of canned, pre-processed and packaged ingredients. As I demonstrated in my previous book *Microwave Cookery for the Housewife*, also published by Pitman, this is a needlessly narrow outlook. Certainly, those ingredients will ensure that the microwave cookery will be speedy and successful, but I feel that this is cheating in support of the manufacturers' purpose – selling microwave ovens. It is as important to know what you *cannot* do with microwave as it is to learn what can be done. Where, therefore, I feel that I cannot honestly recommend a particular commodity for microwave cookery – or for that matter for freezing – I either omit it or point out the shortcomings.

Throughout the recipes I have kept to the same order to avoid confusion, so that the first section gives directions for the preparation of the recipe by microwave cooking, followed by freezer and then serving instructions. If there are no special instructions for serving immediately, you can serve without further ado.

+ + +

Where there is a row of plus signs between the listed ingredients, it indicates that these are to be added at different stages in the preparation of the recipe. When spoons are mentioned, level spoons are meant and spoonfuls should be levelled off with a knife. The metric/imperial conversions for the recipes in this book have been rounded off to the nearest whole figure for ease of measuring. Use either metric or imperial measurements, but *do not interchange them* as this will upset the balance of the recipe.

1 The Microwave Oven

The Microwave Oven

Microwave ovens are rapidly becoming part of the kitchen scene and the indications are that sales will increase very rapidly in the next few years, so that demand will grow as speedily as it did with freezers in the sixties.

Owners soon discover the incredible range of cooking processes that can be carried out in these neat, hygienic and attractive machines. The oven is a compact cabinet with metal linings. It is operated by high frequency radio waves produced by a magnetron (two in the larger ovens) in the top of the oven. The waves travel down a channel and are dispersed by a revolving blade in the top of the cabinet. These broken waves bounce off the sides, top and bottom, and cause the molecules in the food or liquid to rub together. This is the cooking process.

VARIATIONS BETWEEN MODELS

The oven has no temperature control and the only essential dial on the oven is the timer. Some ovens are now equipped with fast, medium or slow settings and automatic defrost buttons which act as an interrupter to stop and start the machine at set intervals. Others have a built-in grill element which can be used simultaneously with the microwave energy, and some of the most recent models have automatic turntables so that dishes do not need to be turned during cooking. These refinements naturally add considerably to the cost, and whereas the basic model is selling at a price that compares with the cost of conventional ovens, it is likely to be a long time before the sophisticated machines fall in price. In the variable control models, the fast or high setting is comparable to the power of cooking and times I have used for the recipes in this book. The medium setting will allow the tougher cuts of meat to be cooked, and the low setting is for defrosting and cooking delicate dishes such as soufflés and meringues. This does open up a field of cookery not previously possible using a microwave, but it is just as easy to cook these dishes in a conventional oven and there is no great saving in time. The defrost button can also be used for cooking tougher meats and similar items where resting between cooking periods will help. If there is no defrost button, put a glass of water in the back of the oven to slow down the cooking.

The recipes in this book have been worked out and tested on an uncomplicated Amana RR5 – 4. This is an average-powered domestic model. Various makes have outputs of between 600 and 750 watts and these should all give satisfactory results using my specified times, but there are variations with every model in the same way as there would be with conventional ovens, some of which may be faster than others. In a conventional oven, the temperature needs to be adjusted – in the microwave you adjust the timing. For example, if you have an 850-watt oven, allow three-quarters of the time given in my recipes, if a 400-watt oven, take approximately one and a quarter times my timings. Commercial microwave ovens are too powerful for cooking and, although they reheat food very quickly, they are not suitable for domestic use.

THE BROWNING SKILLET

Basic microwave ovens without built-in extras are less liable to go wrong than their more elaborate relations. For grilling and browning, it is always possible to use the conventional cooker or a browning skillet can be bought as an optional extra for the microwave oven. These are all made by the Corning Company Limited, but different models of microwave require different sizes of skillet and skillets cannot be used in all microwave ovens. Some shelves or oven bases are constructed of materials which cannot resist the intense heat from the browning skillet and the oven shelf will then melt or scar. Your retailer will advise you on this, but generally speaking, models fitted with toughened glass shelves are suitable, as are high temperature-resistant ceramics. Where a recipe includes the use of a browning skillet and your oven is unsuitable for use with this appliance, either sear the meat under the conventional grill or use the grill built into your microwave oven. Adequate results can be obtained, however, by cooking foods wholly in glass or ceramic ware, which does not need to be pre-heated.

Browning skillets are casseroles that have a specially treated base and are preheated empty in the microwave oven for a few minutes so that their temperature reaches 315°C/600°F. A frying pan would reach this temperature and any food put in immediately sears and browns. The microwave oven is not suitable for deep fat frying, because the temperature cannot be controlled. However, a certain amount of shallow fat frying is possible, provided a minimum of oil is used. Suitable foods for this method of cooking are steaks, sausages if well pricked, coated fish fillets and chicken pieces, sandwiches and Scotch pancakes. Following the preheating of the skillet, 3 or 4 tablespoons oil may be added and then heated for 1 or 2 minutes before the food is added. Switch on the microwave oven and as soon as one side is brown, turn the food over and continue cooking. Cover the dish to prevent spattering or leave uncovered for a crisp result. More oil may be added as necessary. The browning skillet will maintain its heat for 1 or 2 minutes and will be quite hot enough to fry an egg or bacon without further microwave energy.

The browning skillet can become very hot due to the transfer of heat from the contents combined with its own heat-retaining properties, so the use of oven gloves is essential. The hot skillet should not be put directly on a working surface, but should be treated in the same way as a hot frying pan. Searing often causes burns on the bottom of the skillet which can be removed, as if by magic, with an ample quantity of bicarbonate of soda on a nylon scourer or soft cloth. The browning skillet must be preheated in the microwave oven. It can be used for conventional cooking, but because of its high cost, this is inadvisable.

THE ADVANTAGES OF MICROWAVE COOKING

Cooking by microwave, being fast, saves energy and the cost of electricity is reduced by about 75 per cent. The ovens are so easy to clean that they only need a rub over with a cloth dampened with a little washing-up liquid. Some oven bases (shelves) are removable. In my recipes the shelf is described as the oven base even if removable, in which case dishes should never be placed on the oven 'bottom', as the shelf must always be in the oven during cooking periods. In some models there is a dust filter, which must be washed. There are no messy saucepans to clean when cooking by microwave, since you cook in the serving dish or on the plate.

The microwave oven can be placed anywhere there is a 13-amp socket. This makes sick-room cookery easy for the patient, and holiday accommodation, student rooms and offices without kitchens can be equipped with a microwave at minimum cost. The microwave oven can be used instead of a conventional cooker, but some rethinking is necessary in menu planning. To avoid periods of idling, prepare all the ingredients first and where possible arrange them in their dishes before you begin to cook a complete meal in the microwave oven. First cook dishes that are to be served cold, e.g. cold starters or desserts, then cook foods which can be reheated easily (vegetables). Follow this with foods that are likely to hold their heat during a resting period. Joints and casseroles come into this category. During the resting period, the pre-cooked vegetables may be reheated. Items such as fish fillets or eggs should be cooked or reheated last. A rule of thumb is, the longer it takes to cook, the longer it will retain heat after removal from the oven.

USES OF A MICROWAVE OVEN

There are four main uses for a microwave oven: thawing, reheating, 'quick aids', and cooking. Thawing is fast because, unlike the conventional oven, the microwave develops heat directly in the food, whereas in the conventional oven heating is by conduction. Reheated precooked meals, provided that they are covered during cooking, do not dry up, which often occurs in a conventional oven; nor do they go soggy, as can happen if you use a steamer for reheating.

Meals can be plated up ready for late-comers, covered with plastic film and kept in the refrigerator. A single plate will then take only 2 minutes to reheat in the microwave oven. Up to 4 plates may be stacked, using TPX rings, and it will be necessary to cover only the topmost plate. Four plates will take 6 minutes and they should be stacked so that the foods on each plate are staggered for even cooking.

MICROWAVE COOKING TIMES FOR LIQUIDS, ETC.

Water	Time to boiling point
125 ml/¼ pt	1¾ minutes
250 ml/½ pt	3 minutes
500 ml/1 pt	5 minutes

Milk	
125 ml/¼ pt	1½ minutes
250 ml/½ pt	2½ minutes
500 ml/1 pt	4 minutes

Water will boil more quickly in an efficient electric kettle, but often small amounts cannot be boiled owing to safety devices.

Butter or Margarine	To melt
50 g/2 oz	1 minute
75 g/3 oz	1¼ minutes
100 g/4 oz	1½ minutes

To soften: switch on for 5 seconds, rest for 15 seconds, switch on for a further 5 seconds, rest for 15 seconds, and if necessary switch on for 5 more seconds. Precise melting times will depend on the texture of the fat and its starting temperature.

'Quick aids' covers all those tedious, fiddly jobs such as melting small quantities of butter, softening chocolate or dissolving gelatine. Potatoes can be partly cooked by micro-wave before roasting conventionally, saving a saucepan and time, and chipped potatoes can be softened before putting them in the chip basket. Commercial frozen chipped potatoes, slightly thawed in the microwave oven and subsequently dried, will fry more crisply since the temperature of the oil will not be reduced drastically when the chips are put in the pan.

The fourth use, cooking, is related in this book to the freezer. In fact there are many dishes that may be cooked by micro-wave, but which are not suitable for freezing. Recipes for these are to be found in *Microwave Cookery for the Housewife*. They include fried eggs, bacon and egg, steaks, hot sandwiches, tomatoes, baked apples, refrigerator cakes, porridge, jellies and poppadums. The microwave oven is undoubtedly the most useful all-round kitchen aid yet invented.

GENERAL HINTS

Browning occurs naturally in the microwave oven only when foods are cooked for a long time. Where browning from dry heat is required, dishes should be put under the grill. Different items may be cooked in their dishes at the same time either spread out on the base of the oven or stacked one on top of the other. It is likely there will be differing cooking times involved, so as soon as one dish is ready, it must be removed from the oven. Very little time is saved by doing this and as the cooking must be carefully watched, it is inadvisable to leave the kitchen. However, where several foods are of similar structure with identical cooking times, stacking does work satisfactorily and easily.

The build-up of intense heat in foods totally enclosed by their skin or shell, e.g. eggs, apples, tomatoes, etc., will make them burst. Such items must, therefore, be adequately pricked. This also applies to food such as liver, which is covered by a thin, albeit virtually invisible skin. Because of the intense heat, cooking continues in all foods after the energy has been switched off. This is why a resting time is often recommended in the recipes. Some foods may even seem undercooked when they are removed from the oven. An example of this is the baked apple. When taken from the microwave oven, the top may be a different colour from the middle, but after a rest period, the clear green hue will have changed to the softer, cooked colour. The same applies to thin fillets of fish, liver, chops and potatoes. When using plastic film, the heat will similarly build up inside the dish and care must be taken when removing the film, or scalding could occur.

Although less likely than on the conventional hob, the microwave oven can set things on fire. Teacloths could be dried in the oven, but this would be dangerous. Similarly, wet newspapers that may have been delivered in a rainstorm, or indeed any paper, should not be left to cook in the oven. Oil on its own should not be exposed to microwaves for long periods for the same reason. Food should be covered when moist cooking is required, as this will hold in the steam and increase the temperature. Conversely, the moisture in uncovered food will evaporate to provide a crisper effect. In all cases, the recipes in this book state when foods should be cooked covered.

A booklet comes with every oven giving basic instructions on care, cleaning and safety. These should be carefully followed. There are various recommendations given regarding the use of metal. This is a question of care and intelligence. At no time must metal touch the sides, back or bottom of the oven. Metal skewers should only be used in large joints of meat or poultry and only small pieces of metal foil should be wrapped round those parts of the food that cook faster than the remainder. The microwave cannot penetrate metal, so these parts will cook only after unwrapping the foil. Shallow dishes such as TV trays that are less than 2 cm/¾ inch deep, placed centrally on the oven base (shelf), are acceptable because of the shallowness of the food. Remove the foil cover and replace with plastic film to allow the rays to penetrate. In fact, I have frequently taken a chance and used a metal flan ring with good results and no misfortune, but there is always the risk of damaging the magnetron. To be on the safe side, use metal very sparingly in the microwave. You will soon know there is something wrong when flashing and sparking occurs. This can even take place when a dish decorated with gold or silver is used. This form of metal trim is made up of tiny particles which react with one another to cause arcing. Also avoid dishes with metal handles, and do not leave metal forks or spoons in the food after stirring.

Oven gloves should be used when removing dishes from the microwave oven. Regardless of the material from which the containers are manufactured, long cooking and very hot food will transfer the heat, and dishes can sometimes become too hot to handle comfortably.

The microwave oven must never be switched on when it is empty. Always leave a glass of water in the oven, for although you may never switch on inadvertently, a child might. Children are prone to fiddle with switches and in this case the microwave is safer than the electric hob, which can severely burn a tiny hand on the hot plate. Gas cookers are equally hazardous and can set fire to long hair or a dangling sleeve.

The Microwave Oven

However, the microwave can be dangerous if the doors are forcibly bent, which damages the seal, or if a metal object such as a knitting needle is pushed through the grid while the oven is working.

Even the blind are catered for in microwave. The latest Amana model RR–4DW can be obtained with Braille cooking instructions and timer controls. Nothing can really be safer in cookery than the microwave oven.

2 The Freezer

The Freezer

Freezers met with considerable consumer resistance when they first appeared on the market. It was said that vitamins would be destroyed, that deterioration would set in and that flavour would be impaired. When all the old wives' tales were disproved and the true advantages and disadvantages explained rationally, the public realised that money, time and temper could be saved by investing in a freezer. Now freezers are available in many different forms and sizes ranging from enormous, chest-type top-openers to small, front-loading compartments built into the top of the refrigerator.

CHOOSING A FREEZER

Top-opening models conserve more cold air, as warm air rises to the top. They are easy to load, but it is sometimes difficult to reach what you require without lifting out heavy baskets. Because of its size this type of freezer should not be kept in the kitchen. A spare room is the most suitable, but if you keep the freezer in the garage, apply a coat of furniture polish from time to time to prevent the exterior from deteriorating in cold, damp weather. It is the model to choose if you intend to freeze your own garden produce or if you plan to buy meat in bulk.

Front-opening models save space and it is relatively easy to keep a check on the contents, but it is essential to make sure the door is properly closed every time it has been opened as doors do not always swing to automatically. To prevent too much warm air entering, take all the day's requirements out at the same time. This type of freezer often has an automatic defrosting device.

You must, of course, choose the type and size of freezer that suits your particular circumstances. Ignore advice to buy the biggest you can afford, for a half-empty freezer is an inefficient machine. Too much air in a partially filled compartment causes the grids to ice up more quickly and this in turn increases the running costs. So buy a freezer that will accommodate your own family requirements, plus enough space for those of one or two guests. Bulk buy only the items that you are sure to use, as it is no saving at all to purchase a large quantity of meat only to find that it is sub-standard in quality. The ultimate in freezer-owning is to have an upright model which fits comfortably in the kitchen for everyday use and a chest freezer in the garage or similar area for long-term storage.

Not all microwave manufacturers produce freezers. The exceptions are the American Amana, who make extremely attractive freezers in various shapes, colours and finishes, and the European Philips. At present, microwave ovens and freezers are not designed in single units, but all good kitchen shops and stores have experts to advise you on the most suitable choice. The microwave oven can be built into fitted kitchens and Thermidor produce a microwave, warming drawer and conventional oven assembled as one unit.

USING A FREEZER

A freezer is portable in the same way as a microwave oven and only requires a 13-amp outlet. Running costs amount to only a few pence per week, depending on the size of the freezer. Cleaning is relatively easy and the freezer should be defrosted when the frost is 1 cm/$\frac{1}{2}$ inch thick and the contents are low. This should be necessary only two or three times a year. To defrost, switch off the electricity, then scrape the frost into a bowl with a plastic scraper and thaw the remaining ice by putting a bowl or two of very hot water in the cabinet. Wipe out the interior with a solution of bicarbonate of soda and then dry with a soft cloth. Only after this should you switch on the electricity again, otherwise strands of the material will adhere to the sides of the cabinet. Close the door or lid and replace the food only when the temperature reaches −6°C/21°F. The melted ice is a useful substitute for distilled water in your steam iron. During the defrosting, put the food in the refrigerator at its lowest temperature setting or wrap frozen food in several thicknesses of newspaper.

For best results, fresh food should be quick-frozen. This is possible with a freezer marked with the 4 star symbol ****, in which temperatures will reach between −25°C to −30°C/−13°F to −22°F. The reason that food should be frozen as speedily as possible is that ice crystals form during the freezing process which can damage cell structure. The more quickly the process passes freezing point, the less likely this is to happen, so the freezer should be set at its lowest mark for 2 or 3 hours before fresh food is put in the cabinet and maintained at this setting for 24 hours, if a considerable quantity is being frozen at the time. Food should only be put in the freezer when it is quite cold.

Frozen food should only be held for one week in the freezer compartment of a refrigerator marked with 1 star * −6°C/21°F, for 1 month in a 2 star ** −12°C/10°F, and for 3 months in a 3 star *** −18°C/0°F, after which the food begins to deteriorate. However, it is quite permissible to store small quantities of food in the ice-making compartment of a refrigerator for 2 or 3 days.

Special freezer labels and pencils will ensure that the date of storage will not fall off the package or become illegible. Make it a rule always to note either the date when the article went into the freezer or the date it should come out. Prepared dishes have only a short storage life, as can be seen in the chart on

The Freezer

page 21, but the food will not go bad if left in for much longer – it is merely that the taste and texture deteriorate. Wrappings should exclude as much air as possible and there should be no holes in these materials. When freezing liquids, a minimum headspace of $2\frac{1}{2}$ cm/1 inch must be left to allow for the increase in volume which occurs.

Commercially frozen packets of meat, fish and dairy produce must not be refrozen after thawing out completely, because of the multiplication of bacteria which is held in check at freezing point. While some ice crystals remain, the food may be refrozen for a short time, but if all the crystals have melted it must be cooked immediately. Fruit and vegetables may be refrozen after thawing, but the flavour and texture will be impaired.

To clarify the rules for freezing and thawing:

1. Frozen food may be thawed, cooked and then frozen.
2. Thawed animal produce must be cooked at once and may then be frozen.
3. Fresh food may be cooked, frozen and then thawed and reheated (but it is inadvisable to refreeze left-overs).

Remember that the more 'to-ing and fro-ing' from cooking to freezing, the more deterioration takes place, until eventually the point is reached where the food becomes poisonous. Open-freezing means that prepared food is frozen before it is wrapped. This avoids damage to any decorations and enables liquids to solidify first. When frozen, pieces of food can be packed closely together without one item sticking to its neighbour.

If your freezer breaks down, the food will keep for 12 hours provided you do not open the lid. But just in case, make certain that your insurance policy covers this eventuality.

Freezer gloves should be kept near the freezer, so that your hands do not get burnt when removing several items at a time. If fingers are wet, they may stick to the shelves.

FOODS THAT DO NOT FREEZE WELL

Avocado (except as purée)	Fizzy drinks	Pickles
Bananas	Grapes	Radishes, raw
Blue cheese	Ham	Salad vegetables
Cucumbers	Lettuce	Single cream
Custard tarts	Marmalade	Strawberries
Dripping	Marzipan	(unless very
Eggs (in shell and hard-boiled)	Mayonnaise	firm)
	Milk (except	Watercress
Fat	homogenised or skimmed)	

GUIDE TO BEST MONTHS FOR FREEZING FOODS IN THEIR PRIME

JANUARY
Apricots
Bitter oranges
Rhubarb (forced)
Brussels sprouts
Parsnips
Spring greens
Turnips
Haddock
Herrings
Mackerel
Plaice
Scallops
Skate
Goose
Hare

FEBRUARY
Apricots
Rhubarb (forced)
Brussels sprouts
Parsnips
Spring greens
Turnips
Cod
Haddock
Herrings
Mackerel
Plaice
Scallops
Skate
Goose
Hare

MARCH
Rhubarb (forced)
Parsnips
Spring greens
Cod
Mackerel
Plaice
Scallops
Skate
Whitebait

APRIL
Rhubarb (garden)
Cod
Lobster
Mackerel
Plaice
Whitebait

MAY
Apricots
Gooseberries
Peaches
Rhubarb (garden)
Asparagus
Broad beans
Carrots (new)
Potatoes (new)
Crab
Lobster
Mackerel
Salmon
Salmon trout
Whitebait

JUNE
Apricots
Cherries
Gooseberries
Peaches
Strawberries
Asparagus
Broad beans
Carrots (new)
Peas
Potatoes (new)
Crab
Lobster
Salmon
Salmon trout
Whitebait

JULY
Apricots
Blackcurrants
Cherries
Gooseberries
Peaches
Raspberries
Redcurrants
Strawberries

AUGUST
Apricots
Blackberries
Blackcurrants
Gooseberries
Peaches
Plums
Raspberries
Redcurrants

SEPTEMBER
Apples
Blackberries
Damsons
Greengages
Peaches
Plums
Brussels sprouts
Runner beans

The Freezer

JULY
Broad beans
French beans
Peas
Potatoes (new)
Crab
Herrings
Lobster
Salmon
Salmon trout
Whitebait
Venison

AUGUST
Broad beans
French beans
Runner beans
Corn on the cob
Peas
Crab
Herrings
Lobster
Grouse
Venison

SEPTEMBER
Corn on the cob

Peas
Turnips
Crab
Herrings
Scallops
Grouse
Venison

OCTOBER
Cooking apples
Blackberries
Damsons
Quinces
Brussels sprouts
Runner beans
Corn on the cob
Parsnips
Turnips
Crab
Herrings
Scallops
Skate
Whiting
Goose
Grouse
Hare
Partridge
Venison

NOVEMBER
Cooking apples
Cranberries
Quinces
Brussels sprouts
Parsnips
Spring greens
Turnips
Haddock
Herrings
Scallops
Skate
Whiting
Goose
Hare
Partridge
Pheasant
Venison

DECEMBER
Cooking apples
Apricots
Brussels sprouts
Parsnips
Spring greens
Turnips
Haddock
Herrings
Scallops
Skate
Whiting
Goose
Hare
Pheasant
Venison

AVAILABLE ALL THE YEAR ROUND
Avocados, eating apples, oranges and pineapples
Aubergines, beetroot, broccoli, cauliflower, celery and
courgettes
Chicken and rabbit

RECOMMENDED MAXIMUM STORAGE TIMES

Food	Approximate Time In Months
Avocado, purée only	7
Bacon, smoked	1
unsmoked	2
Beef, minced, uncooked	9
roast and steaks, uncooked	12
Biscuits	6
Bread, bought	2
dough, uncooked	2
home-baked	8
Butter, salted	3
unsalted	6
Cakes, batter, uncooked	4
decorated	3
undecorated	6
Cheese, Camembert	6
cottage	4
cream	4
Dutch	12
hard, grated	6
hard, ungrated	3
Chestnuts	1
Chicken, uncooked	12
livers, uncooked	3
Cream, over 40% butterfat	3
Crumbles, cooked or uncooked	6
Duck, uncooked	6
roast	2
Eggs, separated, whites, lightly whipped	9
whole, shelled and lightly beaten with sugar or salt	9
yolks, whisked with sugar or salt	9
Fish, cooked from fresh	2
cooked from frozen	1
raw oily	3
raw white	6
Fruits, citrus and juices	6
other	9
Game, prepared dishes	1
uncooked	6
Goose, roast	2
uncooked	6
Ham (but flavour deteriorates)	3
Ice cream	3

The Freezer

Food	Approximate Time In Months
Lamb, uncooked	12
Margarine	6
Meat, cooked slices	1
dishes made with mince	3
pies	1
roast joints	6
Melon	6
Meringues	Unlimited
Milk, emergency only for pasteurised	$\frac{1}{2}$
homogenised	3
skimmed	3
Mousse	1
with gelatine	3
Offal, prepared dishes	6
uncooked	1
Pancakes	3
Pastry cases, uncooked	9
cooked, filled	4
cooked, unfilled	6
Pasta, cooked	4
Pâté	1
Pork, uncooked	6
precooked dishes	4
Puddings, cooked, steamed, sponge or suet	3
Rabbits, uncooked	6
Rhubarb	12
Rice, cooked	2
Sandwiches, depending on filling	$\frac{1}{2}$–2
Sauces	4
Sausages	1
Sausage rolls	1
Savouries, prepared	1
Scallops, fresh or prepared	1
Shellfish, prepared dishes	1
raw	4
Sorbet	2
Soups	4
Starters, prepared	1
Stocks	4
Stuffings	2
Sweetmeats	6
Turkey, uncooked	6
Veal, uncooked	6

Food	Approximate Time In Months
Vegetables, cooked prepared dishes	3
cooked beetroot	6
cooked jacket potatoes	1
artichokes, globe	
uncooked cauliflower	
celeriac	
celery	
courgettes	6
leeks	
mushrooms	
potatoes, old and chipped	
artichokes, Jerusalem, puréed	
asparagus	
aubergines	
beans, French, broad and runner	
cabbage	
carrots	
corn on the cob	
onions	
parsnips	12
peas	
peppers	
potatoes, new	
spinach	
swedes	
tomatoes, purée only	
turnips	
Venison, cooked	2
uncooked	12
Waffles	6
Yeast	12
Yoghurts	6
Yorkshire pudding, batter	1
cooked	1

Although the above are the recommended times, it is quite safe to keep food for much longer. As a general rule, allow 4 to 6 months for pre-cooked composite dishes.

The Freezer

GUIDE TO THAWING TIMES

The microwave thawing times are only an indication, since
defrosting depends on the starting temperature of the frozen
food. In simple microwave ovens, the dish must be turned or
the food stirred during thawing. Where there is an automatic
defrost button, this is not necessary and although the thawing
process will take twice as long, the resting time is not required.

	Microwave	Conventional
Apples	4 minutes	$\frac{1}{2}$ hour in moderate oven
Apricots	4 minutes	6–8 hours in refrigerator
Artichokes, globe	4 minutes	Boil from frozen
Biscuits, baked	2 minutes	1 hour at room temperature
Bread	2 minutes	5 hours in refrigerator or 2 hours at room temperature
Butter, per lb	Six 10-second bursts with 3-minute rests between	1–2 hours at room temperature
Cabbage	2 minutes	Boil from frozen
Cakes, single layer	3 minutes	1–1½ hours at room temperature
2 layers, angel and sponge	3 minutes	2–3 hours at room temperature
Canapés	10 seconds, then rest for 10 minutes	1 hour at room temperature
Cheese	Two 15-second bursts with 5 minutes rest	5 hours in refrigerator
Cheesecake	Two 15-second bursts with 30 minutes rest	3–4 hours at room temperature
Cherries	4 minutes	8 hours in refrigerator
Chestnuts	4 minutes	3–4 hours in refrigerator

	Microwave	Conventional
Chicken, uncooked	1-minute-per-pound bursts with 10-minute rests between, then repeat until thawed	2–3 hours per 450 g/1 lb at room temperature or 10 hours per 450 g/1 lb in refrigerator
Crab	4 minutes	8–12 hours in refrigerator
Cream, cartons	Unsuitable	1–2 hours at room temperature or 24 hours in refrigerator
decorations	Unsuitable	10–15 minutes at room temperature
Egg whites	Unsuitable	24 hours in refrigerator
yolks	10 seconds, then rest for 10 minutes	3 hours in refrigerator
Flans	3 minutes	$\frac{1}{2}$ hour in hot oven
Fruit	3 minutes (allow no air in during thawing)	8 hours in refrigerator
Fruit juices	5 minutes	8 hours in refrigerator
purées	5 minutes	2–4 hours at room temperature
Goose	As for chicken	3 hours per 450 g/1 lb at room temperature or 10 hours per 450 g/1 lb in refrigerator
Grapefruit, whole fruit, segments or juice	1 minute	3 hours at room temperature or 6 hours in refrigerator
Grouse	As for chicken	2–3 hours per 450 g/1 lb at room temperature or 6–8 hours per 450 g/1 lb in refrigerator
Kidney	$\frac{1}{2}$ minute per lb then rest for 3 minutes	2–3 hours at room temperature or 4–6 hours in refrigerator

The Freezer

	Microwave	Conventional
Lobster	½ minute, rest for 2 minutes, then repeat until thawed	8–12 hours in refrigerator
Meat, joints cooked or uncooked	As for chicken	4–6 hours at room temperature or 8 hours in refrigerator
sliced	As for chicken	2–3 hours in refrigerator
Melon balls	6 minutes, stirring occasionally	2–3 hours in refrigerator
Meringues	Unsuitable	1–2 hours at room temperature
Mousse, with eggs and cream	¼ to ½ minute	1–2 hours at room temperature
with gelatine	½ minute	6 hours in refrigerator
Oranges	1 minute	3 hours at room temperature or 6 hours in refrigerator
Oxtail	As for kidney	45 minutes in moderate oven
Oysters	Unsuitable	10 hours in refrigerator
Pancakes	10 seconds	30 minutes in a moderate oven
Partridge	As for chicken	3 hours at room temperature or 8 hours in refrigerator
Pastry, shortcrust and puff	½ minute	2–3 hours at room-temperature or 8 hours in refrigerator
choux	¼ minute	2 hours at room temperature
Pâtés	4 minutes	1–3 hours at room temperature
Peaches	Unsuitable	1½ hours at room temperature or 6 hours in refrigerator

	Microwave	Conventional
Pears	3 minutes	2–4 hours at room temperature or 6–8 hours in refrigerator
Pies	2 minutes	½ hour in hot oven
Plate meals	5 minutes	40–50 minutes in moderate oven
Plums	1 minute	2–4 hours at room temperature
Prawns	½ minute	3 hours in refrigerator
Puddings	2 minutes	6 hours at room temperature
Quiche	2 minutes	6 hours in refrigerator
Rabbit	As for chicken	6 hours in refrigerator
Raspberries	1½ minutes	6–8 hours in refrigerator
Ratatouille	4 minutes	8 hours in refrigerator
Rolls	15 seconds	1 hour at room temperature
Salmon, whole	½ minute followed by 3 minutes rest, then repeat until thawed	24 hours in refrigerator
portions	As for whole salmon	3 hours at room temperature or 6 hours in refrigerator
Sandwiches	½ minute	4 hours at room temperature or 8 hours in refrigerator
Sausages	Spread out in the microwave and switch on for 2 minutes, turning occasionally	3 hours at room temperature or 6 hours in refrigerator
Sausage rolls	½ minute	3 hours at room temperature or 6 hours in refrigerator
Scallops	2 minutes	10 hours in refrigerator

The Freezer

	Microwave	Conventional
Shrimps	½ minute	1 hour at room temperature or 3 hours in refrigerator
Sorbets	Unsuitable	15 minutes at room temperature
Strawberries	2 minutes	8 hours in refrigerator
Stuffing	Switch on for ½ minute, rest for ½ minute and switch on for further ½ minute	8 hours in refrigerator
Tarts	2 minutes	½ hour in a hot oven
Turkey	As for chicken	10 hours per 450 g/1 lb in refrigerator
Yeast	5 seconds, rest for 5 minutes, then repeat until thawed	20–30 minutes at room temperature
Yorkshire pudding	3 minutes	40–45 minutes at room temperature

3 The Combined Use of Microwave and Freezer

The Combined Use of Microwave and Freezer

The microwave oven and the freezer complement one another so often. The permutations are many – cooking by microwave, freezing and subsequently thawing and reheating by microwave; cooking prime frozen foods; reheating prepared dishes; blanching fruit and vegetables for freezing, thawing and then cooking them.

When cooking by microwave for the freezer, undercook slightly as food is inclined to soften during storage. Pack in suitable portion sizes. If food is frozen in a single lump, it is almost impossible to divide while frozen. Particular care should be taken when freezing chops and steaks. These may be packed in a single bag, provided each is individually wrapped and separated with waxed paper, foil or plastic film. Some dishes can be cooked, frozen and reheated in the same casserole. Freeze in the dish, then dip the base in hot water to loosen the block. This can then be turned into a freezer bag. When you want to thaw the food, the block is still in the right shape to put back into the original dish.

It is a good idea when cooking by microwave to weigh out and cook double the quantity of ingredients required and divide into two. Serve one meal immediately and set aside the other for freezing, so that there is always a wide variety of prepared food ready in the freezer. Ready cooked meals have a relatively short life in the freezer, and it is much more exciting to have a greater selection in penny numbers so you will not be faced with the same things time and again.

COOKING DISHES AND WRAPPINGS

A wide range of materials are suitable for both the microwave and the freezer, but this is not so in every case. Metal, which is only acceptable in the microwave oven under certain circumstances (see page 13) would be included in a list of suitable materials for the freezer. So that although aluminium foil, foil dishes and baking tins are a good choice for the freezer, you could not use them in the microwave oven, as metal is reflective and microwaves cannot pass through. This is why the microwave ovens are metal lined. Even where there is a built-in ceramic shelf, it is concealing the metal bottom of the oven.

Non-metallic cooking dishes allow the microwaves to pass through without slowing the heating process. Plastics are, of course, non-metallic and all plastics are suitable in the freezer as they are non-porous and can be made airtight. The lids can be sealed with special freezer tape. Be sure that they are resistant to low temperatures, for they may crack in these circumstances. The lids can always be replaced with freezer foil if they crack. Tupperware, although guaranteed against low temperatures, can be disastrously deformed in the microwave oven. As a general rule, plastics that are safe in the dishwasher are safe in the microwave, but since it is likely that prime cooking will involve a higher temperature, only food that is to be warmed through should be heated in these containers. Commercially frozen packs sealed in boilable bags can be cooked by microwave provided the bag is pierced to allow steam to escape.

Materials such as polypropylene bowls and Porosan bags that are described as 'boilable' are highly microwave resistant. Very hot syrup or oil can cause scarring, but this will not spoil the efficiency of these bowls. TPX rings of similar material are generally available and can be used for stacking three or four plates of food for simultaneous thawing. If you are in any doubt about plastic containers, you will find that the rigid type is more microwave resistant than the pliable. Melamine, Centura and Corelle should not be used in the microwave oven because they absorb energy rather than allowing it to pass through, and become damaged. Unsuitable freezer containers should not be put in the microwave oven for more than a few moments and if there is syrup in the bottom, not at all.

Plastic film is an ideal material for both the freezer and the microwave. It keeps the moisture in during cooking and gives a good seal. Cellophane will not seal the dishes, but is a good covering and again suitable for both purposes. Although 'roaster bags' are unsuitable for use in the freezer, they may be used for cooking joints or poultry by microwave for extra browning, but they must not have metal edges or metal tags. The bags should be unsealed with the opening raised so that the fat does not seep out over the oven base. Thick-gauge polythene bags, the favourite freezer packaging material, are only used in the microwave oven for thawing. Metal tags must be removed and the bag left open at the top. All materials derived from paper are microwave-proof and include absorbent kitchen towels, greaseproof, non-stick and waxed paper, and cardboard, but only the waxed and non-stick are suitable for the freezer unless they are to be overwrapped.

Heat-resistant glass is more indestructible in the microwave oven than in the conventional oven, because the container is only heated by conduction from the food and not by direct heat. All glass, glass-ceramics including Pyrosil, and pottery, provided they have no metallic decoration, can be used in the freezer and the microwave. Most of my experimental work has been carried out using Denbyware, which has never cracked or crazed.

I would not recommend the rust-coloured oven bricks that are meant for long, slow cooking in the conventional oven.

The Combined Use of Microwave and Freezer

They have to be wet and could crack if dried out by the microwave action.

Pyrex is manufactured in most countries but in differing shapes. Pyrex Patisseries, which include some suitable cake and loaf shapes, are now becoming available in Britain and are excellent for baking. Porcelain fluted flan dishes are also on sale in France and in the UK, and in Britain we are able to obtain some delightful Worcester china soufflé dishes and a wide range of stoneware. But until more manufacturers will produce suitable glass and plastic shapes for cakes, we must use our own ingenuity to create cooking receptacles out of cardboard boxes (see the Introduction to Chapter 12). Paper cases, one inside the other, will give more resistance as the cakes rise, and chocolate or cake boxes are suitable, provided they are not painted with silver or gold. Flan rings can be made from cardboard. Nevertheless, you should test the containers before using them for the first time. Glass, china and pottery should be put into the switched on microwave oven for 20 seconds. They should then be cold or just warm to the touch.

The shells from scallops and other fish are both attractive and resistant to breakage in the microwave oven and can also be frozen if overwrapped. Wood and straw should be exposed to microwaves for short times only, such as when reheating bread rolls, as they are absorbent and will crack.

SUITABLE CONTAINERS AND WRAPPINGS FOR MICROWAVE AND FREEZER

	Microwave	Freezer
Absorbent kitchen paper	Yes	No
Boilable bags	Yes	Yes
Cake boards (silver and gold covered)	No	Yes
Cardboard cartons	Yes	Yes (if over-wrapped)
Cellophane	Yes	Yes
China	Yes (without metal trim)	Yes (with care or for a short time)
Clear rigid commercial dessert containers	No	No
Einoplas plastic tissue	Yes	Yes
Foam plastics	No	Yes (if over-wrapped)

The Combined Use of Microwave and Freezer

	Microwave	*Freezer*
Foil containers	No (unless only $\frac{3}{4}$ inch deep and completely filled with food)	Yes
Freezer film	No	Yes
Freezer foil	No	Yes (double thickness)
Glass	Yes	Yes (leave $2\frac{1}{2}$ cm/1 inch headspace)
Greaseproof paper	Yes	No
Melamine	No	Yes
Natural shells	Yes	Yes (if over-wrapped)
Non-stick paper	Yes	Yes
Paper cake cases	Yes	Yes (if over-wrapped)
Paper plates	Yes	No
Papier maché plates	Yes	No
Plastic containers	Yes (if dish-washer proof)	Yes
Plastic film (Snapwrap, Saran etc.)	Yes	Yes (if double)
Polypropylene bowls and sheets	Yes	Yes
Polythene bags (thick)	Yes (short spells only and open)	Yes
Porcelain	Yes	Yes
Porosan bags	Yes	Yes (when cold)
Pottery (casseroles, dishes and plates)	Yes	Yes
Roaster bags and film	Yes (without metal trim and open)	Yes
Straw	Yes (short spells only)	No
Waxed cartons	Yes	Yes
Waxed paper	Yes	Yes
Wood	Yes (short spells only)	No
Yoghurt pots	No	Yes

The Combined Use of Microwave and Freezer

COOKING AND THAWING

It is always preferable to cook foods of similar density and size together in the microwave oven and if possible, reheating should be carried out in the same way. An example of this is the reheating of a dinner consisting of meat, peas and mashed potato. The potato will remain cool when the meat and peas are hot. Given extra time, the potatoes will become hot, but there is the risk that the other items will have over-cooked. However, whole boiled potatoes would reheat more speedily.

In the recipes there are thawing instructions that are suitable for all ovens, but the recommended timings can only be approximate, for this must depend on the starting temperature of the food. If you have a model with a thaw button, this can be used instead. However, when proving bread, it is inadvisable to give more than 5 seconds of microwave energy at a time and many of the thaw buttons operate at longer set intervals. Merrychef have an exclusive 'Freezing Hot Set' for use in the ordinary microwave oven, which consists of a plate with a lid. The frozen food is placed on the plate, which prevents over-cooking around the edges. When covered with the lid, the energy is concentrated in the centre of the food, which is, of course, the coldest part.

Commercially frozen, ready-prepared dishes which would take a considerable time in a conventional oven can be reheated quickly by microwave. Shallow dishes covered with foil should be taken out of their boxes, the foil covers removed and then put back in the cardboard container. Foods packed in boilable bags may be reheated by microwave, provided the bags are pierced. Reheating times depend on the depth of freezing and the best results will be obtained if frequent rest periods are allowed. The dishes should be turned during cooking for even reheating. I have not included a chart for commercially prepared ready-to-serve dishes as new products are continually reaching the shops. However, depending on the portion size and density, 6 to 10 minutes will suffice.

Learning to cook conventionally takes a long time, but learning to cook by microwave takes only a few hours. It will help to read the introduction to each chapter before using the recipes, which should reduce the initial failures. Inevitably some trial and error, particularly with timings for your own oven, will be necessary when cooking by microwave, but freezing is a more definite process, following fairly fixed rules. The combination of freezer and microwave provides the most exciting potential, and gives the housewife complete control of storage and virtually instant serving, so that she need never be caught unprepared and can cook at the most convenient times.

4 Soups and Stocks

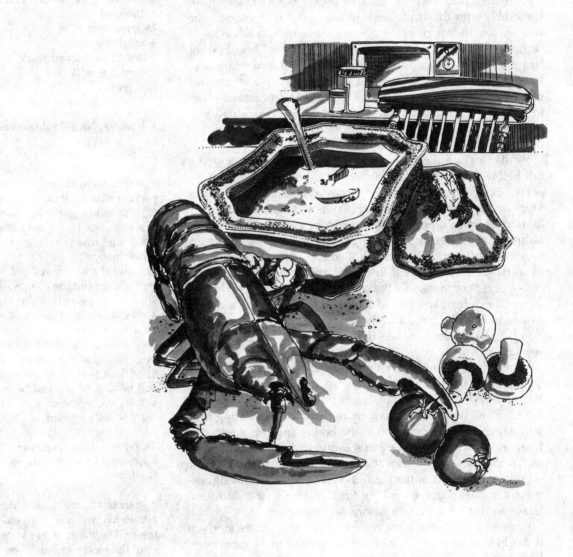

Soups cooked by microwave admirably illustrate the use of a single dish from the preparation stages, through cooking, to service at the table.

The maximum amount of liquid that can be cooked in the microwave oven at one time is 3½ litres/6 pts, but recipes can be stretched by cutting down on the amount of liquid used to cook the solid ingredients. The soup can then be thinned down with more liquid – water, stock or milk – before freezing, or preferably after thawing. Large quantities of *roux*-based soups will require thorough beating when extra milk is added.

Stocks should be cooked on the conventional hob as only lengthy simmering can extract all the flavour and nutrients from bones and vegetables, and it is not possible to use the microwave oven for simmering. The meat and vegetables used for making stock must be in good condition. Poor-quality ingredients will produce a bitter flavour and hasten the deterioration of a soup made with them.

While stocks are cooking, they should never be allowed to fall below simmering point as this could cause souring to occur. Fat and scum should be removed before freezing either stock or soup made with stock. Fish stock is simmered for only 20 minutes, but otherwise stocks can be boiled to reduce the volume before freezing. If they are not to be used or frozen immediately, stocks should be boiled for 5 minutes before use.

To freeze stock, leave it until it is quite cold. Then pour it into freezer containers in the quantities required, leaving 2½ cm/1 inch headspace, and seal. Alternatively, stock may be frozen in ice cube trays and the cubes packed in freezer bags. Soups will keep for 12 weeks in the freezer, stocks for up to 16 weeks.

When thawing and reheating soup in the microwave oven, the bowl(s) should be lightly covered so that the maximum heat is trapped. Ice is a transferring rather than an absorbent material and it is slow to thaw by microwave. Reheating time will depend on the quantity in the bowls and the depth of freezing. A single bowl, or 3 or 4 individual portions, may be put in the microwave oven at a time. Switch on until the soup is bubbling (3 to 6 minutes). Stir to spread the heat throughout the soup and continue cooking for a further 1 or 2 minutes. Leave to rest for a minute before serving.

Canned soups should be mixed with a few tablespoons of water before reheating in individual bowls or in a soup tureen. Powdered soups should be reconstituted with the amount of liquid recommended on the packet. Clear packet soups with suspended vegetables or pasta take about 10 minutes to cook in the microwave oven, and thickened soups take about 4 minutes.

ARTICHOKE SOUP
Serves 6–8

450 g/1 lb Jerusalem artichokes
Lemon juice
1 medium onion, chopped
1 garlic clove, crushed
2 rashers bacon, rinded and chopped
25 g/1 oz butter
8 hazelnuts
1 litre/1¾ pt chicken stock
250 ml/½ pt milk
Salt, pepper

+ + +

6–8 tablespoons double cream

1. Scrub and peel the artichokes. Cut into small cubes and sprinkle with lemon juice to prevent discoloration.
2. Put onion, garlic and bacon in a large bowl with the butter. Cook 4 minutes, stirring occasionally.
3. Add the artichokes and nuts. Cover and cook 5 minutes, stirring occasionally.
4. Pour in half of the stock and cook 20 minutes.
5. Blend in the liquidiser and pour back into the bowl.
6. Stir in the remaining stock and milk. Add salt and pepper to taste and reheat until the soup reaches boiling point.

To serve without freezing Stir a spoonful of cream into each bowl.

To freeze Leave to cool. Pour into individual bowls. Open freeze. Dip bases in hot water until the blocks loosen, then turn into freezer bags. Seal.

To serve from the freezer Remove from bags and put the blocks of soup in the original bowls. Cover and thaw by microwave. Switch on for 5 minutes. Stir, then continue cooking until thoroughly reheated. Stir a spoonful of cream into each bowl before serving.

CREAM OF AVOCADO SOUP
Serves 4

2 ripe avocados
2 teaspoons lemon juice
25 g/1 oz unsalted butter
1 small onion, grated
25 g/1 oz flour
750 ml/1½ pt chicken stock
Celery salt
Pepper

+ + +

1 egg yolk
3 tablespoons double cream

1.   Cut the advocados in half lengthways, remove the stones and peel.
2.   Mash the advocados to a pulp and mix in the lemon juice.
3.   Put the butter and onion in a large bowl. Cook 2 minutes.
4.   Stir in the flour. Cook 1 minute.
5.   Gradually blend in the stock and cook 4 minutes or until the sauce thickens, stirring frequently.
6.   Add the mashed advocado to the sauce. Season with celery salt and pepper. Cook 2 minutes.

To serve without freezing
Blend the egg yolk with the cream. Stir in a ladleful of the hot soup. Return to the bowl, stir, then reheat for ½ minute.

To freeze   Leave to cool. Open freeze in the serving bowl, then dip the base in hot water until

the block loosens. Turn into a freezer bag and seal.

To serve from the freezer
Remove from bag and put the block of soup in the original bowl. Cover and thaw by microwave. Switch on for 5 minutes, stir, then continue cooking until the soup begins to boil. Blend the egg yolk with the cream, stir in a ladleful of hot soup and return to the bowl. Stir, then reheat but do not boil, or the egg yolk may curdle.

AVGOLEMONO
Serves 6

The soup will curdle if the eggs and lemon are added while it is boiling, but it should be cool enough by the time it is removed from the microwave oven to the worktop.

1½ litres/2¾ pt chicken stock
Salt, pepper
50 g/2 oz long-grain rice

+ + +

2 eggs
3 tablespoons lemon juice

1.   Pour the stock into a large bowl, bring to the boil and cook 8 minutes.
2.   Add salt and pepper to taste.
3.   Stir in the rice. Cook 10 minutes.

To serve without freezing
Cook for a further 2 minutes. Beat the eggs, lemon juice and 2 tablespoons water together. Pour into the soup. Stir thoroughly, then reheat for ½ to 1 minute, but do not allow to boil.

To freeze   Cover and leave to cool. Open-freeze in a soup

tureen. Dip base in hot water until the block loosens and turn into a freezer bag. Seal.

To serve from the freezer
Remove from bag and put the block of soup back in the tureen. Thaw by microwave. Cover and switch on for 15 minutes or until boiling, stirring occasionally. Beat the eggs and lemon juice with 2 tablespoons cold water. Pour into the soup. Stir vigorously and serve at once.

BORSCH
Serves 6–8

1 large (175 g/7 oz) beetroot, cooked and peeled
1 celery stalk
1 carrot
1 onion
1 garlic clove
2 tomatoes, skinned
1 litre/1¾ pt hot stock
Salt, pepper
2 teaspoons Worcestershire sauce

+ + +

2 tablespoons double cream

1.   Remove the strings from the celery. Peel the carrot, onion and garlic clove.
2.   Roughly chop all the vegetables and blend in the liquidiser with about 375 ml/¾ pt of the stock.
3.   Transfer to a large bowl. Season to taste with salt and pepper. Add the Worcestershire sauce and the remaining stock.
4.   Cover loosely with plastic film and cook 10 minutes.
5.   Remove the film carefully, taste and adjust the seasoning.

To serve without freezing
Ladle into individual bowls and

Soups and Stocks

garnish each bowl with a little cream.

To freeze Leave to cool. Open freeze in individual portions in the bowls in which the soup will be served. When frozen, dip bases in hot water until the blocks loosen, then turn into freezer bags. Seal.

To serve from the freezer Transfer blocks of soup from freezer bags to the original bowls. To thaw by microwave, cover and switch on for 6 to 8 minutes, stirring as soon as bubbles appear around the edge. Stir a little cream into each bowl.

CARROT SOUP
Serves 4

450 g/1 lb young carrots
1 onion
500 ml/1 pt chicken stock
25 g/1 oz soft margarine
25 g/1 oz flour
250 ml/½ pt milk
Salt, pepper
1 bay leaf

+ + +

2 tablespoons single cream

+ + +

1 teaspoon flour

1. Peel and chop the carrots and onion, and blend in a liquidiser with some of the stock.
2. Put the margarine in a large bowl. Cook until melted, 1 minute.
3. Blend in the flour. Cook ½ minute.
4. Gradually stir in the milk. Cook 3 minutes, stirring frequently.
5. Add the liquidised

vegetables and the remaining stock. Season with salt and pepper and add the bay leaf. Stir well.
6. Cook 10 minutes. Remove the bay leaf.

To serve without freezing Ladle into individual bowls and stir a little cream into each.

To freeze Leave to cool. Blend 1 teaspoon flour with 2 tablespoons water and stir in. Open-freeze in individual bowls, then dip bases in hot water until the blocks loosen. Turn into freezer bags. Seal.

To serve from the freezer Remove from bags and place blocks of soup in the original bowls. To thaw by microwave, cover and switch on for 5 minutes. Stir. Leave to rest for 2 minutes, then continue cooking until thoroughly reheated. Stir a little cream into each bowl.

CRÈME DUBARRY
Serves 6

1 large onion, finely chopped
50 g/2 oz butter
450 g/1 lb cauliflower florettes, fresh or frozen
1 medium potato, chopped
1 litre/1¾ pt vegetable stock
250 ml/½ pt milk
Bouquet garni
Salt, pepper
2 teaspoons cornflour

+ + +

Finely chopped parsley

1. Put the onion in a large bowl with the butter. Cook 2 minutes.
2. Add the cauliflower and potato with 2 tablespoons water.

Cover tightly and cook 5 minutes.
3. Add the vegetable stock, milk, *bouquet garni*, salt and pepper. Cook 4 minutes.
4. Remove the *bouquet garni* and blend the soup in a liquidiser or press through a sieve.
5. Blend the cornflour with a little cold water. Stir into the soup and bring to boiling point.

To serve without freezing Serve hot, each portion garnished with a sprinkling of finely chopped parsley.

To freeze Leave to cool. Open freeze in individual bowls. Dip bases in hot water until the blocks loosen, then turn into freezer bags. Seal.

To serve from the freezer Remove from bags and place the blocks of soup in the original bowls. To thaw by microwave, cover and switch on for 5 minutes. Stir. Continue cooking if necessary until thoroughly reheated. Garnish with parsley.

CRAB BISQUE
Serves 4

500 ml/1 pt fish stock
1 can (300 ml) condensed tomato soup
1 can (200 g) crabmeat
4 tablespoons single cream
Salt, pepper

+ + +

2 tablespoons dry sherry

1. Combine the fish stock, soup, crabmeat, cream, salt and pepper in a suitable serving bowl.

To serve without freezing
Put in the microwave oven and switch on for 4½ to 5 minutes until the soup is hot but not boiling. Stir in the sherry and serve hot.

To freeze Open-freeze in the serving bowl, then dip the base in hot water until the block loosens. Turn into a freezer bag and seal.

To serve from the freezer
Remove from bag. Put the block of soup back in the original bowl, cover and thaw by microwave. Switch on for 5 minutes. Stir, then continue cooking until the soup is thoroughly reheated. Add the sherry just before serving.

SWEET CORN SOUP
Serves 4–6

Exact cooking times for this soup will depend on the temperature of the frozen ingredients. Since it is prepared with frozen foods, there is no purpose in preparing it for freezing.

150 g/6 oz frozen sweet corn
250 ml/½ pt chicken stock
750 ml/1½ pt frozen Béchamel
  sauce (page 140)
125 ml/¼ pt fresh milk
Salt, pepper
          + + +
2 tablespoons single cream

1.   Combine the sweet corn with the chicken stock in a large bowl. Cook 5 minutes.
2.   Add the Béchamel sauce, cover and cook 10 minutes, stirring occasionally.
3.   Blend in a liquidiser or press through a sieve.

4.   Stir in the milk. Cook 4 to 6 minutes until the soup reaches boiling point.
5.   Add salt and pepper to taste. Stir thoroughly and thin with a little more stock or milk if necessary, then reheat for 1 minute.

To serve   Pour into a heated soup tureen and stir in the cream.

ICED CUCUMBER SOUP
Serves 4

1 large cucumber
50 g/2 oz butter
50 g/2 oz flour
500 ml/1 pt milk
4 tablespoons chicken stock
¼ onion
Salt, pepper
          + + +
4 tablespoons single cream

1.   Peel the cucumber. Cut into chunks and blend in the liquidiser.
2.   Put the butter into a large bowl. Cook until melted, 1 minute.
3.   Stir in the flour and cook for 1 more minute.
4.   Gradually add the milk, then continue cooking for 4 minutes until the sauce thickens. Stir every ½ minute.
5.   Add the puréed cucumber, chicken stock, the piece of onion and salt and pepper to taste. Stir. Cook 5 minutes.
6.   Leave until cold before discarding the onion.

To serve without freezing
Stir the cream into the soup, then chill in the refrigerator for 1 hour before serving.

To freeze   Open-freeze in the bowl in which the soup is to be served. When frozen, dip the base of the bowl in hot water. As soon as the block loosens, transfer to a freezer bag. Seal.

To serve from the freezer
Remove from bag and place the block of soup in the original bowl. To thaw by microwave, cover and switch on for 4 to 6 minutes, stirring frequently as the block liquefies. Add a tablespoon of single cream to each portion before serving. If preferred hot, reheat before adding the cream.

LENTIL SOUP
Serves 6

The lentils may be cooked without soaking but the microwave cooking time must then be extended by 30 minutes.

200 g/8 oz red lentils
2 rashers lean bacon, rinded and
  chopped
1 small onion, chopped
1 celery stalk, chopped
15 g/½ oz butter
Black pepper, salt

1.   Wash and drain the lentils. Soak in a large bowl with 500 ml/1 pt cold water for at least 2 hours. *Do not drain.*
2.   Mix the bacon, onion and celery, and put in a dish with the butter. Cook 4 minutes, stirring occasionally. Spoon off surplus fat.
3.   Add the bacon and vegetables to the lentils together with 500 ml/1 pt water (or stock). Cover and cook 20 minutes, stirring occasionally.
4.   Blend in a liquidiser or press

Soups and Stocks

through a sieve. Add pepper and salt if necessary.

To serve without freezing
Reheat in the microwave oven for 3 to 4 minutes (1½ minutes for a single portion).

To freeze Leave to cool. Open freeze in individual bowls. Dip bases in hot water until the blocks loosen, then turn into freezer bags and seal.

To serve from the freezer
Remove blocks from bags and put back in original bowls. Cover and thaw by microwave. Switch on for 5 minutes. Stir, then continue cooking until thoroughly reheated.

MULLIGATAWNY
Serves 6

50 g/2 oz margarine
1 onion, chopped
1 garlic clove, crushed
25 g/1 oz flour
2 teaspoons curry powder
1 tablespoon tomato purée
1 litre/1¾ pt beef stock
1 small dessert apple, chopped
2 teaspoons sweet pickle
25 g/1 oz cornflour
Salt, pepper

+ + +

6 tablespoons cooked rice

1. Put the margarine, onion and garlic in a large bowl. Cook 3 minutes. Stir.
2. Blend in the flour and curry powder. Cook 1 minute, stirring after ½ minute
3. Add the tomato purée. Then gradually stir in half of the stock. Cook 4 minutes, stirring frequently.
4. Add the chopped apple, pickle and the cornflour blended

with a little cold water. Stir, then add the remaining stock. Cook 5 minutes.
5. Press the soup through a sieve into a bowl. Season to taste with salt and pepper.

To serve without freezing
Serve chilled. Or reheat in the microwave oven for 3 to 4 minutes (1½ minutes for a single portion). Stir a spoonful of rice into each bowl.

To freeze Leave soup until cold. Open-freeze in individual bowls, then dip bases in hot water until the blocks loosen. Turn into freezer bags. Seal.

To serve from the freezer
Remove from bags and place the blocks of soup in their original bowls. Cover and thaw by microwave. Switch on for 5 minutes, stirring frequently as the blocks liquefy. Serve chilled or continue cooking until thoroughly reheated. Stir a tablespoon of cooked rice into each bowl and serve.

MUSHROOM SOUP
Serves 4

50 g/2 oz margarine
50 g/2 oz flour
1 litre/1¾ pt chicken stock
100 g/4 oz button mushrooms, finely chopped
Bouquet garni
Salt, pepper

+ + +

2 teaspoons flour
125 ml/¼ pt milk

1. Put the margarine in a large bowl. Cook until melted, 1 minute.
2. Blend in the flour. Cook ½ minute.

3. Gradually stir in the stock. Cook 4 minutes, stirring frequently.
4. Add mushrooms, *bouquet garni*, and salt and pepper to taste. Cook 5 minutes, stirring occasionally.
5. Remove the *bouquet garni* and press the soup through a sieve into a bowl.

To serve without freezing
Reheat the soup in the microwave oven for 3 to 4 minutes (1½ minutes for a single portion).

To freeze Blend 2 teaspoons flour with the milk. Stir into the soup. Open-freeze in individual bowls, then dip the bases in hot water until the blocks loosen. Turn into freezer bags. Seal.

To serve from the freezer
Remove from bags and place the blocks of soup in the original bowls. To thaw by microwave, cover and switch on for 4 minutes. Stir, then continue cooking, uncovered, until thoroughly reheated. Correct seasoning and serve.

FRENCH ONION SOUP
Serves 4

450 g/1 lb large onions, thinly sliced
50 g/2 oz butter
1 litre/1¾ pt beef stock
Salt, pepper

+ + +

4 slices French bread
Butter for spreading
75 g/3 oz Gruyère cheese, grated
Parmesan cheese, grated

1. Combine the onions and butter in a large bowl and cook

10 minutes, stirring occasionally.

2. Add stock, salt and pepper, and cook 10 minutes.

To serve without freezing
Toast bread slices on one side and spread the untoasted side with butter. Sprinkle with Gruyère cheese and grill until melted. Reheat the soup in the microwave oven for 2 to 3 minutes, then pour into individual bowls. Float a slice of toast on each portion and sprinkle with grated Parmesan.

To freeze Cool rapidly. Open freeze in a bowl, then dip base of bowl in hot water until the block loosens. Turn into a freezer bag and seal.

To serve from the freezer
Remove from bag and put the block of soup in the original bowl. Cover and thaw by microwave. Switch on for 8 minutes. Stir, then continue cooking until the soup is thoroughly reheated. Toast bread on one side and spread the untoasted side with butter. Sprinkle this side with Gruyère cheese and toast until melted. Pour soup into individual bowls. Float the toast on top. Serve the Parmesan cheese separately.

ONION AND TOMATO SOUP
Serves 8

50 g/2 oz butter
450 g/1 lb onions, thinly sliced
500 ml/1 pt beef stock
1 small can (200 g) tomatoes
½ teaspoon dried basil
Salt
Coarsely ground black pepper
2 teaspoons cornflour

1. Put the butter in a large bowl. Cook 1 minute.
2. Add the onions and stir. Cook 4 minutes.
3. Add all the other ingredients except the cornflour and bring to the boil, approximately 4 minutes. Then continue cooking for 10 minutes.
4. Blend the cornflour with 2 tablespoons cold water, stir into the soup and cook for a further 5 minutes.

To serve without freezing
Pour into a tureen or ladle into individual bowls.

To freeze Cool and open freeze in the bowls in which the soup is to be served. When frozen, dip bases in hot water and as soon as the blocks loosen, transfer them to freezer bags. Seal.

To serve from the freezer
Remove from bags and place the blocks of soup in their original bowls. To thaw by microwave, cover and switch on for 6 to 8 minutes, stirring as soon as bubbles appear around the edge.

SCOTCH BROTH
Serves 4

200 g/8 oz raw minced lamb
1 carrot, grated
1 small turnip, grated
1 leek, thinly sliced
1 tablespoon finely chopped parsley
2 tablespoons pearl barley
750 ml/1½ pt hot beef stock
Salt, pepper

+ + +

1–2 tablespoons single cream

1. Put all the ingredients into a

large bowl. Cover loosely and cook 35 minutes.

To serve without freezing
Ladle into individual bowls and serve garnished with a little cream.

To freeze Cool rapidly. Open freeze in individual bowls. When frozen, dip bases in hot water until the blocks loosen, then turn into freezer bags. Seal.

To serve from the freezer
Remove from bags and place the blocks of soup in their original bowls. To thaw by microwave, cover and switch on for 6 to 8 minutes, stirring as soon as bubbles appear around the edge. Just before serving, stir a little cream into each bowl.

CREAM OF SPINACH SOUP
Serves 6–8

When making soup it is easier to use frozen spinach, so there is no purpose in freezing this soup after preparation

1 packet (400 g) frozen chopped spinach
50 g/2 oz butter
50 g/2 oz flour
500 ml/1 pt milk
250 ml/½ pt hot chicken stock
Salt, pepper

+ + +

4 tablespoons sour cream

1. Put the butter into a large bowl. Cook until melted, 1 minute.
2. Blend in the flour and cook ½ minute.
3. Gradually add the milk and cook 3 minutes, stirring frequently.

4. Stir in the chicken stock, salt and pepper.
5. Add the block of spinach, cover and cook 10 minutes, stirring occasionally.
6. Blend the soup in a liquidiser or press through a sieve into a bowl.

To serve Reheat in the microwave oven for 3 to 4 minutes (1½ minutes for a single portion). Stir and pour into individual bowls, adding 1 tablespoon sour cream to each portion.

STILTON SOUP
Serves 4

450 g/1 lb potatoes, peeled and grated
1 onion, grated
100 g/4 oz Stilton or other blue cheese, crumbled
1 can (400 ml) consommé
125 ml/¼ pt single cream

+ + +

16 to 20 croûtons (page 44)

1. Combine the potatoes and onion in a large bowl and add just enough water to cover. Cover and cook 10 minutes.
2. Blend in a liquidiser and make up to 1 litre/1¾ pt with water.
3. Combine with the cheese and consommé. Cook 3 to 4 minutes until the cheese has just melted. Stir and add the cream.

To serve without freezing
Pour into individual heated bowls and garnish with croûtons.

To freeze Cool the soup. Pour into individual bowls. Open freeze, then dip bases in hot

water until blocks loosen. Turn into freezer bags and seal.

To serve from the freezer
Remove from bags and put each block in one of the original bowls. Cover. To thaw by microwave, switch on for 4 minutes. Stir and continue cooking until thoroughly reheated. Serve with croûtons.

CREAM OF TOMATO SOUP
Serves 6

50 g/2 oz margarine
1 rasher bacon, rinded and chopped
1 onion, finely chopped
50 g/2 oz flour
1 litre/1¾ pt beef stock
1 small can (75 g) tomato purée
Bouquet garni
Salt, pepper

+ + +

6 tablespoons single cream

+ + +

1 teaspoon flour

1. Put the margarine, bacon and onion in a large bowl. Cook 3 minutes, stirring occasionally.
2. Blend in the flour. Cook ½ minute.
3. Gradually add 500 ml/1 pt stock and the tomato purée. Mix thoroughly. Cook 4 minutes, stirring every minute.
4. Add *bouquet garni* and the remaining stock. Season with salt and pepper. Cook 5 minutes.
5. Leave to rest for ½ hour, then remove the *bouquet garni* and press the soup through a sieve.

To serve without freezing
Reheat in the microwave oven

for 3 to 4 minutes (1½ minutes for a single portion). Stir a tablespoon of cream into each bowl just before serving, and accompany with croûtons (page 44) if desired.

To freeze Cool the soup. Blend flour with 1 tablespoon cold water. Stir into the soup. Open freeze in individual bowls, then dip bases in hot water until the blocks loosen. Turn into freezer bags. Seal.

To serve from the freezer
Remove from bags and place the blocks of soup in their original bowls. To thaw by microwave, cover and switch on for 5 minutes, stirring frequently as the soup liquefies. Continue cooking until thoroughly reheated. Stir 1 tablespoon cream into each bowl and serve with croûtons (page 44) if desired.

VICHYSSOISE
Serves 4

4 small leeks, white parts only, chopped
1 onion, minced
25 g/1 oz butter
1 large potato, peeled and diced
1 litre/1¾ pt hot chicken stock
1 tablespoon finely chopped parsley
Salt, pepper

+ + +

4 tablespoons single cream
1 tablespoon lemon juice
2 tablespoons finely chopped chives

1. Put the leeks, onion and butter in a large bowl. Cook 3 minutes, stirring occasionally.
2. Add potato, chicken stock,

parsley, salt and pepper. Bring to the boil and cook 10 minutes.
3. Blend in a liquidiser or press through a sieve into a bowl.

To serve without freezing
Chill in the refrigerator for at least 1 hour. Mix the cream and lemon juice together, and stir into the soup. Garnish each portion with chives.

To freeze Cool and pour into individual bowls. Open freeze. Dip bases in hot water until the blocks loosen, then turn into freezer bags. Seal.

To serve from the freezer
Remove from bags and put the blocks of soup back in their original bowls. Cover and thaw by microwave. Switch on for 4 minutes, stir, then leave at room temperature until the blocks have melted. Mix the cream and lemon juice together. Stir a spoonful into each bowl and sprinkle with chives.

BEEF STOCK

450 g/1 lb freshly bought marrow bones
1 bay leaf
Salt, pepper

1. Ask the butcher to chop up the bones.
2. Wash the bones in cold water and put them in a large pan with the bay leaf, salt, pepper and 1 litre/1¾ pt cold water.
3. Cover, bring to the boil and simmer for 2 hours, or until the liquid is reduced by a quarter.
4. Strain and cool the stock, then chill in the refrigerator.
5. Remove any fat from the surface when it has solidified. Makes about 750 ml/1¼ pt.

CHICKEN STOCK

Carcass of 1 roast chicken or chicken bones and flesh, raw or cooked
1 bay leaf
Salt, pepper

1. Put the ingredients in a large saucepan with 1 litre/1¾ pt cold water.
2. Bring to the boil. Lower heat and simmer, covered, for 2 hours, or until the liquid is reduced by a quarter.
3. Strain, cool and chill in the refrigerator until the fat has solidified on the surface.
4. Remove the fat and use the stock as required. Makes about 750 ml/1¼ pt.

VEGETABLE STOCK

1 kg/2¼ lb mixed vegetables: carrots, celery, celeriac, spinach, turnip, cauliflower, onion, tomatoes
2 teaspoons salt
2 bay leaves

1. Scrub the vegetables clean but do not peel them. Dice the vegetables.
2. Put vegetables in a large pan with the salt and bay leaves, and cover with 1 litre/1¾ pt cold water.
3. Bring to the boil and simmer for 2 hours, or until the liquid is reduced by a quarter, skimming as necessary.
4. Strain through a sieve and press gently with a wooden spoon to extract as much liquid as possible. Discard the pulp. Makes about 750 ml/1¼ pt.

FISH STOCK

225 g/8 oz fresh fish bones and trimmings
1 teaspoon salt
8 peppercorns
1 small onion, quartered
1 celery stalk
2 bay leaves
Pinch of dried mixed herbs

1. Put all the ingredients in a large saucepan and add 500 ml/1 pt water.
2. Bring to the boil slowly, lower heat and simmer for 15 to 20 minutes.
3. Strain and use or freeze immediately. Makes about 500 ml/1 pt.

COURT BOUILLON

1 onion, sliced
1 small carrot, thinly sliced
2 tablespoons malt vinegar
2 bay leaves
Salt, pepper

1. Put all the ingredients in a large pan with 1 litre/1¾ pt cold water.
2. Bring to the boil and simmer for 10 minutes. Cool and strain.
3. Alternatively, cook for 10 minutes in the microwave oven. Makes about 1 litre/1¾ pt.

To freeze stock When the stock is quite cold, pour it into freezer containers in the quantities required, leaving 2½ cm/1 inch headspace, and seal.

CROÛTONS
Makes enough for 18 portions

Drop a few croûtons into piping hot soup just before serving. To make them spicier, toss them with 2 teaspoons sweet paprika.

6 thick slices white bread
100 g/4 oz butter

1. Remove the crusts and cut the bread into cubes.
2. Place them in a single layer on a sheet of non-stick paper in the microwave oven. Cook 5 or 6 minutes, tossing the croûtons frequently until they are hard but not coloured.
3. Put the butter in a large bowl and cook until melted, $1\frac{1}{2}$ minutes.
4. Immediately toss the hot croûtons into the butter and mix well until all the butter is absorbed.

To serve without freezing
Drop a few croûtons into individual bowls of soup. Keep the remainder in an airtight container for a few weeks or freeze for longer storage.

To freeze Leave to cool. Pack into a freezer bag. Seal.

To serve from the freezer
Thaw the quantity required in the microwave oven. Switch on for 1 or 2 minutes. *Do not overcook.*

SOUP PUFFBALLS (CHOUX PASTRY)
Makes 50

Prepare the choux pastry and bake puffballs by microwave. Cream buns and éclairs made with the same pastry will have to be baked in a conventional oven at 220°C/425°F/Gas 7 for 25 to 35 minutes.

40 g/scant $1\frac{1}{2}$ oz plain flour
Pinch of salt
25 g/1 oz butter
1 egg

1. Sift the flour and salt together on to a sheet of paper.
2. Put the butter and 5 tablespoons water in a large bowl. Cook until the water is boiling and the butter has melted, approximately $1\frac{1}{2}$ minutes.
3. When the liquid is boiling fast, remove from the oven and toss in the flour all at once. Stir vigorously until it forms a ball and the mixture comes away from the sides of the bowl.
4. Leave to cool a few minutes.
5. Add the egg and beat thoroughly until the mixture is thick and shiny.
6. Transfer the mixture to a piping bag fitted with a 1-cm/$\frac{1}{2}$-inch plain nozzle.
7. Pipe 50 tiny dots on to a piece of non-stick paper.
8. Put the paper in the oven and cook for 7 to 8 minutes, turning the paper occasionally.

To serve without freezing
Drop a few puffballs into hot or cold soup just before serving.

To freeze Open-freeze. Pack into a freezer bag. Seal.

To serve from the freezer
Drop a few puffballs into piping hot soup. They will thaw quickly in the steaming liquid. Puffballs may be partially thawed in the microwave oven for serving with cold soup. Switch on for a few seconds only.

5 Starters

Starters

Starters, otherwise known as Hors d'Oeuvre, should be appetising, for their purpose in the meal is to stimulate the taste buds in anticipation of the main course. They should not be too filling, otherwise they will take the edge off your appetite, and should be easy to serve, so as not to take up too much of the cook's time and energy. At a formal meal, starters may be served in addition to soup.

In choosing a starter, bear the main course in mind. Heavy meals should be preceded by a light starter and the ingredients should not be repeated. For example, serving prawn tartlets before a main course meat pie would involve pastry twice over.

The microwave oven is a helpful means of preparing either hot or cold first courses. Those based on vegetables can be cooked easily without having to use a saucepan, and in most cases vegetable starters can be precooked by microwave for serving later. Stuffed vegetables will keep their shape well, and their fillings may be cooked separately if preferred. Starters to be served hot may be attractively arranged on the serving dish at preparation stage, thus eliminating the need to add the finishing touches at the last minute. Pâtés and terrines cook very quickly by microwave, so if necessary a last-minute pâté is now possible. Starters reheat very quickly, especially if they have been taken out of the freezer to thaw for at least an hour before serving. They can then be reheated by the hostess during the time it takes for the guests to be seated.

ARTICHAUTS AU BEURRE
Serves 2

This is one of the classic ways of serving artichokes hot. If you wish to serve them cold, substitute a vinaigrette sauce for the melted butter.

2 artichokes, fresh or frozen
1 tablespoon lemon juice
1 teaspoon vegetable oil
75 g/3 oz butter
Salt, pepper

1. Wash fresh artichokes thoroughly in cold water. Remove lower leaves. Snip off leaf tips and trim stems level with the base.
2. Put the artichokes in a dish. Pour in the lemon juice and oil mixed with 125 ml/¼ pt water.
3. Cover and cook 10 minutes for fresh artichokes, 7 minutes for frozen, turning them over halfway through the cooking time.
4. Leave to rest for 2 minutes. Drain thoroughly.
5. Put the butter in a jug. Cook until melted, 1 minute.
6. Season butter with salt and pepper.

To serve Pour the melted butter over the hot artichokes and serve immediately.

CREAMED ARTICHOKE HEARTS
Serves 4

Fresh cooked artichoke hearts may be substituted for canned. The heart is the soft, fleshy part left when the leaves of the artichoke have been pulled away and the fuzzy chokes have been scraped out.

1 can (400 g) artichoke hearts
25 g/1 oz butter
25 g/1 oz flour
Artichoke liquor made up to
   250 ml/½ pt with milk
Salt, pepper
2 tablespoons single cream

+ + +

1 slice ham (50 g/2 oz), chopped
2 tablespoons grated Cheddar
   cheese

+ + +

2 teaspoons flour
2 tablespoons milk

1.   Put the butter in a large
bowl and cook until melted, 1
minute.
2.   Blend in the flour and cook ½
minute.
3.   Gradually stir in the mixed
artichoke liquor and milk. Cook
2 minutes or until the sauce
thickens, stirring frequently.
4.   Add salt and pepper to
taste, and stir in the cream.

To serve without freezing
Put the artichoke hearts in a dish
and sprinkle with the ham.
Cook in the microwave oven for
3 minutes. Pour over the sauce
and reheat for ½ minute.
Sprinkle with grated cheese and
brown under the grill.

To freeze   Blend the flour with
the milk and stir into the sauce.
Arrange the artichoke hearts
and ham in a freezer container
and pour the sauce over the top.
Seal. Wrap the cheese in a twist
of freezer film. Put the container
and cheese parcel in a freezer
bag and seal.

To serve from the freezer
Remove wrappings and turn the
artichoke mixture into a dish.
Cover lightly and thaw by
microwave. Switch on for 2
minutes. Stir. Cook for a further

2 minutes, stir again, then
continue cooking until the sauce
is warmed through. Sprinkle
with grated cheese and brown
under the grill.

AUBERGINE BOATS
Serves 4

2 large aubergines
Salt
200 g/8 oz lean minced beef
2 onions, finely chopped
1 teaspoon dried basil
8 medium tomatoes, skinned
   and quartered
Pepper

+ + +

4 tablespoons fresh
   breadcrumbs
4 tablespoons grated cheese

1.   Cut the aubergines in half
lengthways. Score the cut flesh
with a sharp knife, sprinkle with
salt and leave for 1 hour.
2.   Put the minced beef and
onions in a casserole. Cook 3
minutes.
3.   Drain off any surplus fat.
4.   Add the basil and tomatoes,
and season with salt and
pepper. Cover and cook 2
minutes.
5.   Rinse the aubergines and
scoop out the flesh, leaving
shells intact.
6.   Chop the aubergine flesh
and add to the casserole. Cook 6
to 8 minutes, stirring
occasionally, until the
aubergines are soft.
7.   Pile mixture into aubergine
shells.

To serve without freezing
Sprinkle with breadcrumbs and
grated cheese, and brown under
the grill.

To freeze   Leave to cool. Wrap
boats separately in freezer film
and overwrap with freezer foil.

To serve from the freezer
Remove wrappings and arrange
the aubergine halves in a
shallow dish. To thaw by
microwave, cover and switch on
for 4 minutes. Remove cover,
sprinkle with breadcrumbs and
cheese, and brown under the
grill.

CIDER FONDUE
Serves 4

250 g/10 oz Cheddar cheese,
   grated
Salt, pepper
Garlic powder, 1 shake
250 ml/½ pt dry white cider
2 tablespoons cornflour
2 tablespoons Kirsch

+ + +

1 small French loaf

1.   Mix the cheese, salt, pepper
and garlic powder together.
Place in a dish and cover with
cider. Cook until melted, about
1½ minutes.
2.   Blend the cornflour with the
Kirsch and 4 tablespoons water.
3.   Stir into the melted cheese
and cook until creamy, about 3
minutes.

To serve without freezing
Quickly cut the bread into thick
cubes and place in a bowl in the
centre of the table. Turn the hot
fondue into a heatproof bowl
and rest on a table heater. Serve
immediately, supplying each
guest with a fondue fork to
spear the bread for dipping into
the hot fondue.

To freeze   Leave to cool in the

dish, cover with freezer film, overwrap and freeze.

To serve from the freezer
Cut the bread into thick chunks. Thaw fondue by microwave. Switch on for 1 minute, give the dish a ¼ turn, then repeat 3 times more. As soon as the fondue is thawed, turn into a heatproof dish and complete the heating over a spirit lamp, adding more cider if necessary to thin down the mixture.

CORN ON THE COB
Serves 4

The silk and outer husks should be removed before cooking fresh corn, which should have firm, cream-coloured kernels. Cook fresh corn for 4 minutes prior to freezing.

4 frozen corn cobs
50 g/2 oz butter
Salt, pepper

1. Arrange frozen corn cobs in two layers in a deep casserole.
2. Dot with butter and cover tightly. Cook for 10 to 12 minutes, giving the dish a ¼ turn every 2½ minutes.
3. Season with salt and pepper and serve.

COURGETTES PROVENÇAL
Serves 6

450 g/1 lb small courgettes
2 large onions, sliced
½ garlic clove, crushed
2 tablespoons vegetable oil
1 large can (400 g) tomatoes
Salt, pepper

2 tablespoons grated Parmesan cheese

+ + +

1 tablespoon grated Parmesan cheese

1. Put the onions and garlic in serving dish with the oil and cook 3 minutes.
2. Top and tail the courgettes, and slice thinly. Add to the dish. Cover and cook 3 minutes.
3. Add the tomatoes, salt, pepper and cheese.

To serve without freezing
Cook for a further 2½ minutes, then sprinkle with the remaining Parmesan and brown under the grill.

To freeze Cover the dish with freezer film and overwrap with freezer foil.

To serve from the freezer
Remove the foil wrapping but leave the plastic film covering. Thaw by microwave. Switch on for 8 minutes, giving the dish a ¼ turn every 2 minutes. Sprinkle with remaining cheese and brown under the grill.

SCRAMBLED EGGS WITH ONIONS AND TOMATOES
Serves 4

Four eggs and 4 tablespoons milk will take 2½ minutes to cook by microwave, 2 eggs and 2 tablespoons milk will take 1¼ minutes.

1 small onion, finely chopped
2 tablespoons vegetable oil
550 g/1¼ lb tomatoes, skinned and deseeded
Salt, pepper

25 g/1 oz butter
8 eggs
8 tablespoons milk

+ + +

1 tablespoon finely chopped parsley

1. Put the onion and oil in a dish. Cook 3 minutes.
2. Chop the tomatoes finely and stir in. Cook 5 minutes, stirring occasionally. Add salt and pepper to taste.
3. Put the butter in a large bowl. Cook until melted, 1 minute.
4. Add the eggs and milk, and beat lightly. Cook 2½ minutes, stir, then cook for a further 1½ minutes. Stir. Season to taste.

To serve Place a portion of egg on each warmed plate. Spoon the tomato mixture in the centre. Sprinkle with parsley.

FARMER'S TERRINE
Serves 6

450 g/1 lb belly pork
200 g/8 oz pigs' liver
1 small onion
2–3 sprigs parsley
2 tablespoons flour
1 garlic clove, crushed
Salt, pepper
1 egg, beaten
6 rashers streaky bacon, rinded

1. Put the pork, liver, onion and parsley through a mincer, using the fine disc.
2. Blend in the flour and garlic, and season with salt and pepper. Bind with the beaten egg.
3. Stretch bacon rashers out thinly with the side of a knife blade.
4. Line the base and sides of a

22½ by 12½ cm/9 by 5 inch dish with bacon rashers.

5. Fill with the meat mixture and press down well.

6. Cover with plastic film and cook 8 minutes, giving the dish a ¼ turn every 2 minutes. Pour off any surplus fat.

To serve without freezing
Place a heavy weight on top of the plastic film and leave the terrine to cool in the dish. As soon as it is cool, put in the refrigerator. Leave the weight on top until just before serving. Turn out on to a dish and slice with a sharp knife. Serve with thin triangles of toast and pats of butter.

To freeze Leave to cool. Cover with freezer film and overwrap with freezer foil.

To serve from the freezer
Remove wrappings and put the terrine on a serving dish. Thaw by microwave. Switch on for 5 minutes. Leave to thaw completely in the refrigerator. Slice with a sharp knife and serve.

4 C FLASH COOKED SALAD
Serves 6

1 cucumber
¼ red cabbage
2 large carrots
1 celery heart
Salt
6 tablespoons wine vinegar
4 tablespoons vegetable oil
1 teaspoon freshly ground black pepper
1 teaspoon sugar
1 tablespoon finely chopped parsley

1. Wash the cucumber and cabbage. Top and tail and scrape the carrots. Remove the strings from the celery.

2. Shred all the vegetables finely, using an electric shredder if available.

3. Sprinkle liberally with salt and leave for 1 hour.

4. Rinse and shake away any surplus water.

5. Mix the vinegar, oil, pepper, sugar and parsley together, and mix into the vegetables. Cover and cook 4 minutes, stirring frequently.

To serve without freezing
Leave to cool, but do not chill.

To freeze Turn into a freezer container and seal.

To serve from the freezer
Put in a serving dish. Cover and thaw by microwave. Switch on for 4 minutes, stirring occasionally. Leave at room temperature until completely thawed.

BAKED GRAPEFRUIT
Serves 4

Any whole unused grapefruit can be deep frozen successfully. They need only be placed in a freezer bag. No other preparation is necessary.

2 frozen grapefruit
2 tablespoons Orange Velvet Sauce (page 155)
1 tablespoon chopped fresh mint

1. Partially thaw the grapefruit in the microwave oven for 2 minutes.

2. Halve the grapefruit and segment them. Place the

segments in suitable dishes or saucers.

3. Pour the sauce over each serving and cook 3 to 4 minutes.

4. Sprinkle with the mint and serve hot.

HAM MOUSSE
Serves 4–6

Evaporated milk whips more readily if it has been chilled in the refrigerator for 12 hours.

150 g/6 oz cooked ham, minced
125 ml/¼ pt Béchamel sauce (page 140), coating consistency
2 eggs
125 ml/¼ pt chicken stock
25 g/1 oz powdered gelatine
½ teaspoon made English mustard
125 ml/¼ pt evaporated milk

+ + +

1 tablespoon shredded sweet red pepper

1. Put the sauce in a jug and warm in the microwave oven for ½ minute.

2. Separate the eggs and beat the yolks into the sauce.

3. Heat the chicken stock in the microwave oven for 1 minute. Sprinkle with the gelatine and stir until dissolved.

4. Mix the sauce, stock, ham and mustard together. Leave until cold but not set.

5. Whisk the evaporated milk and fold in.

6. Beat the egg whites until stiff but not dry. Stir 1 tablespoon into the ham mixture, then fold in the remainder.

7. Pour into individual soufflé dishes.

To serve without freezing
Garnish with shredded red pepper and serve with melba toast and pats of butter.

To freeze Open-freeze. Overwrap each dish with freezer foil.

To serve from the freezer
Remove the foil. Thaw by microwave. Arrange, well spaced out, in the microwave oven. Switch on for 1 minute, then leave to thaw at room temperature. Garnish with shredded red pepper and serve with melba toast and pats of butter.

KIPPER PÂTÉ
Serves 6

Serve this pâté with melba toast and butter cylinders. To make butter cylinders, cut through a block of butter with an apple corer dipped in hot water.

3 pairs kippers, boned
125 g/5 oz butter
2 tablespoons double cream
2 tablespoons lemon juice
1 teaspoon paprika
Freshly ground black pepper

+ + +

Black olives
Lemon slices

1. Arrange the kippers in a shallow dish. Cover with plastic film and cook 6 minutes.
2. Remove the skin and any remaining bones from the fish and leave to cool.
3. Flake the fish, then mash until smooth with the butter, cream, lemon juice, paprika and pepper to taste.

To serve without freezing
Pile into a dish and decorate with black olives and thin slices of lemon.

To freeze Pack into a freezer container, cover with plastic film. Seal.

To serve from the freezer
Remove wrapping and place pâté in a serving dish. Thaw by microwave. Switch on for 1 minute, then leave to thaw out completely in the refrigerator. Garnish with black olives and thin slices of lemon.

LEEK FLAN
Serves 4

Leeks are at their best from September to April. It is essential that the pastry flan case has no cracks for the filling to seep through.

150 g/6 oz white parts of leek,
    sliced and washed
15 g/½ oz butter
1 egg
125 ml/¼ pt milk
1 tablespoon finely grated
    Cheddar cheese
White pepper
15–cm/6–inch pastry case, fully
    baked

1. Put the leeks and butter in a dish, add 4 tablespoons water, cover with plastic film and cook 5 minutes. Drain.
2. Beat the egg and milk together.
3. Add the grated cheese, pepper and leeks.
4. Stand the pastry case on a plate and fill with the mixture.
5. Cook 4 minutes, giving the dish a ½ turn after 2 minutes.

To serve without freezing
Leave to cool and serve with a green salad.

To freeze Let the flan cool at room temperature. Cover the flan and plate with plastic film and freeze rapidly. Remove the flan from the plate, overwrap with two sheets of foil and replace in the freezer on a flat surface.

To serve from the freezer
Remove wrappings, stand the flan on a plate and thaw by microwave. Switch on for ½ minute, rest for 2 minutes, give the plate a ¼ turn, then repeat resting and thawing until completely thawed.
To serve hot, switch on for a further 2 minutes.

MUSHROOM VOL-AU-VENTS
Serves 2–3

It may be necessary to reshape vol-au-vent cases while they are cooking, as they tend to topple over as they rise, but this in no way spoils the results. Overcooking will cause burning inside the pastry.

Six 7½-cm/3-inch frozen
    vol-au-vent cases
25 g/1 oz butter
25 g/1 oz flour
125 ml/¼ pt milk
100 g/4 oz frozen button
    mushrooms
2 teaspoons mushroom ketchup
Salt, pepper

1. Leave the vol-au-vent cases at room temperature until they begin to thaw (30 minutes).
2. Cook 3 at a time close together on the base of the

microwave oven for 2 or 3 minutes, or until the cases stop quivering.

3. Put the butter in a bowl and cook until melted, 1 minute.

4. Blend in the flour. Cook ½ minute.

5. Gradually stir in the milk. Cook 1½ minutes, stirring occasionally.

6. Add the mushrooms, ketchup, salt and pepper. Cook 4 minutes, stirring occasionally.

7. Fill vol-au-vent cases and brown under the grill if desired. Serve immediately.

ONION COSIES
Serves 2

Add salt sparingly since Parmesan cheese tends to be salty.

450 g/1 lb potatoes, peeled and cubed
Salt
2 Spanish onions, peeled
25 g/1 oz butter
2 tablespoons grated Parmesan cheese
Pepper
½–1 beaten egg
Flour
75 g/3 oz almonds, chopped

+ + +

250 ml/½ pt Parsley sauce (page 142)

1. Put the potatoes in a casserole, cover with water and salt lightly. Cover with plastic film and cook 10 to 12 minutes, stirring occasionally. Drain.

2. Prick the onions with a fork and put them in an empty dish. Cover with plastic film. Cook 5 minutes, turning the dish once during cooking. Test for cooking with a sharp knife. Leave to cool.

3. Mash the potatoes with the butter, cheese and pepper. Bind with the beaten egg.

4. With floured hands, mould half of the mashed potatoes round each onion so that it is completely enclosed.

5. Gently roll the onion parcels in the chopped almonds. Brown under the grill.

To serve without freezing
Heat the sauce in a jug or sauceboat in the microwave oven for 2 minutes. Stir. Serve the onions on warmed plates and hand the sauce separately.

To freeze Wrap onions carefully in freezer film. Overwrap, taking care not to squash them. Freeze the sauce separately in a rigid container.

To serve from the freezer
Remove wrappings. Thaw by microwave. Switch on for 2 to 3 minutes. Leave to stand for 5 minutes while thawing the sauce, then continue cooking until thoroughly reheated. To thaw the sauce in the microwave oven, switch on for 5 minutes, break up the lumps with a fork, then continue cooking until thoroughly reheated. Stir well before serving.

PÂTÉ DE FOIE AU COGNAC
Serves 4

You may hear a popping sound as the livers cook in the microwave oven – this is quite normal with any liver dish.

50 g/2 oz butter
½ bunch spring onions, white parts only
250 g/10 oz chicken livers

2 tablespoons brandy
Pinch of dried mixed herbs
Salt, pepper
250 g/10 oz cooked chicken, finely minced

+ + +

Watercress leaves

1. Put the butter in a suitable dish. Cook until melted, 1 minute.

2. Add the chopped spring onions and cook 1 minute longer.

3. Add the chicken livers. Toss.

4. Add the brandy, herbs and seasoning. Cover and cook 4 minutes. Stir well and cook for another 4 minutes.

5. Blend a small quantity at a time in a liquidiser or press through a fine sieve.

6. Beat in the minced chicken.

To serve without freezing
Divide the pâté between 4 ramekin dishes and press down well. Cover with foil and refrigerate for 3 to 4 hours. Remove the foil and garnish each dish with watercress leaves.

To freeze Line 4 ramekin dishes with foil, fill with the liver pâté, cover with foil and overwrap. When frozen, the pâté can be removed from the dishes and wrapped in foil so that the dishes can be re-used.

To serve from the freezer
Unwrap the foil parcels. Replace the pâté in the ramekins. Thaw by microwave. Switch on for 1 minute per dish (4 minutes for 4 dishes), then leave in the refrigerator until completely thawed. Garnish with watercress leaves.

SAVOURY PRAWN SLICE
Serves 4

To make a flan ring suitable for use in a microwave oven, cut a piece of stiff card 60 cm/24 inches long and fix the ends with freezer tape.

Pastry

150 g/6 oz plain flour
1 teaspoon salt
50 g/2 oz soft margarine
50 g/2 oz grated Cheddar cheese
½ teaspoon dry mustard
1 tablespoon beaten egg
1–2 tablespoons milk

Filling

2 eggs
125 ml/¼ pt milk
100 g/4 oz shelled, cooked prawns
1 small onion, grated
1 small green pepper, deseeded and finely chopped
2 tomatoes, skinned and chopped
50 g/2 oz frozen peas
Salt, pepper
2 tablespoons grated Cheddar cheese

1. Sift the flour and salt together, and rub in the margarine.
2. Stir in the grated cheese and mustard, and mix to a dough with the beaten egg and a little milk.
3. Wrap and chill in the refrigerator.
4. Put a flan ring 18 cm/7 inches in diameter on a plate. Roll the pastry to fit, cover with a piece of kitchen paper and stand a 15 cm/6 inch plate on top. Cook 3 minutes. Remove the plate and paper.
5. Beat the eggs and milk together. Add the prawns and

vegetables, and season with salt and pepper.
6. Pour into the pastry flan and sprinkle with the grated cheese. Cook 4 minutes, giving the dish a ¼ turn every minute.

To serve without freezing
Remove the flan ring and carefully transfer the flan to a serving dish.

To freeze Leave to cool. Open freeze, then wrap in freezer film and overwrap with foil.

To serve from the freezer
Remove wrappings. Thaw by microwave. Switch on for 2 minutes, giving the dish a ¼ turn every ½ minute. Test, then continue cooking if necessary until thoroughly reheated, taking care not to overcook.

PRAWN TARTLETS
Makes 18 tartlets

Pastry

75 g/3 oz cream cheese
2 tablespoons double cream
125 g/5 oz butter
150 g/6 oz flour
½ teaspoon salt

Filling

200 ml/8 fl oz double cream
2 eggs, beaten
200 g/8 oz cooked and shelled prawns
75 g/3 oz Cheddar cheese, grated
1 garlic clove, crushed
1 teaspoon dried marjoram
Salt, pepper

1. Beat the cream cheese, cream and butter together. Sift the flour and salt together, and

gradually stir them in to make a dough. Roll into a ball and wrap in plastic film. Chill for 2 hours.
2. Roll out and line 18 patty tins. Prick well and bake blind in a pre-heated (conventional) 180°C/350°F/Gas 4 oven for 20 minutes. Leave to cool before turning out.
3. Mix the filling ingredients together and divide between the baked patty cases.
4. Cook in the microwave oven, 4 at a time, for 2 minutes.

To serve without freezing
Leave tartlets to cool or, if serving hot, keep the tartlets in a warming drawer or in the conventional oven set at 100°C/200°F/Gas 2, until all are cooked.

To freeze Layer tartlets between sheets of greaseproof paper in a shallow freezer container. Seal.

To serve from the freezer
Remove from the freezer container and thaw by microwave, reheating 4 at a time, well spaced out, for 2 minutes. If serving hot, continue cooking for 1 more minute, until heated through. Keep warm in a conventional oven until all tartlets are reheated.

SPINACH TART
Serves 4–6

The three parts of this recipe can be prepared and frozen separately, then combined later. Prepare the pastry, freeze it, then cook before adding the filling. Prepare the sauce, adding 1 teaspoon of flour blended with 1 tablespoon cold water, and freeze. Store a block of spinach in the freezer.

Pastry

150 g/6 oz plain flour
½ teaspoon salt
75 g/3 oz soft margarine
1½–2 tablespoons cold milk

Filling

25 g/1 oz butter
25 g/1 oz flour
250 ml/½ pt milk
2 tablespoons grated cheese
Salt, pepper
150 g/6 oz frozen chopped
   spinach

1. Sift the flour and salt together, rub in the margarine and add sufficient milk to bind.
2. Roll the pastry out and line a round dish 20 cm/8 inches in diameter. Cover with a piece of absorbent paper and stand a 15-cm/6-inch plate on top. Cook 3 minutes. Remove the plate and paper.
3. Put the butter in a bowl. Cook until melted, 1 minute.
4. Blend in the flour. Cook ½ minute.
5. Gradually add the milk and cook 3 minutes, stirring frequently. Add the grated cheese and season with salt and pepper.
6. Put the spinach in the microwave oven in its package, provided that this is not a metallic one. Cook 4 to 5 minutes.
7. Blend the spinach with the sauce and pour into the pastry case.

To serve without freezing
Serve straight from the dish and cut into 4 to 6 wedges. Serve hot or leave to cool.

To freeze Cover with freezer film and overwrap with freezer foil, taking care not to crush the pastry.

To serve from the freezer
Remove wrappings. Thaw by microwave. Switch on for 4 minutes, giving the dish a ¼ turn every minute. Then continue cooking if necessary until quite thawed out. Serve hot or cold.

SUCCOTASH
Serves 3–4

Lima beans (fresh butter beans) can replace broad beans when obtainable. Serve as a starter or as a vegetable. The dish may also be sprinkled with breadcrumbs and grated cheese, and browned under the grill.

200 g/8 oz frozen broad beans
200 g/8 oz frozen sweet corn
50 g/2 oz butter
½ teaspoon paprika
Salt

+ + +

125 ml/¼ pt cream

1. Put beans in a casserole and add 4 tablespoons water. Cover and cook 6 minutes. Drain and chop roughly.
2. Return the beans to the casserole with the sweet corn, butter, paprika and salt. Cook uncovered for 6 minutes. Leave to rest for 5 minutes to allow the residual heat to complete the cooking.

To serve Stir in the cream and adjust seasoning before serving.

STUFFED VINE LEAVES
Serves 4–6

16 fresh or canned vine leaves
450 g/1 lb minced lean beef
100 g/4 oz short-grain rice
1 onion, finely chopped
Salt, pepper
1 tablespoon vegetable oil
15 g/½ oz butter

1. If using fresh vine leaves, blanch them, rinse in cold water and drain thoroughly. Rinse and drain canned vine leaves.
2. Mix together the beef, rice, onion, salt, pepper and oil.
3. Divide the mixture between the leaves and roll up as follows: fold the stem end over the filling, then fold in the sides and roll up tightly.
4. Pack the rolls tightly side by side in a large dish and dot with butter.
5. Cover with 750 ml/1½ pt boiling water and cook uncovered for 15 minutes, or until the water is absorbed.

To serve without freezing
Leave until completely cold. Serve 3 to 4 rolls per portion.

To freeze Cool rapidly. Wrap carefully in freezer film, making sure that the rolls are not touching one another, and overwrap with freezer foil.

To serve from the freezer
Remove the foil and thaw by microwave in the film wrapping. Switch on for 4 minutes, giving the package a ¼ turn every minute. Leave to rest for 5 minutes, then complete thawing in the refrigerator.

TUNA FLAN
Serves 4–6

Pastry

150 g/6 oz plain flour
½ teaspoon salt
75 g/3 oz soft margarine
1½–2 tablespoons cold milk

Filling

25 g/1 oz butter
25 g/1 oz flour
250 ml/½ pt milk
Salt, pepper
1 can (200 g) tuna fish, flaked
2 tablespoons frozen peas,
  cooked
4 tablespoons grated Cheddar
  cheese
2 tablespoons fresh white
  breadcrumbs

1. Sift the flour and salt
together, rub in the margarine
and add enough milk to make a
dough.
2. Roll out the pastry and line a
round flan dish 20 cm/8 inches
in diameter with it. Cover with a
piece of absorbent paper and
stand a 15-cm/6-inch plate on
top. Cook 3 minutes. Remove
the plate and paper.
3. To make the filling, put the
butter in a bowl and cook until
melted, 1 minute.
4. Blend in the flour and cook ½
minute.
5. Gradually add the milk and
cook 3 minutes, stirring
frequently. Season with salt and
pepper.
6. Stir in the tuna fish, peas
and 2 tablespoons cheese.
7. Turn the mixture into the
pastry case, sprinkle the
remaining cheese and crumbs
on top, and brown under the
grill.

To serve without freezing
Serve the flan straight from the
dish, cut into 4 or 6 wedges.

To freeze Cool rapidly. Freeze
in the dish and cover with
freezer foil.

To serve from the freezer
Remove foil wrapping. Thaw by
microwave. To serve hot, switch
on for 4 minutes, giving the dish
a ¼ turn every minute. If the flan
is to be served cold, thaw by
microwave for 2 minutes only.

HOT VERMICELLI COCKTAIL
Serves 4

To make a lemon butterfly, cut
thin slices of lemon and remove
a v-shaped wedge from each
side.

200 g/8 oz vermicelli
Salt
1 small can (200 g) tomatoes
1 small can (200 g) tuna
1 tablespoon finely chopped
  parsley
Pepper

+ + +

4 tablespoons thick mayonnaise
4 lemon butterflies (see above)

1. Put the vermicelli in a large
casserole. Pour over 1 litre/1¾ pt
boiling water and add 1
teaspoon salt. Cook 6 minutes.
Stir. Cover the casserole and
leave for 8 minutes. Drain.
2. Rub the contents of the can
of tomatoes through a sieve into
a bowl.
3. Drain the tuna, reserving 1
tablespoon of the oil. Remove
any stray pieces of skin and flake
the fish.

4. Mix together the tomato
purée, tuna, reserved oil and
parsley, and season with salt
and pepper.
5. Combine the vermicelli with
the mixture and divide between
individual stemmed wine
glasses.

To serve without freezing
Reheat in the microwave oven
for 2 minutes. Just before
serving, top each glass with a
spoonful of mayonnaise and
decorate with a lemon butterfly.

To freeze Cover each glass
with freezer film.

To serve from the freezer To
thaw by microwave, put the
glasses, well spaced out, on the
base of the microwave oven.
Switch on for 5 minutes. Leave
to rest for 5 minutes. Remove
film, stir, then continue cooking
until thoroughly reheated. Top
each glass with a spoonful of
mayonnaise and decorate with a
lemon butterfly.

6 Fish and Shellfish

Fish and Shellfish

I can confidently claim that the microwave oven cooks fish better than any other method. Maximum flavour is retained because it cooks in its own juices. However, care must be taken not to overcook it, otherwise it will become tough and dry. The oven should be switched off as soon as the flesh can be flaked with a fork. If the fish is to be reheated, leave it slightly undercooked to allow for the further time it will spend in the oven.

Arrange the fish in the oven so that its depth is as uniform as possible. Thicker parts should be turned towards the outside of the oven. If no other ingredients are to be added, it will take 4 minutes to cook 450 g/1 lb fish. If other ingredients are added, the total weight should be used for calculating the cooking time. A plaice fillet takes about 1 minute, but the exact time will depend on the thickness and 'density' of the flesh. Covering the fish with plastic film will shorten the cooking time.

If flat fish, such as plaice, is buttered before cooking, the butter should be spread over the entire surface, rather than dabbed on. This is because the parts of the fish shielded by dabs of butter would not cook as quickly as the unbuttered flesh. When cooking whole round fish, score the skin with a knife to prevent spattering.

All shellfish may be cooked by microwave, either shelled or cooked and served in the shell. There is no need to allow extra cooking time for the shell.

Fish is a high-protein food and the value is not lost during freezing. It can be cooked by microwave from its frozen state, but in this case it must be turned over during cooking, otherwise the outside will be done before the inside has thawed out.

For best results, frozen fish should be thawed before cooking, but take care not to overthaw it or you will find that some parts have begun to cook. The best way is to give the frozen fish 15-second bursts of microwave energy, followed by 2-minute rests, repeated until it is completely thawed, then proceed according to the recipe. The rest periods give the heat a chance to spread evenly through the fish. If your oven is fitted with a defrost button, 2 to 3 minutes should be sufficient.

To separate frozen fish fillets, place the packet (first checking that the wrappings do not include foil) in the oven and switch on for 2 minutes per 450 g/1 lb fish, turning the packet over once during this time.

Use only the best-quality fresh fish for dishes which are to be deep-frozen. The storage life of prepared dishes in the freezer is 8 weeks if made with fresh or canned fish, but only 4 weeks if cooked fish or left-overs have been used. Raw white and oily fish have a storage life of 6 months.

COD IN SHRIMP AND CHEESE SAUCE
Serves 4

450 g/1 lb cod fillet
Salt, pepper
25 g/1 oz butter
25 g/1 oz flour
250 ml/½ pt milk
75 g/3 oz shrimps, shelled
1 small onion, grated
4 tablespoons grated cheese
4 tablespoons single cream

+ + +

2 tablespoons grated cheese
2 tablespoons fresh
  breadcrumbs

+ + +

2 teaspoons flour
2 tablespoons milk

1. Season the fish fillet with salt and pepper and arrange in a shallow dish. Cover and cook 2 minutes, giving the dish a ½ turn after 1 minute.
2. Put the butter in a large bowl. Cook until melted, 1 minute.
3. Blend in the flour and cook ½ minute.
4. Gradually stir in the milk. Cook 3 minutes, stirring frequently.
5. Add the shrimps, onion, cheese and cream.

To serve without freezing
Pour the sauce over the fish and cook 2½ minutes, giving the dish a ½ turn halfway through cooking. Sprinkle with a mixture of grated cheese and breadcrumbs, and brown under the grill.

To freeze Blend flour with milk and stir into the sauce. Lay the fish in a shallow container. Pour the sauce over the fish and seal the container.

To serve from the freezer
Turn into a serving dish and cover with plastic film. Thaw by microwave. Switch on for 1 minute. Leave to rest for 2 minutes. Cook for a further 3 to 4 minutes, giving the dish a $\frac{1}{4}$ turn after each minute. Mix the breadcrumbs with the cheese and sprinkle on top, then brown under the grill.

COQUILLES SAINT-JACQUES
Serves 4–6

Use the deep shell of the scallops for cooking and freezing.

8 scallops, about 50 g/2 oz each (shelled weight)
125 ml/$\frac{1}{4}$ pt white vermouth
$\frac{1}{2}$ teaspoon salt
Pepper
$\frac{1}{2}$ bay leaf
1 small onion, grated
200 g/8 oz mushrooms, sliced
50 g/2 oz butter
50 g/2 oz flour
175 ml/7 fl oz milk
125 ml/$\frac{1}{4}$ pt single cream
1 egg yolk
$\frac{1}{4}$ teaspoon lemon juice

+ + +

4 tablespoons grated Cheddar cheese

1. Combine the vermouth, salt, pepper, bay leaf and onion in a large bowl, and cook 3 minutes.
2. Add the scallops and mushrooms, cover and cook 5 minutes. Set aside. Remove the bay leaf.
3. Put the butter in a large bowl and cook until melted, 1 minute.
4. Blend in the flour. Cook $\frac{1}{2}$ minute.

5. Gradually stir in the milk and cook 4 minutes, until the sauce thickens, stirring frequently.
6. Stir in the cream and egg yolk, and add the lemon juice.
7. Add the sauce to the scallop mixture, stir well. Cook 2 minutes.

To serve without freezing
Divide the mixture between the greased scallop shells. Sprinkle with grated cheese and brown under the grill. The shells should not be too close to the grill element.

To freeze Grease scallop shells and divide the mixture between them. Cool rapidly, cover with plastic film and overwrap with freezer foil. Make sure the shells do not tip over while they are freezing.

To serve from the freezer
Remove wrappings. Thaw in the microwave oven. Switch on for 2 minutes for each shell (6 minutes for 4 shells). Sprinkle with cheese and brown under the grill.

FISH PIE
Serves 3–4

If you are in a hurry, substitute potato granules, reconstituted according to the directions on the packet, for the mashed potato.

450 g/1 lb white fish fillet, skinned
Salt, pepper
1 tablespoon lemon juice
250 ml/$\frac{1}{2}$ pt Parsley sauce (page 142)
450 g/1 lb cooked mashed potato

25 g/1 oz butter
1 egg yolk

1. Lay fish in a shallow dish and sprinkle with salt, pepper and lemon juice. Cover with plastic film. Cook 4 minutes, giving the dish a $\frac{1}{2}$ turn after 2 minutes.
2. Remove bones, and flake fish.
3. Mix with Parsley sauce and place in a shallow serving dish. Cook 2 minutes.
4. Mix mashed potato with butter, egg yolk and salt and pepper to taste.
5. Pipe over the fish mixture.

To serve without freezing
Brown the finished dish under the grill before serving.

To freeze Prepare the pie in a shallow freezer container and open freeze. Seal the container.

To serve from the freezer
Transfer the pie to a serving dish. Thaw by microwave. Cover and switch on for 4 minutes, giving the dish a $\frac{1}{4}$ turn every minute. Leave to rest for 5 minutes. Continue cooking until thoroughly reheated. Brown under the grill.

FILLETS OF HADDOCK VERONIQUE
Serves 4

A sterilised hair grip may be used for removing grape pips. Insert the rounded end lengthways into the grape, hook around the pips and pull out.

450 g/1 lb haddock fillet
2 tablespoons seasoned flour
25 g/1 oz butter

50 g/2 oz white grapes, skinned
 and depipped
2 tablespoons dry white wine

1. Skin the fish and remove
any stray bones.
2. Spread the flour on a piece
of greaseproof paper.
3. Cut the fish into portions,
coat with seasoned flour and
place in a large dish so as to
avoid any overlapping.
4. Dot the fish with butter,
arrange the grapes on top and
pour over the wine.
5. Cover with plastic film and
cook 5 minutes, turning the dish
once during cooking.

To serve without freezing
Remove the plastic film and
serve straight from the dish.

To freeze Cool rapidly,
transfer to a shallow freezer
container, cover with freezer
film and overwrap.

To serve from the freezer
Remove wrappings. Place the
fish in a dish and thaw in the
microwave oven. Switch on for $\frac{1}{2}$
minute, give the dish a $\frac{1}{2}$ turn
and cook for a further minute.
Separate the pieces of fish if
necessary, making sure that
they do not overlap. Cover with
plastic film and reheat for 2 to 3
minutes.

SOUSED HERRING
Serves 4

Mackerel, which is also an oily
fish, may be soused in the same
way as herring. Serve as a
supper dish or in small portions
as an hors d'oeuvre.

**4 herrings, gutted and cleaned
1 onion, chopped**

$\frac{1}{4}$ teaspoon dried fennel
$\frac{1}{4}$ teaspoon turmeric
2 bay leaves
Salt, pepper
125 ml/$\frac{1}{4}$ pt dry white wine

1. Arrange the herrings in a
shallow dish.
2. Sprinkle with onion, fennel,
turmeric, bay leaves, salt and
pepper, and pour the wine over.
3. Cover with plastic film.
Cook 4 minutes, giving the dish
a $\frac{1}{4}$ turn every minute.
4. Leave to stand for 10
minutes. Turn the fish over and
leave until cold.

To serve without freezing
Gently lift the fish from the dish
with a fish slice. Remove bay
leaves. The onions and herbs
may be served with the fish.

To freeze Put the fish in a
shallow freezer container lined
with plastic film. Pour the liquor
over. Seal.

To serve from the freezer
Remove wrappings and place
the herrings and frozen liquor in
a serving dish. Thaw by
microwave. Cover and switch
on for 4 minutes, giving the dish
a $\frac{1}{4}$ turn every minute. Leave to
rest for 4 minutes, then continue
cooking until completely
thawed. Drain before serving.

LOBSTER

Live lobster is a blackish-blue
colour. When it is cooked, it
turns bright red and the flesh
becomes opaque.

To kill Pierce the head with a
sharp knife through the cross
marked on the head.

To cook Put the lobster in a
large casserole. Add
750 ml/1$\frac{1}{2}$ pt boiling water.
Cover and cook 5 minutes for a
550 g/1$\frac{1}{4}$ lb lobster, 8 minutes for
a 1 kg/2$\frac{1}{4}$ lb one. Turn the lobster
twice during cooking. Drain and
cool.

To dress Cut through from the
cross on the head down to the
tail. Turn the lobster and split
through the head. Remove the
dark thread along the tail and
the sac from the top part of the
head. Crack open the claws and
remove the meat. Remove the
meat from the tail with a
sharp-pointed knife. Clean the
shell and rub with oil.

To serve without freezing
Follow any recipe for cooked
lobster meat, using the shells if
required.

To freeze Pack the lobster
meat in a freezer container. Seal.
Freeze the shells separately.

To serve from the freezer
Put the lobster meat in a dish.
Cover and thaw by microwave.
Switch on for 1 to 2 minutes
until the meat will separate,
then use in any recipe suitable
for lobster meat.

LOBSTER THERMIDOR
Serves 4

A lobster weighing 750 g/1$\frac{1}{2}$ lb
yields about 200 g/8 oz meat.

**200 g/8 oz frozen lobster meat,
 thawed (see above)
25 g/1 oz butter
2 spring onions, chopped
2 tablespoons dry white wine
$\frac{1}{2}$ teaspoon French mustard
250 ml/$\frac{1}{2}$ pt Béchamel sauce (page**

140), coating consistency
**6 tablespoons grated Gruyère
cheese**
**2 tablespoons grated Parmesan
cheese**
1 egg yolk

1. Put the butter and onions in a dish. Cook 2 minutes.
2. Add the lobster meat, wine and mustard. Cook 2 minutes.
3. Put the sauce in a jug. Heat 2 minutes.
4. Beat in half of the cheese and the egg yolk.
5. Fold the lobster mixture into the sauce.
6. Divide the mixture between 4 lobster shell halves or put into fireproof dishes.
7. Sprinkle with the remaining cheese and brown under the grill.

FILETS DE PLIE AUX CHAMPIGNONS
Serves 2

If this dish is not being prepared for the freezer you may use frozen fish, in which case allow an additional minute during the final stage of cooking.

2 fillets of plaice or flounder, about 150 g/6 oz each
25 g/1 oz butter
25 g/1 oz flour
250 ml/½ pt milk
Salt, white pepper
50 g/2 oz button mushrooms, chopped

1. Put the butter in a large bowl. Cook until melted, 1 minute.
2. Blend in the flour. Cook ½ minute.
3. Slowly blend in half of the milk. Cook 2 minutes.

4. Season with salt and white pepper and beat in the remaining milk. Fold in the mushrooms and cook uncovered 5 minutes.
5. Lay the plaice fillets in a serving dish and cover with the sauce. Cook 4 minutes, turning the dish once.

To serve without freezing
Serve straight from the dish with sauté potatoes and green peas.

To freeze Cover with freezer wrap and cool rapidly. Overwrap and freeze.

To serve from the freezer
Remove wrappings. Thaw by microwave. Switch on for 2 minutes, turn the dish and cook for a further 2 minutes. Leave to rest for 5 minutes, then continue cooking until the fish and sauce are thoroughly reheated, about 3 minutes.

FILETS DE PLIE PRINTEMPS
Serves 2

Overcooking makes fish tough. A popping noise could be a signal that this is occurring.

2 fillets of plaice or flounder, about 150 g/6 oz each
1 bunch spring onions
50 g/2 oz butter
50 g/2 oz flour
375 ml/¾ pt milk
Salt, pepper

1. Trim the stems and roots from the spring onions. Slice the white bulbs thinly.
2. Put them in a serving dish with the butter and cook 4

minutes, stirring once during cooking.
3. Blend in the flour. Cook 1 minute, then stir.
4. Blend in 250 ml/½ pt milk and cook for a further 2 minutes. Season with salt and pepper.
5. Add the remaining milk and cook 1 minute.
6. Lay the seasoned fish fillets on top of the sauce. Cover with plastic film. Cook 2 minutes, turning the fish once.

To serve without freezing
Remove the plastic film and serve straight from the dish.

To freeze Cool rapidly and freeze in the serving dish. Dip the base in hot water briefly to loosen the fish from the dish. Wrap in freezer foil and immediately replace in the freezer.

To serve from the freezer
Remove the wrappings and place the block upside down in the original dish. Cover with greaseproof paper. Thaw by microwave. Switch on for 2 minutes, then give the dish a ½ turn and cook for a further 2 minutes. Leave to rest for 5 minutes, then continue cooking until the fish and sauce are thoroughly reheated, about 3 minutes.

PRAWN-FILLED RED PEPPERS
Serves 2

2 large sweet red peppers, deseeded
1 small onion, finely chopped
2 tablespoons vegetable oil
¼ teaspoon Tabasco sauce
¼ teaspoon ground ginger
1 tablespoon tomato purée

½ teaspoon sugar
2 tablespoons red wine
Salt, pepper
1 tablespoon cornflour
100 g/4 oz cooked and shelled
  prawns

+ + +

150 g/6 oz cooked rice, fresh or
  frozen and thawed

1. Cut off the tops of the red
peppers and reserve them.
Wash and core the peppers, and
remove the seeds.
2. Stand the peppers in a dish,
cover and cook 2 minutes.
3. In another dish, mix the
onion with the oil. Cook 3
minutes.
4. Add the Tabasco sauce,
ginger, tomato purée, sugar and
wine, and salt and pepper to
taste. Cook 1 minute.
5. Blend the cornflour
smoothly with 2 tablespoons
cold water and add to the sauce.
Cook 2 minutes, stirring
occasionally.
6. Mix in the prawns.
7. Pack the peppers with the
prawn filling. Replace the tops
on the peppers. Cook 4 minutes.

To serve without freezing
Serve on a platter surrounded
by a border of cooked rice.

To freeze Cool rapidly. Wrap
each pepper in freezer film and
overwrap with freezer foil. Keep
the peppers upright until they
are fully frozen.

To serve from the freezer
Remove wrappings. To thaw by
microwave, put the peppers in a
serving dish, cover and switch
on for 4 minutes, giving the dish
a ½ turn after 2 minutes. Leave to
rest for 5 minutes, then continue
cooking until thoroughly
reheated. Garnish with cooked
rice.

DARNES OF SALMON
Serves 4

Scotch salmon is at its cheapest
in mid-summer. Freeze it in
convenient portions, then cook
as instructed below. The texture
and taste will be far superior to
frozen salmon bought at a
freezer centre. Allow extra time
for cooking from the frozen state.

4 cutlets fresh or thawed frozen
  salmon, about 150 g/6 oz each
1 tablespoon malt vinegar
1 onion, thinly sliced
1 small carrot, thinly sliced
Bay leaf
Salt, pepper

+ + +

Mayonnaise (page 145)

1. Combine 500 ml/1 pt water
with the vinegar, onion, carrot,
bay leaf, salt and pepper in a
large shallow dish. Cook 5
minutes.
2. Wash the salmon in cold
water, removing any blood clots
with salt. Rinse and dry the
cutlets with kitchen paper.
3. Put the salmon in the liquor,
cover and cook 4 to 6 minutes,
basting once during cooking.
Give the dish a ¼ turn every
minute. When the fish is pink all
the way through and the flesh
comes away easily from the
bone, remove from the
microwave oven.
4. Cover and leave to cool in
the liquor.

To serve without freezing
Lift the cutlets out carefully with
a fish slice and remove the skin
with the tines of a fork. Serve
with a mixed salad and hand
mayonnaise separately.

To freeze Drain the cutlets

thoroughly. Wrap them
individually in freezer film and
pack in a freezer bag. Seal.

To serve from the freezer
Remove wrappings and arrange
the salmon cutlets in a shallow
serving dish. To thaw by
microwave, cover and switch on
for 2 minutes, giving the dish a ½
turn after 1 minute. Leave to rest
for 4 minutes, then continue
cooking until thawed but still
cold. Serve with a mixed salad
and hand mayonnaise
separately.

SALMON TROUT

Salmon trout is similar to
salmon in flavour and colour,
but the texture is more like trout.
Only small fish can be cooked
whole by microwave.

1 salmon trout weighing
  1 kg/2¼ lb after head is
  removed and fish is gutted
Salt, pepper
2 bay leaves
1 tablespoon lemon juice
50 g/2 oz soft margarine

+ + +

½ cucumber, peeled and sliced
  thinly

1. Make 3 or 4 diagonal slashes
on both sides of the fish.
2. Season with salt and
pepper, lay bay leaves inside the
fish and sprinkle with lemon
juice.
3. Rub the margarine over the
fish, pressing it into the slashes.
4. Wrap in non-stick paper and
place diagonally on the base of
the oven. Cook 1 minute.
5. Give the fish a ¼ turn and
cook 1 minute.
6. Turn the fish over and give a
¼ turn. Cook 1 minute.

7.   Give the fish a $\frac{1}{4}$ turn and cook for a final 1 minute.

To serve without freezing
Remove the bay leaves, unwrap the fish and slide on to a serving dish. Decorate with a border of cucumber slices.

To freeze   Cool rapidly. Leave the fish in the non-stick wrapping and completely enclose in freezer foil.

To serve from the freezer
Remove the foil wrapping. Thaw the fish by microwave. Switch on for $\frac{1}{2}$ minute, give the fish a $\frac{1}{4}$ turn and cook for $\frac{1}{2}$ minute. Turn the fish over and cook a further $\frac{1}{2}$ minute, giving the dish a $\frac{1}{4}$ turn once.
Leave to rest for 5 minutes. To serve hot, continue cooking and turning for 1 or 2 more minutes. Remove the non-stick wrapper and serve the fish on a platter with a border of cucumber slices.

SCALLOPED FISH TARRAGON
Serves 2

To make herbed vinegar: pack a vinegar bottle a quarter full with fresh herbs of your choice; top up with hot white wine vinegar or malt vinegar and cork. Leave for at least a month before straining.

150 g/6 oz frozen white fish steaks
3 tablespoons vegetable oil
1 tablespoon tarragon vinegar
Garlic powder, a shake
$\frac{1}{4}$ teaspoon dry mustard
Salt, pepper
$\frac{1}{4}$ cucumber, thinly sliced
Few lettuce leaves, shredded

Small piece of chicory, thinly sliced
1 hard-boiled egg, chopped

+ + +

Lettuce leaves
8 anchovy fillets

1.   Thaw and cook the fish steaks between 2 plates in the microwave oven for 2 minutes. Leave to rest for 5 minutes. Turn the fish steaks over, then cook for a further $2\frac{1}{2}$ minutes, or until the fish is opaque.
2.   Flake the fish.
3.   Mix the oil, vinegar, garlic powder, mustard, salt and pepper together.
4.   Add the fish, cucumber, lettuce, chicory and egg, and toss lightly until thoroughly mixed.

To serve   Pile in to a serving dish lined with a few lettuce leaves and arrange a lattice of anchovy fillets on top.

SEAFOOD GRATINÉE
Serves 3–4

This dish may be frozen in individual portions in scallop shells if preferred, as these are suitable for use in the microwave oven.

250 ml/$\frac{1}{2}$ pt dry white wine
1 small onion, chopped
1 bay leaf
Salt, pepper
3 fresh or 6 frozen and thawed scallops
150 g/6 oz white fish, skinned and boned, and cut into large chunks
100 g/4 oz button mushrooms
100 g/4 oz cooked prawns
50 g/2 oz butter
50 g/2 oz flour
250 ml/$\frac{1}{2}$ pt milk

2 egg yolks
Lemon juice

+ + +

6 tablespoons Edam cheese, grated
6 tablespoons dried breadcrumbs

1.   Combine the wine, onion and bay leaf with salt and pepper to taste in a large bowl. Cook 1 minute. Set aside until cold.
2.   Cook a further $2\frac{1}{2}$ minutes, or until the wine comes to the boil.
3.   Lay the scallops in a large dish and strain the wine mixture over them. Add enough water to cover. Cover the dish and cook 2 minutes.
4.   Add the fish and mushrooms. Cook covered for 4 minutes.
5.   Add the prawns, cook 2 minutes. Strain, reserving the liquor.
6.   Put the butter in a bowl. Cook until melted, 1 minute.
7.   Blend in the flour. Cook $\frac{1}{2}$ minute.
8.   Gradually stir in 250 ml/$\frac{1}{2}$ pt reserved fish liquor and 125 ml/$\frac{1}{4}$ pt milk. Cook 4 minutes, stirring frequently.
9.   Beat the egg yolks with the remaining milk. Add to the sauce. Cook 3 minutes, stirring frequently. Season with salt, pepper and a squeeze of lemon juice.
10.   Arrange the seafood mixture in a dish and pour the sauce over the top.

To serve without freezing
Sprinkle the fish with a mixture of grated cheese and breadcrumbs. Brown under the grill.

Fish and Shellfish

To freeze   Cool rapidly. Cover with freezer film. Overwrap.

To serve from the freezer
Remove wrappings and thaw by microwave. Switch on for 4 minutes, turning the dish occasionally. Sprinkle with the cheese and breadcrumbs, and brown under the grill.

CREAMED SHRIMP PANCAKES
Serves 4

The pancakes may either be freshly made or frozen and thawed for this dish. Cook the sauce in advance and freeze it, or prepare it just before use. Fresh shrimps should be used if cooking for the freezer, frozen shrimps if the dish is to be served immediately.

25 g/1 oz butter
25 g/1 oz flour
125 ml/¼ pt milk
125 ml/¼ pt single cream
150 g/6 oz shelled shrimps

+ + +

8 pancakes
15 g/½ oz butter
2 tablespoons grated mild cheese

1.   Put the butter in a bowl. Cook until melted, 1 minute.
2.   Stir in the flour. Cook ½ minute.
3.   Gradually blend in the milk and cream. Bring to boiling point, about 3 minutes.
4.   Mix in the shrimps. Cook 2 minutes.

To serve without freezing
Divide the mixture between the pancakes and roll up the pancakes. Place these close together in a heatproof dish. Dot

with butter, sprinkle with grated cheese and brown under the grill.

To freeze   Cool the mixture rapidly and turn into a freezer bag. Seal. Layer pancakes individually in waxed paper, overwrap with freezer foil and seal.

To serve from the freezer
Remove frozen mixture from bag. Put the block in a deep dish and thaw by microwave. Switch on for 5 minutes. Stir. Continue cooking until thoroughly reheated. To thaw pancakes, put stack in the microwave oven and switch on for ½ minute. Leave until completely thawed and pliable before separating. Divide the mixture between the pancakes and roll up. Place the pancakes close together in a heatproof dish. Dot with butter, sprinkle with grated cheese and brown under the grill.

SMOKED FISH CHARLOTTE
Serves 4

Ring the changes on this dish by substituting smoked cod or mackerel for the haddock.

450 g/1 lb smoked haddock fillet
25 g/1 oz butter
25 g/1 oz flour
250 ml/½ pt Herbed Milk (page 142)
Salt, pepper
75 g/3 oz fresh white breadcrumbs
4 tomatoes, skinned and thickly sliced
25 g/1 oz melted butter

1.   Put the fish in a shallow dish

and cover with plastic film. Cook 4 minutes.
2.   Remove the skin and any bones. Flake the fish.
3.   Put the butter in a large bowl. Cook until melted, 1 minute.
4.   Blend in the flour. Cook ½ minute.
5.   Strain the milk and gradually stir it in. Cook 3 minutes, stirring frequently. Season with salt and pepper.
6.   Layer the crumbs, fish and sauce in a serving dish, finishing with a layer of crumbs.
7.   Arrange the tomatoes on top and pour over the melted butter. Cook 4 minutes.

To serve without freezing
Serve immediately. This dish is best when piping hot.

To freeze   Cool rapidly. Cover the dish with freezer film and overwrap with freezer foil.

To serve from the freezer
Remove foil wrapping. To thaw by microwave, switch on for 4 minutes, giving the dish a ¼ turn every minute. Leave to rest for 5 minutes, then continue cooking until thoroughly reheated.

DOVER SOLE
Serves 1

Dover sole should either be home-frozen uncooked, with the dark skin removed, or purchased frozen from the freezer centre. To cook 2 fish, arrange them side by side in a shallow dish and cook as directed below, giving the dish a ¼ turn every minute.

1 frozen Dover sole, about

225 g/8 oz, cleaned and
gutted weight
2 teaspoons butter
Salt, pepper
Lemon juice

1. Put the frozen sole in a dish.
Cook ½ minute.
2. Turn the fish over and cook
½ minute. Leave to rest for 5
minutes.
3. Spread the butter over the
fish and sprinkle with salt,
pepper and lemon juice. Cover
with plastic film. Cook 1 minute.
4. Give the dish a ½ turn and
cook for 1 more minute. Leave to
rest for 3 minutes, by which time
the flesh should be opaque and
tender, but not shrunken away
from the bone.

To serve Serve whole or
filleted from the bone.

TOMATO GEFÜLLTE FISH
Serves 2–3

Quantities in this recipe may be
doubled and the dish cooked for
6 minutes. The same size can of
soup will be enough.

200 g/8 oz white fish fillet
1 onion
1 carrot
1 celery stalk
1 tablespoon finely chopped
   parsley
2 tablespoons ground almonds
4 tablespoons fresh white
   breadcrumbs
Salt, pepper
1 egg, beaten
1 can (425 ml) cream of tomato
   soup

1. Put the fish, onion, carrot
and celery stalk through a
mincer fitted with a fine disc.
2. Add the parsley, almonds,
breadcrumbs and seasoning,

and bind with the beaten egg.
3. Form into 6 balls and
arrange around the edges of a
shallow serving dish.
4. Pour the soup over the fish
balls so that they are coated.
Cook 4 minutes, giving the dish
a ¼ turn every minute. Leave to
rest for 5 minutes, then continue
cooking until hot.

To serve without freezing
Serve directly from the dish,
spooning some of the hot sauce
over each ball.

To freeze Transfer the fish
balls and sauce to a shallow
freezer container. Seal.

To serve from the freezer
Remove from the container and
replace in the original dish.
Cover with plastic film. Thaw by
microwave. Switch on for 4
minutes, giving the dish a ¼ turn
every minute. Leave to rest for 5
minutes, then continue cooking
until thoroughly reheated.

TROUT WITH ALMONDS
Serves 2

Frozen trout may be used for
this dish but the package should
be thawed by microwave for 2
minutes before cooking.

2 small trout, cleaned and
   gutted
75 g/3 oz butter
50 g/2 oz flaked almonds
Salt, pepper
1 tablespoon lemon juice
125 ml/¼ pt single cream

1. Put the butter in a shallow
dish. Cook until melted, 1
minute.
2. Stir in the flaked almonds

and cook until lightly browned,
1 to 2 minutes, then remove.
3. Lay the trout side by side in
the dish, baste with butter,
season with salt and pepper,
and sprinkle with lemon juice.
Cook 2 minutes.
4. Turn the fish over and cook
for a further 2 minutes. Test for
cooking with the point of a
knife, which should easily
puncture the thickest part of the
flesh.
5. Stir in the cream and cook 15
seconds.

To serve without freezing
Coat fish with the sauce and
scatter the flaked almonds on top.

To freeze Cover with freezer
wrap, cool rapidly, overwrap and
freeze. Freeze almonds
separately.

To serve from the freezer
Remove wrappings and thaw in
the microwave oven. Switch on
for 2 minutes. Leave to rest for 5
minutes, then cook for a further
3 minutes, turning the dish
once. Serve with the sauce and
almonds spooned over the fish.

TRUITE SUPRÈME
Serves 2

Trout vary in size, the smallest
ones weighing about 150 g/6 oz.
Rainbow trout are available
throughout the year, but the
season for brown trout is from
March to September.

2 small trout, cleaned and
   gutted
4 tablespoons medium-dry
   sherry
8 tablespoons milk
Salt, pepper

Stuffing

50 g/2 oz butter
**50 g/2 oz fresh white
    breadcrumbs**
**2 teaspoons dried crumbled
    parsley**
¼ teaspoon dried chervil
¼ onion, finely chopped
Salt, pepper

1.   Lay the trout side by side in a dish that just fits. Pour the sherry over and leave to marinate for at least 12 hours, basting occasionally.
2.   To make stuffing, put the butter in a bowl. Cook until melted, 1 minute.
3.   Add the remaining stuffing ingredients and 2 tablespoons cold water, mix well and return to the microwave oven. Cook 1 minute.
4.   Remove fish from the dish and fill the cavities with the stuffing.
5.   Add the milk to the sherry and season to taste.
6.   Replace the stuffed trout in the dish and baste with the milk and sherry mixture.
7.   Cook in the microwave oven 4 minutes, turning dish once.

To serve without freezing
Serve 1 trout per person, moistened with a few spoonfuls of the liquor.

To freeze   Cover with freezer film and cool rapidly. Overwrap and freeze.

To serve from the freezer
Remove wrappings. Thaw in the microwave oven. Switch on for 2 minutes. Leave to rest for 5 minutes, then cook for a further 3 minutes, turning the dish once. Serve straight from the dish, spooning a little of the liquor over each trout.

TUNA LOAF
Serves 6

Canned tuna has a dryer texture than the more expensive canned salmon, but it may be used as a substitute in recipes for fish moulds, rings or loaves.

1 can (200 g) tuna
1 can (200 g) sweetcorn
**3 celery stalks, very finely
    chopped**
Salt, pepper
Grated rind of 1 lemon
25 g/1 oz softened butter
**50 g/2 oz fresh white
    breadcrumbs**
250 ml/½ pt milk
2 eggs

+ + +

Anchovy sauce (page 141)

1.   Mash the tuna and mix with the sweetcorn, celery, salt, pepper, lemon rind and butter.
2.   Put the milk and breadcrumbs in a bowl. Cook 2 minutes.
3.   Beat the eggs and add to the mixture.
4.   Stir in fish mixture and turn into a greased 20 by 10 cm/8 by 4 inch loaf-shaped container. Cook 6 minutes, giving the dish a ¼ turn every 1½ minutes.

To serve without freezing
Leave to stand for 10 minutes before turning out on to a hot platter. Slice with a sharp knife and serve with Anchovy sauce.

To freeze   Leave to cool. Open freeze, then turn out on to a piece of freezer foil. Wrap tightly.

To serve from the freezer
Remove wrapping. Thaw by microwave. Switch on for 1 minute. Leave to rest a few minutes, then slice while still partially frozen. Reheat on dinner plates, allowing 1 or 2 minutes for each portion. Serve with Anchovy sauce.

7 Meat

Meat

The microwave oven will not tenderise a tough cut of meat so ideally only prime cuts should be cooked by microwave. If the meat does need some form of softening, this should be done before cooking. It may be pricked all over with a fork, sprinkled with tenderising powder and left for 30 minutes before cooking. Another way of breaking down tough tissue is to pound the meat with a meat hammer, a rolling pin or the side of a heavy cleaver. Marinating in oil and vinegar for several hours will improve flavour as well as texture, and even brushing the meat with lemon juice just before cooking it will help. Tough meat may also be chopped or minced.

Most cuts of veal are suitable for microwave cooking. Leg or shoulder is excellent stuffed. Fillet may be cut into escalopes, and chops or cutlets can be cooked using the oven's browning skillet or grill, if available, for browning.

Any cuts of beef which would normally be grilled or fried can be cooked by microwave. Fillet, sirloin and rump are best because of their natural tenderness. The oven will brown a large joint, but small pieces such as steaks are best seared and browned in a browning skillet. If the oven has a built-in grill, a joint may be cooked and also browned, otherwise the use of a roaster bag will ensure some browning on large joints.

Cuts of lamb suitable for cooking by microwave are loin, chump and best end neck, which can be cooked whole or cut into chops. The top or fillet end of the leg can be cooked whole or cut into cubes for kebabs. If the leg is cooked in one piece, the bone end should be shielded with a piece of foil half way through the cooking time. Shoulder is also good cooked by microwave.

Prime cuts of pork are leg, loin, spare rib and belly. The fillet end of the leg, the fillet and tenderloin, belly and chops are the best cuts to choose for cooking by microwave.

All cuts of bacon, ham and gammon may be cooked by microwave except for collar, butt, hock and slipper.

Types of offal recommended for microwave cookery are liver, tongue, brains, sweetbreads and lambs' kidneys.

When meat is cooked by microwave, shape is of vital importance. When cooking chops, for example, they should be arranged so that thicker parts are facing towards the edges of the dish, with thinner parts in the middle. Joints should be as evenly shaped as possible. If you have to cook an uneven piece, cover the thinner part with a piece of foil for about half of the cooking time to protect it from overcooking.

Rolled joints should be tied with string. Metal skewers should be used with great care and only when the joint is large, for if the metal touches the back or sides of the oven, the magnetron will be damaged.

Joints should be cooked resting on an upturned (undecor-

ROASTING FRESH MEAT BY MICROWAVE

1. Put the roast, fat side down, on an upturned saucer in a large dish. Cover with a piece of greaseproof paper. Cook for half of the cooking time.
2. Spoon away surplus fat and leave to rest for 20 minutes.
3. Turn the joint over and cook for the remaining time. If the joint is to be frozen and then reheated, undercook by 3 or 4 minutes. Alternatively, cut total cooking time by a third; transfer joint to a flameproof dish and brown briskly on all sides under a preheated hot grill. A 1½- to 1¾-k/3- to 4-lb joint will take 10 to 15 minutes.
4. Leave to stand for 15 minutes before carving.

To freeze Wrap the cold joint in freezer foil and pack into a freezer bag. Seal. If the meat is to be minced or sliced, do so before freezing. Wrap slices interleaved with freezer film.

To serve from the freezer Remove wrappings and transfer joint to a large, shallow dish. Thaw by microwave. Cover and switch on for 1 minute per 450 g/1 lb. Leave to rest for 5 minutes, then repeat until the meat is thoroughly thawed. Continue cooking 2 minutes per 450 g/1 lb if the joint is to be served hot. Cooked sliced or minced beef should be thawed by microwave before using in recipes.

BEEF JAMAICA
Serves 3–4

300 g/12 oz tender beef, cut into
  thin strips
4 tablespoons vegetable oil
2 tablespoons cornflour,
  seasoned with salt and
  pepper
125 ml/¼ pt red wine
1 large banana

+ + +

Boiled rice

+ + +

Lemon juice

1. Pour the oil into a shallow dish. Cook 2 minutes.
2. Toss the strips of meat in the seasoned cornflour.
3. Put the coated meat strips in the dish and baste with the oil. Cook 3 minutes, stirring once during cooking.
4. Add the wine. Cook 5 minutes, stirring occasionally.
5. Peel the banana and cut into 2½ cm/1 inch chunks.
6. Add to the meat, cover with plastic film and cook 2 minutes.

To serve without freezing
Remove the plastic film, spoon on to heated plates and surround with a border of hot boiled rice.

To freeze Cool rapidly and transfer to a freezer container, sprinkling the banana chunks with lemon juice. Overwrap.

To serve from the freezer
Remove wrappings, transfer to a bowl and cover loosely. Thaw by microwave. Switch on for 3 minutes, then continue cooking until thoroughly reheated. Serve on heated plates surrounded by a border of hot boiled rice.

ated) saucer in a casserole, covered so that any spattering is confined to the casserole. The lid may be removed after part of the cooking time to release steam, which would prevent the surface becoming brown. The fat which drips from the joint as it cooks will collect in the bottom of the casserole and should be drained off regularly for if left in, it will slow down cooking. Joints should not be salted before cooking. Salt extracts the meat's juices and causes the exterior to dry out.

Large joints cook better if they are allowed to 'rest' for 20 minutes halfway through. They should then be left for 15 minutes on the serving dish before carving to allow juices to 'settle'. If you use a meat thermometer to test the meat, do so after it has had its final resting time. Never cook a joint with a thermometer stuck in it.

Meat should be removed from its wrappings as soon as it is brought home and stored on a plate, loosely covered, in the refrigerator. Joints will keep for 5 days, steaks and chops 4 days, cut-up meat 2 days, sausages 3 days and cooked ham 5 days. Minced meat does not keep well because so much of the surface is exposed, allowing decomposition to set in, and should be cooked or frozen as quickly as possible. Offal should be refrigerated on a plate lightly covered with greaseproof paper and stored for a maximum of 24 hours before cooking or freezing.

If a joint is to be frozen, first wrap greaseproof paper or foil round any sharp bones, then wrap the joint closely in freezer film or foil so that no air is trapped inside, and seal in a polythene bag.

To thaw a frozen joint by microwave, switch on for 2 minutes per 450 g/1 lb meat, then give it a 10-minute rest. Turn the joint over and repeat as necessary. Chops and thin pieces of meat should be thawed by removing any wrappings and giving them a burst of a few seconds of microwave energy only. Then leave them until completely thawed before cooking.

Because of their size, joints of meat cannot be cooked by microwave from their frozen state. The meat will cook to a depth of about 5 cm/2 inches before the centre has had a chance to thaw. Further cooking will only result in a joint which is overdone on the outside but still raw in the middle. Only if your oven has an automatic defrost button can meat be cooked from frozen. In this case, allow 2½ times the recommended time.

Meat

MICROWAVE ROASTING CHART

Meat	Minutes per 450 g/1 lb			Temperature in middle after final resting time		
	Rare	Medium	Well Done	Rare	Medium	Well Done
Beef	6½	7½	8½–9	135°F	150°F	170°F
Veal	–	–	9	–	–	165°F
Lamb	–	8½	9½	–	165°F	180°F
Pork	–	–	10	–	–	170°F

PATAK'S BEEF CURRY
Serves 4

All Indian spices and pastes are obtainable from Patak (Ltd), Drummond Street, London NW1, who will also send a list of stockists by post. Curry pastes are available in different strengths. Curry base is a mixture of tomatoes, onions and spices. A small can of tomatoes may be substituted.
If using frozen onions, cooking will take 10 minutes at Step 2.

300 g/12 oz lean beef
100 g/4 oz onions, sliced
3 tablespoons vegetable oil

Curry Ingredients

2 tablespoons curry paste
2 tablespoons curry base
2 cardamom pods
Garlic powder, a shake
Cayenne pepper, a shake
Ground ginger, a shake
2 cloves
2 tomatoes, roughly chopped
1 can (140 g) tomato purée
Salt, pepper

1. Combine all the curry ingredients in a bowl. Add 125 ml/¼ pt water, cover and cook 4 minutes.
2. Put the onions and oil in a dish, and cook 5 minutes until soft and golden, stirring occasionally. Mix into the curry sauce.
3. Put the beef in a shallow serving dish. Pour the sauce over, cover and leave in the refrigerator for 2 to 12 hours. Baste the beef with the sauce occasionally.
4. Cook 15 minutes, giving the dish a ¼ turn several times during cooking.

To serve without freezing
Serve with boiled rice, chapattis and a side salad of diced cucumber steeped in natural yoghurt.

To freeze Cool and turn into a polythene bag resting in a bowl. Seal. When frozen, remove the bowl and overwrap the bag with freezer foil.

To serve from the freezer
Remove wrappings and place in a bowl. To thaw by microwave, cover and switch on for 10 to 12 minutes, stirring after 5 minutes. Leave to rest for 5 minutes, then continue cooking until thoroughly reheated.

ROAST BEEF IN PEPPER SAUCE
Serves 4

Beef cooked previously by microwave is suitable in this dish.

450 g/1 lb roast beef, cubed or sliced
1 onion, finely chopped
1 green pepper, finely chopped
1 garlic clove, crushed
125 ml/¼ pt French dressing
Few drops Tabasco sauce
2 tablespoons Worcestershire sauce
Salt, pepper
1 bay leaf
250 ml/½ pt beef stock

1. Put the onion, pepper and garlic in a large bowl, cover with plastic film and cook 3 minutes, stirring occasionally.
2. Add all the other ingredients except the beef. Cook, uncovered, for 5 minutes.

To serve without freezing
Add the beef and cook for an

additional 2 or 3 minutes, until the beef is thoroughly hot.

To freeze Put the meat in a freezer container and pour the sauce over it. Seal.

To serve from the freezer
Transfer to a serving dish. To thaw by microwave, cover and switch on for 5 minutes. Stir. Leave to rest for 5 minutes, stir again, then continue cooking until thoroughly reheated.

BEEF STROGANOFF
Serves 4

450 g/1 lb lean frying steak
25 g/1 oz flour
Salt, pepper
4 tablespoons vegetable oil
1 large onion, finely chopped
1 can (285 g) cream of chicken soup
200 g/8 oz button mushrooms, sliced
2 tablespoons tomato purée

+ + +

125 ml/¼ pt sour cream

+ + +

1 teaspoon flour

1. Pound the meat with a tenderiser or rolling pin. Cut into thin strips.
2. Season the flour with salt and pepper, and coat the meat with this mixture.
3. Preheat the browning skillet for 5 minutes, add the oil and toss in the meat, stirring rapidly. Cook 3 minutes. Stir.
4. Add the onion. Cook 2 minutes, stirring once.
5. Add the soup, 125 ml/¼ pt hot water, the mushrooms and tomato purée. Cook 2 minutes, stirring frequently.

To serve without freezing
Stir in the sour cream and serve on heated plates with a bed of boiled rice.

To freeze Cool rapidly. Blend 1 teaspoon flour with 2 tablespoons water and stir in. Turn into a freezer container. Seal.

To serve from the freezer
Transfer the stroganoff to a serving dish. Cover and thaw by microwave. Switch on for 5 minutes, stirring occasionally. Leave to rest for 5 minutes, then continue cooking until thoroughly reheated. Stir in the sour cream.

BEEFBURGER SPECIAL
Serves 4

Polypropylene (TPX) rings for stacking plates in a microwave oven are available at shops stocking microwave ovens. Home-made rings can be constructed from corrugated card, sewing the ends together or securing them with a wooden cocktail stick. Do not use paper clips. It will take 1 minute to reheat individual covered plates.

4 frozen beefburgers
4 rashers bacon
1 large can (400 g) baked beans

1. Preheat the browning skillet for 5 minutes.
2. Quickly brown the beefburgers on both sides, then continue cooking in the microwave oven for 2 minutes. Remove from the skillet and drain on absorbent paper.
3. Lay the rashers of bacon in the skillet, cover with a piece of

paper and cook 2½ minutes. Drain.

4. Open the can of baked beans and spoon on to individual plates. Lay a beefburger and a bacon rasher on top. Stack plates, using ovenproof rings, and cover the top plate with a piece of paper. Reheat for 2½ minutes.

BURGUNDY MINCE

Serves 3

Wine for cooking need not be of the best quality. Left-over cooking wine may be frozen for later use.

**300 g/12 oz lean minced beef
1 medium onion, sliced
2 carrots, thinly sliced
2 tablespoons flour
1 large can (400 g) tomatoes
½ teaspoon dried mixed herbs
1 Oxo cube
125 ml/¼ pt red wine
Salt, pepper**

1. Put the minced beef and onion in a dish, and cook 2 minutes.
2. Add the carrots. Cook 1 minute.
3. Stir in the flour. Cook 1 minute.
4. Add the contents of the can of tomatoes and the herbs. Crumble in the stock cube, add the wine and season with salt and pepper. Cook for 15 minutes, stirring occasionally.

To serve without freezing
Serve hot with boiled rice, creamed potatoes or a topping of freshly boiled noodles.

To freeze Cool rapidly, pack in a freezer bag, seal and freeze.

To serve from the freezer
Remove from freezer bag and turn the contents into a serving dish. To thaw by microwave, cover dish loosely and cook for 6 minutes or until thoroughly reheated. Stir once during cooking.

CORNED BEEF SOUTH AMERICAN STYLE

Serves 4

**1 can (450 g) corned beef
1 onion, minced
1 garlic clove, crushed
¼ teaspoon compound chilli powder
¼ teaspoon ground cumin
Salt, pepper
Juice of 1 orange
4 courgettes
15 g/½ oz butter**

1. Mash the corned beef in a suitable serving dish. Add the onion, garlic, chilli and cumin, salt and pepper. Squeeze the orange juice over the top. Cover and cook 4 minutes, turning the dish every minute.
2. Cut the courgettes in 4 lengthways and arrange on top. Dot with butter, cover and cook for a further 4 minutes.

To serve without freezing
Serve immediately with sauté potatoes and grilled tomatoes.

To freeze Cool rapidly. Cover with freezer film and overwrap with freezer foil.

To serve from the freezer
Remove the foil wrapping. To thaw by microwave, switch on for 5 minutes and leave to rest for 5 minutes. Then continue cooking until thoroughly reheated.

HAMPSTEAD PIE

Serves 6–8

Minced cooked beef and vegetables baked in a pastry case make a one-dish main course and no extra vegetables need be served. Mango chutney has a sweet taste. For those who prefer a sharper flavour, substitute bottled sauce. Two-crust pies should be frozen in the dish in which they were cooked, as they cannot easily be removed whole. The potatoes can be parboiled conventionally or parcooked in the microwave oven for 4 minutes.

**450 g/1 lb cooked minced beef
200 g/8 oz onions, fresh or frozen
200 g/8 oz frozen peas
200 g/8 oz potatoes, quartered and parboiled
Salt, pepper
2 tablespoons finely chopped parsley
4 tablespoons mango chutney
Shortcrust pastry made with 200 g/8 oz plain flour (page 120)
Milk**

+ + +

Basic Brown sauce (page 143)

1. Pass the beef, onions, peas and parcooked potatoes through the mincer, using a fine disc.
2. Season with salt and pepper, and add the parsley. Moisten with 2 tablespoons water and blend in the mango chutney.
3. Line a 25-cm/10-inch round, ovenproof glass pie dish with half of the pastry. Cover with a piece of absorbent paper and put a 20-cm/8-inch plate on top. Cook 4 minutes, giving the dish a ½ turn after 2 minutes. Remove

plate and paper, and leave to rest for 5 minutes.

4. Fill the pastry case with the meat mixture. Roll out the remaining pastry to form a lid. Lift on to the pie and seal the edges.

5. Brush the top of the pie with milk and decorate with leaves made from the pastry trimmings. Cook 6½ to 7 minutes. Brown under the grill.

To serve without freezing
Serve hot or cold in the pie dish with a green salad tossed in French dressing. Hand hot Brown sauce separately.

To freeze Cool rapidly. Overwrap with plastic film and freezer foil.

To serve from the freezer
To thaw by microwave remove the wrappings and switch on for 4 minutes, turning the pie every minute. Test the pie and, if necessary, allow extra cooking time. *The pie can now be eaten hot or cold but must not be reheated a second time.* Serve with Basic brown sauce.

MEAT BALLS WITH EGG AND LEMON SAUCE
Serves 4

Ring the changes with this dish by using veal or lamb instead of beef.

450 g/1 lb stewing beef, cut in chunks
1 onion
1 carrot
1 slice white bread
1 teaspoon ground cumin
Salt, pepper
1 egg, beaten

500 ml/1 pt hot stock
25 g/1 oz butter
25 g/1 oz cornflour

+ + +

2 egg yolks
4 tablespoons lemon juice

1. Put the beef on a dish, cover and cook 5 minutes.
2. Mince the beef, onion, carrot and bread.
3. Mix in the cumin, season with salt and pepper, and add the juices from the meat. Bind with the beaten egg.
4. Form into 6 or 8 balls and arrange round the edge of a shallow dish. Cover and cook 6 minutes, turning the dish halfway through the cooking time.
5. Pour the stock into a large bowl and add the butter. Cook 2½ minutes.
6. Blend the cornflour with 2 tablespoons cold water and add to the hot stock. Stir thoroughly and continue cooking for 2 minutes, stirring frequently, until the sauce thickens. Add seasoning to taste.

To serve without freezing
Reheat the meat balls for 3 minutes. Lightly beat the egg yolks with the lemon juice, add a generous spoonful of the hot sauce, then pour back into the sauce. Stir vigorously and reheat for 15 seconds. Pour over the meat balls and serve immediately.

To freeze Lay the meat balls in a shallow freezer container and pour the sauce over them. Seal.

To serve from the freezer
Put block in a serving dish, cover and thaw by microwave. Switch on for 2 minutes, turning the dish after 1 minute. Leave to

rest for 5 minutes, then continue cooking until thoroughly reheated. Remove the meat balls from the dish. Cook the sauce until it boils. Beat the egg yolks and lemon juice together, add a generous spoonful of the hot sauce, then pour back into the sauce. Stir vigorously and cook ¼ minute. Pour over the meat balls and serve.

MOUSSAKA
Serves 3–4

Substitute sliced boiled potatoes for the aubergine if preferred.

1 medium-size aubergine
Salt
6 tablespoons vegetable oil
200 g/8 oz minced beef (or lamb)
1 medium onion, finely chopped
150 g/6 oz mushrooms, finely chopped
2 tablespoons tomato purée
Pepper
1 egg yolk
250 ml/½ pt Béchamel sauce, coating consistency (page 140)

+ + +

2 tablespoons grated cheese
2 tablespoons breadcrumbs

1. Slice the aubergine, sprinkle the slices with salt and leave to drain in a colander for at least 30 minutes. Rinse and pat dry.
2. Preheat the browning skillet for 5 minutes. Add 4 tablespoons of the oil, toss in the aubergines and brown quickly on both sides.
3. Cover and cook 2 minutes.
4. Remove the aubergines and blot with absorbent paper.
5. Wipe out the browning skillet and reheat for 5 minutes.

6. Add 2 tablespoons oil and stir in the beef and onion. Cover and cook 2 minutes.

7. Add the mushrooms, tomato purée, salt and pepper. Stir. Cover and cook 2 minutes.

8. Beat the egg yolk and add to the Béchamel sauce.

9. Put the meat in a dish and cover with the aubergines, then pour the sauce on top.

To serve without freezing
Sprinkle with the grated cheese and breadcrumbs, and brown under the grill.

To freeze Cover the dish with freezer film and overwrap with freezer foil.

To serve from the freezer
Remove wrappings. To thaw by microwave, switch on for 5 minutes, giving the dish a ¼ turn every minute. Leave to rest for 5 minutes, then sprinkle with the grated cheese and breadcrumbs, and brown under the grill.

CÔTELETTES AU JAMBON, SAUCE PIQUANTE
Serves 4

4 thick lamb cutlets
1 egg, beaten
50 g/2 oz ham, finely chopped
2 tablespoons freshly toasted breadcrumbs
25 g/1 oz butter
1 small carrot, chopped
1 small onion, chopped
25 g/1 oz flour
250 ml/½ pt beef stock
8 button mushrooms
½ teaspoon yeast extract
2 teaspoons malt vinegar
2 teaspoons Worcestershire sauce
2 small gherkins

1 tablespoon capers
1 blade of mace
Salt, pepper
200 g/8 oz mashed potatoes

+ + +

1 teaspoon flour

1. Trim the cutlets, dip in the beaten egg and coat with a mixture of ham and breadcrumbs.

2. Preheat the browning skillet for 5 minutes. Add the butter and quickly brown the cutlets on both sides. Cook 6 minutes, turning the cutlets over after 3 minutes. Remove from the skillet.

3. Cook the carrot and onion in the fat remaining in the skillet for 4 minutes, stirring occasionally.

4. Blend in the flour, then add all the other ingredients. Cover and cook 6 minutes, stirring occasionally.

5. Remove the mushrooms and blend the sauce in a liquidiser or press through a sieve into a bowl.

To serve without freezing
Pipe a border of mashed potatoes on a suitable platter. Arrange the cutlets in the middle. Decorate with the mushrooms. Pour the sauce over the cutlets and reheat the entire dish in the microwave oven for 3 minutes, giving the dish a ½ turn after 1½ minutes.

To freeze Arrange the chops in a freezer container. Blend 1 teaspoon flour with 2 tablespoons cold water, stir into the sauce and pour over the meat. Add the mushrooms. Seal.

To serve from the freezer
To thaw by microwave, transfer to a serving dish, cover and switch on for 6 minutes, giving the dish a ¼ turn every 1½ minutes. Leave to rest for 5 minutes, then continue cooking until thoroughly reheated. Pipe a border of freshly mashed potatoes around the edge of the dish.

LAMB CUTLETS BRUNOISE
Serves 4

8 lamb cutlets (best end neck)
25 g/1 oz margarine
Salt, pepper
2 onions, diced
2 carrots, diced
2 celery stalks, thinly sliced
2 tablespoons tomato purée
250 ml/½ pt brown meat stock (made with an Oxo cube)

1. Preheat the browning skillet for 5 minutes. Add the margarine and brown the cutlets on both sides. Arrange the chops with the bones towards the centre of the dish. Cover and cook 5 minutes.

2. Remove the cutlets from the skillet. Season with salt and pepper, and put aside.

3. Stir the vegetables into the fat remaining in the skillet. Cover and cook 5 minutes, stirring once during cooking.

4. Stir in the tomato purée and stock. Place the chops on top, cover and cook 12 to 16 minutes, or until the cutlets are tender, giving the dish a ½ turn twice during cooking.

To serve without freezing
Serve directly from the skillet or on a heated platter.

To freeze Cool rapidly. Turn into a shallow freezer container. Seal.

To serve from the freezer
Remove block from container and place upside down in a serving dish. To thaw by microwave, cover and switch on for 8 minutes, giving the dish a ¼ turn every 2 minutes. Leave to rest for 5 minutes, then continue cooking until thoroughly reheated.

SPICY CRUMBED LAMB CHOPS
Serves 4

Serve this dish with carrots, leeks and creamed potatoes, accompanied by a sweetish fruity sauce.

4 lamb chops (loin), about 100 g/4 oz each
8 tablespoons toasted breadcrumbs
Salt, pepper
½ teaspoon curry powder
2 tablespoons sultanas, chopped
1 egg, beaten
50 g/2 oz margarine

1. Mix the breadcrumbs with salt, pepper, the curry powder and sultanas.
2. Trim the chops, dip in beaten egg and coat thickly with the crumbs.
3. Preheat the browning skillet for 5 minutes. Add the margarine and chops, and seal on both sides.
4. Arrange the chops with the bones towards the centre of the dish and cook, uncovered, for 8 to 10 minutes.

To serve without freezing
Drain on kitchen paper and serve immediately.

To freeze Cool chops rapidly. Wrap individually in freezer foil.

To serve from the freezer
Remove wrappings and arrange chops on a dish. To thaw by microwave, switch on for 2 minutes for 1 chop, 3½ minutes for 2 chops and 6 minutes for 4 chops, giving the dish an occasional turn. Leave to rest for 5 minutes. Cook for a further few minutes if necessary until hot.

CÔTELETTES DE PORC ZINGARA
Serves 4

4 pork cutlets, trimmed
15 g/½ oz butter
4 slices ham, cut to the shape of the cutlets
4 tablespoons dry white wine
125 ml/¼ pt Espagnole sauce (page 143)
4 tablespoons tomato ketchup
8 button mushrooms

1. Preheat the browning skillet for 5 minutes. Add the butter and seal the cutlets quickly on both sides. Cover with a piece of greaseproof paper and cook 4 minutes.
2. Spoon off any surplus fat.
3. Lay 1 slice of ham on each chop.
4. Mix together the wine, Espagnole sauce and ketchup, and stir in 2 tablespoons water. Pour over the chops. Cook 6 minutes, giving the dish a ¼ turn every 1½ minutes and basting occasionally with the sauce.
5. Garnish with the mushrooms and cook 2 minutes.

To serve without freezing
Serve from the skillet or transfer to a heated platter.

To freeze Cool rapidly. Arrange in a shallow freezer container. Seal.

To serve from the freezer
Transfer block to a serving dish. Thaw by microwave, cover and switch on for 8 minutes, giving the dish a ¼ turn every 2 minutes. Leave to rest for 5 minutes, then continue cooking until thoroughly reheated.

PORK SPARE RIBS IN BARBECUE SAUCE
Serves 2

The sauce may be stored in a closed jar in the refrigerator for a few days.

2 pork spare rib chops, about 200 g/8 oz each
4 tablespoons vegetable oil
125 ml/¼ pt tomato ketchup
2 tablespoons brown sugar
2 tablespoons Worcestershire sauce
Garlic powder, a shake
4 tablespoons vinegar
Juice of ½ lemon
½ teaspoon paprika
1 teaspoon soy sauce
25 g/1 oz butter

1. Put all the ingredients except the spare ribs and 2 tablespoons of the oil in a bowl with 1 tablespoon water. Cook 3 minutes. Stir.
2. Brush the spare ribs with remaining oil.
3. Preheat the browning skillet for 5 minutes. Put in the spare ribs and quickly seal on both sides.
4. Cover and cook for 4 minutes.
5. Turn chops over and pour in the sauce. Cook 3 minutes. Give the dish a ½ turn and cook for a further 3 minutes.

To serve without freezing
Serve direct from the skillet or transfer to a heated platter.

To freeze   Cool rapidly. Turn into a shallow dish. Cover with freezer film and overwrap with freezer foil.

To serve from the freezer
Remove wrappings. To thaw by microwave, cover and switch on for 6 minutes, giving the dish a ¼ turn every 1½ minutes. Leave to rest for 5 minutes, then continue cooking if necessary until thoroughly reheated.

SAUSAGE AND BACON HOT POT
Serves 4

450 g/1 lb pork sausage meat
Flour
12 rashers streaky bacon
1 large onion, finely chopped
1 carrot, thinly sliced
25 g/1 oz cornflour
2 tablespoons tomato purée
750 ml/1½ pt beef stock
Salt, pepper

1.   With floured hands, roll the sausage meat into 12 balls.
2.   Remove rind and any bone or gristle from the bacon. Stretch each rasher with the back of a knife and roll up tightly.
3.   Arrange the sausage balls and bacon rolls in a casserole. Cover and cook 4 minutes, stirring occasionally. Remove from the casserole.
4.   Add onion and carrot to the fat remaining in the casserole, stir and cook uncovered for 4 minutes.
5.   Drain the surplus fat from the dish.
6.   Stir in the cornflour. Add the tomato purée and stock, and season with salt and pepper. Cook 4 minutes.
7.   Return the sausage balls and

bacon rolls to the casserole, and baste with the sauce. Cover and cook 6 minutes.

To serve without freezing
Skim off any fat that may have accumulated on the surface of the sauce. Serve hot with boiled potatoes and cauliflower.

To freeze   Cool rapidly. Turn into a freezer container. Seal. Remove any remaining fat when the dish is frozen, then reseal and return to the freezer.

To serve from the freezer
Transfer to a serving dish. To thaw by microwave, cover and switch on for 8 minutes, giving the dish a ¼ turn every 2 minutes. Leave to rest for 5 minutes, then continue cooking if necessary to reheat thoroughly.

ESCALOPES OF VEAL FLORIDA
Serves 4

4 escalopes of veal, about
    150 g/6 oz each
125 ml/¼ pt vegetable oil
4 tablespoons wine vinegar
4 cloves
Salt, pepper
2 large oranges
2 teaspoons cornflour
2 teaspoons clear honey

1.   Marinate the veal in a mixture of oil, vinegar, cloves, salt and pepper for 2 to 12 hours. Drain.
2.   Preheat the browning skillet for 5 minutes. Seal the slices of veal quickly on both sides, then cover and cook 8 minutes, giving the skillet a ¼ turn every 2 minutes.
3.   Slice one of the oranges thinly. Press the juice from the

other and blend in the cornflour. Make up to 250 ml/½ pt with water.
4.   Cook in a large bowl for 2¼ minutes, stirring frequently. Stir in the honey.
5.   Pour sauce over the veal, garnish with the orange slices and cook 2 minutes.

To serve without freezing
Serve direct from the skillet or transfer to a heated platter.

To freeze   Arrange the veal in a shallow dish with the orange slices on top. Cover with freezer film and overwrap with freezer foil.

To serve from the freezer
Remove wrappings and thaw by microwave. Switch on for 4 minutes, giving the dish a ¼ turn every minute. Leave to rest for 5 minutes, then continue cooking until thoroughly reheated.

HUNGARIAN GOULASH
Serves 4

This stew, which always contains paprika, can also be made with chicken or pork.

450 g/1 lb veal, cubed
50 g/2 oz butter
1 large onion, finely chopped
1 garlic clove, crushed
1 tablespoon flour
1 tablespoon cornflour
1 tablespoon sweet paprika
6 tablespoons tomato purée
375 ml/¾ pt hot chicken stock
Salt and freshly ground black
    pepper
200 g/8 oz potatoes, peeled and
    quartered

+ + +

125 ml/¼ pt sour cream

1. Preheat the browning skillet for 5 minutes.
2. Add the butter, toss in the veal cubes and stir quickly to seal them on all sides.
3. Add the onions and garlic, and cook 5 minutes.
4. Blend in flour and cornflour. Add paprika, tomato purée and stock, and season with salt and pepper. Stir thoroughly.
5. Cover and cook 6 minutes, stirring occasionally.
6. Stir in potatoes. Cook 4 minutes.
7. Leave to stand for 5 minutes. Cut a veal cube in half to test. It should be an even colour throughout. Stir and cook the goulash for a few minutes longer if necessary.

To serve without freezing
Stir the sour cream into the hot goulash before serving.

To freeze Cool rapidly. Turn into a freezer container. Seal.

To serve from the freezer
Transfer to a serving dish. To thaw by microwave, cover and switch on for 10 minutes, separating the cubes as the dish defrosts. Stir thoroughly. Leave to rest for 10 minutes, then continue cooking until thoroughly reheated. Stir in the sour cream and serve.

LIVER AND BACON SLICE
Serves 2

A quick television sandwich which needs no cutlery. When cooked, the liver should still be slightly pink inside. Overcooking will cause it to toughen.

100 g/4 oz (2 slices) lambs' liver
4 rashers back bacon
French mustard

1. Remove the rinds from the bacon, and reserve them.
2. Spread mustard on both sides of the liver and sandwich each slice between 2 rashers of bacon. Place side by side on a piece of folded kitchen paper.
3. Lay the bacon rinds on top, cover with plastic film and cook for 1½ minutes, giving the dish a ½ turn once during cooking.
4. Remove wrappings and discard rinds.

To serve without freezing
Leave to stand for 2 or 3 minutes before serving, as intense heat develops inside the slices.

To freeze Cool slices rapidly and wrap them individually in freezer film.

To serve from the freezer
Thaw and reheat by microwave. Leave in the wrappings and switch on for 1 or 2 minutes. Alternatively, remove wrappings, sandwich liver slices between 2 slices of bread and reheat for the same length of time.

LIVER AND TOMATO SAVOURY
Serves 2

4 slices lambs' liver
1 small can (200 g) tomatoes
Salt, pepper
8 tablespoons dried
   breadcrumbs
1 teaspoon finely chopped
   parsley
50 g/2 oz butter
2 tablespoons tomato ketchup

1. Lay the slices of liver in a dish. Cover with the drained tomatoes and half of their liquor. Reserve the remaining liquor.
2. Season with salt and pepper, and cover with a mixture of breadcrumbs and parsley. Dot with butter.
3. Cover and cook 2½ minutes, turning the dish once. Test with the point of a sharp knife. The liver should be pink inside, but not moist.
4. Remove the cover and brown the savoury under the grill.
5. Blend the tomato ketchup with a tablespoon of the remaining liquor and spread over the top.

To serve without freezing
Serve directly from the dish.

To freeze Cool rapidly, then cover the dish with freezer wrap and overwrap.

To serve from the freezer
Remove wrappings, cover the dish and thaw in the microwave oven. Switch on for 4 minutes, turning the dish once. Leave to stand for 3 minutes, then continue cooking if necessary until thoroughly reheated.

LAMBS' SWEETBREADS IN APPLE PURÉE
Serves 4

450 g/1 lb lambs' sweetbreads
Salt
1 tablespoon vinegar
25 g/1 oz flour
Pepper
25 g/1 oz butter
200 g/8 oz dessert apples,
   stewed and puréed
2 tablespoons brown sugar

Meat

2 teaspoons lemon juice
4 tablespoons chicken stock

+ + +

4 tablespoons double cream
2 tablespoons brandy

1. Soak the sweetbreads in
cold, salted water for 1 hour.
Drain.
2. Remove the tubes, fat and
membranes, keeping the
sweetbreads whole.
3. Put sweetbreads in a large
bowl. Cover with boiling water
and add vinegar and 1 teaspoon
salt. Cover and cook 5 minutes.
4. Drain the sweetbreads,
refresh with cold water and cut
into slices 1 cm/½ inch thick.
5. Dredge sweetbreads lightly
with flour seasoned with salt
and pepper.
6. Put the sweetbreads in a
serving dish with the butter.
Cook 3 minutes, stirring
occasionally.
7. Stir in the apples, sugar,
lemon juice and stock. Cook 6
minutes, stirring frequently.

To serve without freezing
Stir in the cream and brandy just
before serving.

To freeze Cool rapidly. Turn
into a freezer container. Seal.

To serve from the freezer
Transfer the sweetbread mixture
to a serving dish. To thaw by
microwave, cover and switch on
for 5 minutes, breaking up the
lumps as the mixture defrosts.
Leave to rest for 5 minutes, then
continue cooking until
thoroughly reheated. Stir in the
cream and brandy.

TONGUE
1 kg/2¼ lb tongue serves 4–6

Ask the butcher to remove the
root of the tongue for you.
Tongue should be skinned while
hot. If the skin is difficult to
remove, more cooking is
needed. Serve tongue cold with
aspic jelly or hot spread with
chutney and sprinkled with
toasted breadcrumbs.

1 cured beef tongue
1 onion, chopped
1 carrot, chopped
Bouquet garni

1. Soak the tongue in cold
water for 6 hours.
2. Drain it and put in a large
casserole with the other
ingredients.
3. Cover the tongue with 1 to
1½ litres/2 to 3 pt boiling water.
water.
4. Cover with a lid and cook
until tender, giving the dish a ¼
turn 4 times while it is cooking.
Allow 20 minutes cooking time
per 450 g/1 lb.
5. Drain tongue and skin it.

To serve without freezing
Slice tongue and serve hot or fit
into a round serving dish, cover
with a plate, put a weight on top
and leave until cold.

To freeze Fit the tongue into a
round dish. Cover with a plate
and put a weight on top. When
cold, cut into slices, wrap each
one separately in freezer film,
then pack in a freezer bag.
Alternatively, the tongue may
be frozen whole, wrapped in
freezer film and overwrapped
with freezer foil.

To serve from the freezer
Remove wrappings and thaw

the slices on a covered plate in
the microwave oven. Switch on
for 1 or 2 minutes for each slice.
A whole tongue should be put in
a round dish. To thaw by
microwave, cover and switch on
for 6 minutes, giving the dish a ¼
turn every 1½ minutes. Leave to
rest for 5 minutes, then continue
reheating if required.

8 Poultry and Game

Poultry and Game

POULTRY

All kinds of poultry can be cooked by microwave but like meat, only birds which are naturally tender will cook successfully. A young frying or roasting chicken is excellent cooked by microwave, but a tough old boiling fowl will inevitably turn out dry and leathery.

Most of the chickens sold today are frozen, factory-farmed birds which must be thawed thoroughly before stuffing and cooking. To thaw a frozen chicken by microwave, first unwrap it. The legs and wings should be tied to the body. If metal skewers are used to truss the chicken, make sure they cannot touch the sides or back of the oven, or the magnetron will be damaged. Put the chicken in the oven and switch on for 1 minute per 450 g/1 lb, i.e. 3 minutes for a 1¼-kg/3-lb bird, until the flesh feels warm to the touch. Then leave to rest for 5 minutes to allow the heat to spread through the meat. Repeat thawing and resting until the chicken is completely defrosted. After the second resting period, it will be possible to remove the bag of giblets (cook these conventionally). This makes it easier to tell when the chicken has thawed out completely by putting your hand in the cavity. A 1¼-kg/3-lb chicken will take 30 to 40 minutes to thaw by microwave, making it possible to produce a freezer-to-table roast dinner in 48 minutes.

A microwave oven fitted with a defrost button will automatically thaw a chicken before cooking it. Nevertheless, the two processes should be kept separate. The total oven time is 2½ times that necessary for a fresh thawed bird, so the freezer-to-table time for a 1¼-kg/3-lb chicken is still only 48 minutes.

To cook a chicken by microwave, rest it on an upturned (undecorated) saucer in a suitable dish or casserole to allow fat to drip off as the bird cooks. Too much fat slows down the cooking, so the more you spoon off, the better. Salt the cavity of the chicken and rub the skin with turmeric or paprika to give it colour. You may like to put a piece of onion in the cavity for added flavour.

To ensure even, thorough cooking, turn the chicken four times while it is in the oven so that it rests on its breast, backbone and each side for equal lengths of time. Parts such as wing tips, which will be ready first, may be covered with twists of foil for part of the cooking time to prevent them overcooking, but as always, care must be taken when using metal in a microwave oven. Cover the dish to prevent spattering. Although some browning will occur, if more is required the chicken may be finished off under the grill. Alternatively, poultry may be cooked in an unsealed roaster bag for added browning, but check first that the bag does not have metal in the edging.

FRIED CHICKEN IN EGG AND ALMOND SAUCE
Serves 4

Good-quality ingredients produce the best results. Freshly boned chicken breasts in a delicious nutty sauce make this recipe suitable for a dinner party.

4 boned chicken breasts, about 150 g/6 oz each
75 g/3 oz golden breadcrumbs
1 teaspoon paprika
¼ teaspoon cayenne pepper
1 egg white (save yolk for sauce)

Sauce

15 g/½ oz butter
50 g/2 oz flaked almonds
2 tablespoons flour
White pepper
Grated nutmeg
250 ml/½ pt hot chicken stock
½ teaspoon lemon juice
½ teaspoon grated lemon rind
4 tablespoons single cream
1 egg yolk

1. Mix the breadcrumbs with the paprika and cayenne.
2. Beat the egg white with 1 tablespoon water.
3. Coat the chicken breasts with egg white and breadcrumbs, and arrange them in a dish so that the pieces are not overlapping. Cook 6 minutes, giving the dish a ¼ turn every 1½ minutes.
4. To make the sauce, put the butter in a large bowl and cook until melted, 1 minute.
5. Stir in the almonds and cook 1 minute.
6. Add the flour, pepper and nutmeg, and blend to a smooth paste.
7. Slowly stir in the stock, lemon juice, lemon rind and

cream. Cook 2 to 3 minutes, stirring occasionally.

8. Leave to cool a little, then blend in the egg yolk.

To serve without freezing
Reheat the chicken in a serving dish in the microwave oven for 1½ minutes. Pour the sauce over and serve with green beans, peas and mashed potato.

To freeze Place the chicken in a shallow container and coat with the sauce. Cool rapidly, cover and overwrap.

To serve from the freezer
Remove wrappings and place block in a serving dish. To thaw by microwave, switch on for 2 minutes. Leave to rest for 5 minutes. Separate the pieces, then cook for a further 3 to 4 minutes until the chicken is thoroughly reheated. If the sauce has become too thick, stir in a little fresh milk and serve.

CHINESE CHICKEN AND BEANSPROUTS

Serves 3

450 g/1 lb raw boned chicken meat, lean breast and thigh
1 garlic clove, peeled and cut in half
Salt, pepper
2 tablespoons vegetable oil
2 celery stalks, thinly sliced
1 onion, finely chopped
1 tablespoon cornflour
½ teaspoon ground ginger
3 tablespoons soy sauce
1 tablespoon sweet sherry

+ + +

1 can (285 g) beansprouts or 150 g/6 oz fresh beansprouts, rinsed
Boiled rice

TURKEY

A turkey of about 4½ kg/10 lb dressed weight, which takes 1 kg/2¼ lb stuffing, is the ideal size for cooking by microwave, although there is room in a 650-kw microwave oven for a bird of up to 8 kg/18 lb.

Slow conventional thawing is essential for frozen turkeys if the multiplication of bacteria is to be avoided. Remove plastic wrappings, put the turkey on a plate, cover loosely with foil and leave to thaw in the refrigerator. A large turkey may take as long as 3 days.

Thawing by microwave is considerably quicker. The procedure is much the same as for chicken. Give the turkey 1 minute of microwave energy per 450 g/1 lb, followed by a rest of 20 minutes, and repeat until the bird is fully thawed, turning it over and removing the bag of giblets as soon as it can be detached from the cavity walls. A 4½-kg/10-lb bird will take about 50 minutes, an 8-kg/18-lb bird about 2 hours. If your oven has an automatic defrost button, the same rules apply as for chicken (see above).

Salt the cavity and rub the skin with turmeric or paprika if you wish to give it colour. Cook the turkey resting on an upturned plate in a casserole, turning it over and draining off the fat at regular intervals. A large turkey may also be cooked in a brown paper bag, but surplus fat must still be drained off as it cooks.

Tender parts such as wing tips should be protected with foil for part of the cooking time to prevent them overcooking. If any brown spots appear on the breastbone during cooking, these, too, should be covered to stop the microwaves reaching that part of the flesh any longer.

As time on Christmas day is precious, it is a good idea to cook the turkey by microwave the day before, then take out the stuffing and store the two separately, covered, in the refrigerator. The following day, reheat them both by microwave, the turkey for 15 minutes and the stuffing for 6 minutes. Alternatively, if a hot oven is available, the turkey may be reheated by microwave for 10 minutes, then transferred to the conventional oven to finish reheating and brown the skin.

OTHER POULTRY

Other poultry is thawed and cooked by microwave like chicken. Duck and goose are fatty birds, so it is particularly important to drain off the fat frequently as they cook.

Poultry and Game

MICROWAVE COOKING TIMES FOR FULLY THAWED POULTRY

	Cooking time per 450 g/1 lb	Resting time before carving
Chicken	6½ mins	10 mins
Turkey	7½ mins	15 mins
Duck	6½ mins	10 mins
Goose	6 mins	10 mins

The temperature taken in the centre of the breast at the end of the resting time should read 85°C/180°F.

GAME

The microwave oven is most suitable for cooking game. With the exception of rabbit, all game must first be hung for the flavour to develop and the flesh to soften. A bird is ready for cooking when the tail feathers can be plucked out easily.

Overcooking spoils game, so be sure to weigh a bird before it goes into the oven. Cooking times per 450 g/1 lb will be the same as for chicken. Rabbit is also cooked like chicken. For hare and venison, follow the timings for beef on page 68.

There is very little point in freezing fresh poultry unless you are rearing the birds yourself. The giblets should be frozen separately and uncooked poultry should not be frozen with stuffing already in the cavity.

Game should always be hung, plucked (or skinned) and drawn before freezing. Rabbit and hare are best jointed and frozen in separate portions. Thaw game birds and small animals like chicken and cuts of venison as you would meat.

1. Rub the surface of the chicken with garlic. Discard the garlic.
2. Dice the chicken and season lightly with salt and pepper, bearing in mind that soy sauce, which is to be used in the dish, is itself very salty.
3. Preheat the browning skillet for 5 minutes. Add the oil and chicken, and stir rapidly. Cook 3 minutes.
4. Mix in celery and onion, cover and cook 3 minutes, stirring occasionally.
5. Blend the cornflour with the ginger, soy sauce, sherry and 4 tablespoons water. Pour over the chicken, cover and cook 2 minutes, stirring frequently.

To serve without freezing
Drain the beansprouts. Heat in a bowl in the microwave oven for ½ minute, then turn out on to a heated platter. Top with the chicken mixture and surround with a border of boiled rice.

To freeze Cool rapidly. Turn into a freezer container. Seal.

To serve from the freezer
Transfer to a bowl. To thaw by microwave, cover and switch on for 5 minutes. Leave to rest for 5 minutes, then continue cooking until thoroughly reheated. Drain the beansprouts, and put them in a serving dish. Heat for 2 minutes in the microwave oven. Pour chicken mixture on top. Serve with boiled rice.

CHICKEN CLAVERLEY
Serves 6

Do not be put off by the pallid appearance of this dish, for the flavour is both delicate and smooth. It is perfect for a summer's day, served with colourful vegetables and small new potatoes.

4 fresh chicken breasts, about 150 g/6 oz each, skinned
4 fresh chicken thighs, about 100 g/4 oz each, skinned
4 tablespoons vegetable oil
1 onion, chopped
25 g/1 oz cornflour
Salt, pepper
250 ml/½ pt dry white wine

1. Preheat the browning skillet for 5 minutes. Add the oil. Quickly add the chicken breasts and seal on both sides. Remove from the skillet.
2. Reheat the skillet for 5 minutes, then seal the chicken thighs.
3. Replace the chicken breasts in the browning skillet, arranging them around the outside and leaving the thighs in the middle.
4. Sprinkle the onion over the chicken, cover and cook 5 minutes, giving the dish a ½ turn after 2½ minutes.
5. Mix the cornflour, salt and pepper with a little of the wine. Add the remaining wine and 250 ml/½ pt water.
6. Pour the wine mixture over the chicken. Cook 10 minutes, turning the joints over after 5 minutes.

To serve without freezing
Serve from the skillet or transfer to a heated serving dish.

To freeze Leave to cool. Arrange in a shallow freezer container with the thighs in the middle and the breasts around the edges. Seal.

To serve from the freezer
Transfer to a serving dish. To thaw by microwave, cover and switch on for 2 minutes. Leave to rest for 2 minutes. Then cook for a further 5 minutes, giving the dish a ½ turn after 2½ minutes.

CHICKEN GINGER
Serves 4

The sauce for this dish is very lightly spiced. Add more ginger if a more pronounced flavour is desired.

4 chicken portions, about 200 g/8 oz each
50 g/2 oz flour
2 teaspoons ground ginger
Salt, pepper
50 g/2 oz butter
500 ml/1 pt hot chicken stock

+ + +

2 pieces preserved ginger

1. Mix together the flour, ground ginger and seasoning, and coat the chicken portions with some of this mixture, reserving the remainder.
2. Preheat the browning skillet for 5 minutes. Add the butter.
3. Immediately lay the chicken pieces in the skillet and cook 6 minutes. Turn the pieces over and cook for a further 5 minutes.
4. Remove the chicken pieces and brown under a hot grill. Meanwhile, complete the sauce by microwave.
5. Add the remaining seasoned flour to the skillet. Mix well, then stir in the hot stock. Cook 4 minutes until the sauce begins to thicken, stirring occasionally.

To serve without freezing
Arrange the chicken pieces on a heated platter and cover with

the sauce. Chop the ginger finely and sprinkle over the top just before serving.

To freeze Cool the chicken rapidly. Lay the pieces flat on freezer foil, slide into a polythene bag and seal. Freeze the sauce separately in a freezer container.

To serve from the freezer
To thaw by microwave, turn the sauce into a bowl, cover and switch on for 5 minutes. Break up the lumps with a fork, then continue cooking for 2 minutes. Remove sauce from the microwave oven while thawing the chicken. Unwrap the chicken and put in a suitable serving dish. Cover and switch on for 5 minutes. Separate the pieces, give the dish a ½ turn and continue cooking for a further 5 minutes, or until thoroughly reheated. Leave to stand, covered. Stir the sauce and reheat in the microwave oven for 2 or 3 minutes. Meanwhile, chop the ginger finely. Pour the hot sauce over the chicken and sprinkle with the chopped ginger.

CHICKEN NOODLES KOWLOON
Serves 4

To enhance the characteristic flavour of Chinese food, add a pinch of monosodium glutamate. Although there is no time saved in freezing cooked noodles, there will be no saucepan to wash up when reheating this dish.

450 g/1 lb chicken meat, skinned, boned and cubed (prepared weight)

Poultry and Game

1 teaspoon ground ginger
1 tablespoon cornflour
Salt, pepper
2 tablespoons vegetable oil
1 onion, chopped
1 garlic clove, crushed
100 g/4 oz mushrooms, sliced
1 green pepper, chopped
3 tablespoons soy sauce
1 tablespoon tomato purée
1 tablespoon sherry

Noodles

150 g/6 oz noodles
1 teaspoon salt
1 teaspoon vegetable oil

1. Toss the chicken cubes in a mixture of ginger, cornflour, salt and pepper.
2. Preheat the browning skillet for 5 minutes. Add the oil and toss in the chicken cubes. Cook 1 minute.
3. Stir in the onion and garlic. Cook 4 minutes.
4. Add the mushrooms and green pepper. Cook 2 minutes. Stir.
5. Stir in the soy sauce, tomato purée and sherry. Cover and cook 2 minutes.
6. Put the noodles in a large casserole, add 1 to 1½ litres/1¾ to 2½ pt boiling water, salt and oil. Cook 6 minutes.
7. Cover casserole and leave to stand for 8 minutes.

To serve without freezing
Reheat the chicken mixture for 2 minutes while the noodles are resting. Drain the noodles and pile on top of the chicken. Serve at once.

To freeze Drain and rinse the noodles under cold running water until they separate. Turn into a freezer bag and seal. Cool the chicken rapidly and freeze in a separate container.

To serve from the freezer
Remove noodles from bag and put on a serving dish. To thaw by microwave, cover and switch on for 5 minutes. Leave to rest for 5 minutes. Stir. Remove the chicken from container and place on top of the noodles. Cover and cook for 5 minutes. Leave to rest for 5 minutes, then continue cooking until thoroughly reheated.

CHICKEN À LA PAYSANNE
Serves 4

Stock freezes well and may be reduced to a concentrate by fast boiling and then freezing in ice cube trays. When required, it should be reconstituted with water.

1 chicken, about 1½ kg/3¼ lb, jointed
375 ml/¾ pt chicken stock
200 g/8 oz white parts of leek, sliced
2 celery stalks, sliced
200 g/8 oz small new potatoes
2 carrots, sliced
Salt, pepper
1 medium can (400 g) tomatoes

1. Pour the stock into a large casserole and cook to bring to the boil, 5 minutes.
2. Add the leeks, celery, potatoes, carrots and seasoning. Cook 5 minutes.
3. Arrange the chicken joints in the casserole. Add the tomatoes, cover and cook 20 minutes, or until the chicken is tender, turning the dish occasionally.

To serve without freezing
Serve directly from the casserole or transfer to a heated serving dish.

To freeze Cool rapidly. Freeze in the covered casserole, then dip the base in hot water to loosen the block. Turn it out, wrap in freezer film, overwrap with freezer foil and return to the freezer.

To serve from the freezer
Remove wrappings, replace the block in the original casserole, cover and thaw by microwave. Switch on for 4 minutes, give the dish a ¼ turn and cook for 2 minutes longer. Stir and repeat until the chicken is thoroughly reheated.

PERSIAN CHICKEN RISOTTO
Serves 3

A risotto is an economical dish making use of left-overs. Only 150 g/6 oz of chicken is required to serve 3. Ring the changes with turkey, veal or ham.

50 g/2 oz butter
1 onion, chopped
75 g/3 oz mushrooms, sliced
100 g/4 oz long-grain rice
375 ml/¾ pt chicken stock
25 g/1 oz chopped mixed nuts
25 g/1 oz sultanas
1 teaspoon ground cumin
Salt, pepper

+ + +

150 g/6 oz cooked chicken, diced

1. Put the butter in a large bowl. Cook until melted, 1 minute.
2. Mix in the onion and cook 1 minute. Stir.
3. Add the mushrooms and cook 3 minutes.
4. Wash and drain the rice, and add to the other ingredients

in the bowl, together with the stock. Add the cumin and season sparingly with salt and pepper. Cook 10 minutes, stirring occasionally.

5. Add the nuts and sultanas. Cook 2 minutes. Cover and leave to rest for 5 minutes.

To serve without freezing
While the rice is resting, put the diced chicken in a bowl, cover and reheat in the microwave oven for 1 minute. Stir, then continue heating for a further minute. Mix chicken into the rice and serve immediately.

To freeze Cool rice. Mix in the chicken. Turn into a freezer container and seal.

To serve from the freezer
Put the risotto in a serving dish. Cover lightly with greaseproof paper. To thaw by microwave, switch on for 2 minutes. Leave to rest for 5 minutes. Stir, then continue cooking until thoroughly reheated.

CHICKEN POLONAISE
Serves 4

The browning skillet may be used at Step 4 for extra crispness.

**4 chicken breasts, about
    150 g/6 oz each
2 tablespoons dry white wine
2 tablespoons lemon juice
75 g/3 oz golden crumbs
3 tablespoons grated Parmesan
    cheese
1 teaspoon finely chopped
    parsley
Salt, pepper
Grated nutmeg
1 egg, beaten
2 tablespoons vegetable oil**

1. Marinate the chicken pieces in the mixture of wine and lemon juice for 1 to 2 hours.
2. Mix together crumbs, cheese, parsley, salt, pepper and nutmeg.
3. Remove the chicken pieces from the marinade. Dip them in beaten egg and coat with the crumb mixture.
4. Pour the oil into a large, shallow dish and cook 1 minute.
5. Lay the chicken pieces side by side in the dish. Cook 4 minutes, giving the dish a ½ turn after 2 minutes.
6. Turn the chicken pieces over and cook for a further 4 minutes, giving the dish a ½ turn after 2 minutes.
7. Leave to rest for 5 minutes. Test with the point of a sharp knife and if the chicken is not ready, cook for a further 2 minutes.

To serve without freezing
Serve hot with French fried potatoes and poached courgettes, or leave until cold and serve with salad.

To freeze Cool rapidly. Carefully wrap the chicken pieces individually in freezer film so they will keep their shape, then package them together in freezer foil.

To serve from the freezer
Remove wrappings and put chicken pieces on a plate. Thaw by microwave. To serve cold, switch on for 2 minutes per portion, then leave to stand until thawed. If thawing more than 2 portions, give the plate a ¼ turn every 2 minutes. To serve hot, switch on for 2 minutes, leave to rest for 2 minutes, then cook for 4 minutes, or until thoroughly reheated. Serve as above.

POULET AU VIN BLANC
Serves 4

The flavours of the green and red peppers blend together to produce this colourful and succulent chicken dish.

**4 chicken breasts, about
    150 g/6 oz each
50 g/2 oz butter
200 g/8 oz mushrooms, sliced
1 small red pepper, quartered,
    seeded and cored
1 small green pepper,
    quartered, seeded and cored
50 g/2 oz flour
2 teaspoons cornflour
Salt, pepper
250 ml/½ pt dry white wine
250 ml/½ pt chicken stock**

1. Put the butter, mushrooms and peppers in a large square dish or in the browning skillet. Cover and cook 4 minutes, stirring occasionally.
2. Blend the flour, cornflour, salt and pepper with a little of the wine. Stir in the remaining wine and the stock. Pour over the vegetables and mix thoroughly. Cook, uncovered, until the sauce thickens, 4 to 5 minutes, stirring occasionally.
3. Arrange the chicken breasts on top of the mixture, making sure they are not overlapping. Cover with greaseproof paper and cook 9 minutes, giving the dish a ¼ turn every 2¼ minutes.

To serve without freezing
Serve straight from the dish with mashed potatoes or boiled rice and Baked Tomatoes (page 95).

To freeze Cool rapidly. Transfer to a shallow freezer container and seal.

Poultry and Game

To serve from the freezer
Remove the chicken from the container and replace in the original cooking dish. To thaw by microwave, switch on for 2 minutes, then rest for 5 minutes. Cook for a further 6 minutes or until the chicken is thoroughly reheated giving the dish a ¼ turn each minute. Serve as above.

ROAST CHICKEN FLAMBÉ
Serves 4

Fennel, which has the flavour of aniseed, gives this dish an unusual taste.

**1 roasting chicken, about
1 kg/2¼ lb
1 tablespoon vegetable oil
White pepper
125 ml/¼ pt dry white wine
6 small leeks, thinly sliced
2 carrots, thinly sliced
½ teaspoon dried fennel
Salt
4 tablespoons brandy**

1. Pierce the chicken skin with a sharp knife, rub the chicken with oil, sprinkle with pepper and put it in a large casserole breast side up. Cook 8 minutes.
2. Turn the chicken breast side down. Baste with the fat in the casserole and spoon off any surplus fat.
3. Pour the wine over the chicken and arrange the leeks and carrots around it. Sprinkle with dried fennel.
4. Cover the chicken with a piece of non-stick paper. Cook 8 minutes. Sprinkle with salt.
5. Remove the casserole from the microwave oven. Turn chicken on its back again. Leave to rest for 10 minutes. The chicken is properly cooked when the temperature in the

centre of the breast taken with a meat thermometer reads 85°C/180°F.
6. Warm the brandy in a small pan on the hob. Set alight and pour over the chicken.

To serve without freezing
Transfer to a heated platter and serve immediately.

To freeze Cool the chicken rapidly. Place in a freezer container with the vegetables, and spoon the juices over them. Seal.

To serve from the freezer
Replace chicken in the original casserole. To thaw by microwave, cover and switch on for 3 minutes, leave to rest for 3 minutes, then repeat until the chicken is completely defrosted. Turn the chicken over on to its breast and cook for 5 minutes or until it is thoroughly reheated. Reheat the vegetables in a separate bowl for 2 or 3 minutes. Turn the chicken breast side up again, surround with the reheated vegetables and serve.

ROAST CHICKEN PIQUANTE
Serves 6

Cooking times vary with the weight, shape and age of the chicken. Allow 6 to 7 minutes per pound, but do not overcook. Protect the wing tips and legs with twists of foil for the first 15 minutes.

**1 roasting chicken, about
2 kg/4½ lb
1 tablespoon vegetable oil
2 medium onions, chopped
125 ml/¼ pt tomato purée**

**2 tablespoons sweet pickle
2 tablespoons sweet white wine
Salt, pepper**

+ + +

125 ml/¼ pt sour cream

1. Prick the chicken skin with a sharp knife and brush the chicken with the oil.
2. Heat the browning skillet for 5 minutes.
3. Put in the chicken, breast side down, and quickly brown. Turn the chicken over and add the onions. Cover with non-stick paper and cook 10 minutes.
4. Mix together the tomato purée, pickle and wine, and season with salt and pepper.
5. Spoon the mixture over the chicken and lay it on its breast again. Cover with the paper and cook 10 minutes, basting occasionally.
6. Turn the chicken on to one side. Cook 5 minutes, then cook 5 minutes on the other side. Remove the paper and leave the chicken to stand for 10 minutes. Test with a meat thermometer, which should register 85°C/180°F in the centre of the breast.

To serve without freezing
Transfer the chicken to a serving dish. Stir the sour cream into the sauce and pour into a heated sauceboat or jug.

To freeze Remove the chicken from the dish and skim off any surplus fat from the sauce. Put the chicken in a freezer container. Pour over the sauce. Cool and seal.

To serve from the freezer
Put the chicken and sauce in a serving dish. Cover and thaw by microwave. Switch on for 3 minutes, then leave to rest for 3

minutes. Give the dish a ¼ turn. Repeat until the chicken is completely defrosted. Turn the chicken over on to its breast and cook for 5 minutes, or until thoroughly reheated. Transfer the chicken to a heated dish, breast side up. Stir the sour cream into the sauce and pour into a heated sauceboat.

DUCK WITH CHERRY SAUCE
Serves 4

Duck is more fatty than chicken and frequent draining is necessary to prevent spattering.

1 duck, about 2 kg/4½ lb, cut into 4 joints
1 large can (400 g) pitted black cherries
125 ml/¼ pt port wine
1 tablespoon potato flour
375 ml/¾ pt beef stock
¼ Oxo cube, crumbled
1 garlic clove, crushed
25 g/1 oz butter
Salt, pepper
1 tablespoon redcurrant jelly

1. Drain the cherries and soak overnight in port wine.
2. Arrange the duck joints in a shallow dish. Cover with greased greaseproof paper and cook 20 minutes, giving the dish a ¼ turn every 5 minutes. Drain off the surplus fat.
3. Cook a further 20 minutes, continuing to turn the dish every 5 minutes.
4. Transfer the duck to a heated serving platter and keep warm.
5. Prepare the sauce. Strain the wine into a large bowl and put aside the cherries.
6. Blend the potato flour smoothly with a few

tablespoons of the wine, then stir it into the bowl, together with the beef stock, Oxo cube, garlic, butter, salt and pepper. Cook 3 minutes.
7. Stir in the redcurrant jelly. Cook 1 minute.
8. Mix in the cherries.

To serve without freezing
Pour the hot sauce into a heated sauceboat and hand separately.

To freeze Cool rapidly. Place duck in a freezer container and pour over the sauce. Seal the container.

To serve from the freezer
Place the duck and sauce in a serving dish. To thaw by microwave, cover and switch on for 3 minutes. Leave to rest for 3 minutes, then repeat until the duck is completely thawed, turning the pieces occasionally. Continue cooking for 7 minutes, or until thoroughly reheated.

ROAST GOOSE
Serves 4–6

Goose is rich and is best served with a fruit sauce. When pricked, the juice of a cooked goose is a white colour.

1 goose, about 2½ kg/5½ lb dressed weight
Salt, pepper

1. Wash and clean the goose. Discard the giblets and rub salt inside the bird. Tie the legs and wings to the body. Wrap small pieces of foil around the legs and wings.
2. Rest the goose, breast down, on an upturned soup plate in a casserole, making sure that the foil does not touch the

sides or the back of the microwave oven. Cover with a piece of greaseproof paper and cook 15 minutes.
3. Remove the goose from the oven and drain off any surplus fat. Remove the foil from the legs and wings.
4. Turn the goose over, replace in the casserole, season with salt and pepper, and cook 15 minutes.
5. Remove the bird from the casserole and stand it on absorbent paper to soak up excess grease.

To serve without freezing
Leave to rest for 10 minutes before carving.

To freeze Cool rapidly. Wrap in freezer foil and place in a large freezer bag. Seal.

To serve from the freezer
Remove wrappings and place the goose in a serving dish. To thaw by microwave, switch on for 3 minutes, then leave to rest for 3 minutes. Repeat this procedure 4 times, or until the goose is warm to the touch. Continue cooking for 5 minutes, or until thoroughly reheated.

ROAST TURKEY

Allow 450 g/1 lb purchased weight of turkey per serving, but half this quantity for a cleaned and dressed bird. A 4½ kg/10 lb turkey will require 1 kg/2¼ lb sausage meat for stuffing and will serve 10. For cooking times, see the chart at the beginning of the chapter.

1 oven-ready turkey, thawed
Stuffing (see above)

Poultry and Game

1. Remove the giblets and rub the inside of the turkey with salt.
2. Stuff the turkey and secure the openings with skewers. Wrap small pieces of foil around the legs and wings, and tie the legs and wings to the body.
3. Place the turkey breast side down on an upturned soup plate in a large casserole and put in the oven, making sure that neither the skewers nor the foil touch the sides or back of the oven.
4. Cook for a quarter of the total cooking time.
5. Baste, turn on one side and cook for a further quarter of the total cooking time.
6. Take the turkey out of the casserole, remove the foil wrappings and drain away any surplus fat.
7. Replace the turkey on its other side in the casserole and cook for a further quarter of the total cooking time. Baste.
8. Turn the turkey on to its back and complete cooking.
9. Remove turkey from the oven. Cover with foil and leave to stand for 15 minutes before carving.

TURKEY CUTLETS
Serves 4

It is economical to buy a larger turkey than you need for one meal, then make use of the left-overs in dishes that can be stored in the freezer. Large birds have more flesh in ratio to bone.

200 g/8 oz cooked turkey, minced
25 g/1 oz butter
25 g/1 oz plain flour
125 ml/¼ pt poultry stock

Salt, pepper
1 teaspoon lemon juice
2 teaspoons grated lemon rind
2 eggs, beaten separately
100 g/4 oz dried breadcrumbs
125 ml/¼ pt vegetable oil

1. Put the butter in a large bowl. Cook until melted, 1 minute.
2. Blend in the flour. Cook ½ minute.
3. Gradually stir in the stock. Cook 2 minutes, stirring after 1 minute. Season with salt and pepper.
4. Mix in the turkey, lemon juice and rind, and bind with 1 beaten egg.
5. Shape into 4 cutlets. Dip into remaining beaten egg and coat with breadcrumbs, pressing them well in.
6. Heat the browning skillet for 5 minutes.
7. Quickly add the oil and the cutlets. Cook 2 minutes.
8. Turn the cutlets over and cook 2 minutes.
9. Drain on absorbent paper.

To serve without freezing
Serve hot with fresh spinach and duchesse potatoes.

To freeze Cool cutlets rapidly. Open-freeze, then wrap individually in plastic film and put into a freezer bag. Seal.

To serve from the freezer
To thaw by microwave, unwrap cutlets and place on a piece of absorbent paper, well spread out, on the base of the microwave oven. Switch on for 2 minutes. Turn the cutlets over and cook for a further 1½ minutes. Leave to rest for 2 minutes, then continue cooking if necessary until thoroughly hot.

TWELFTH NIGHT TURKEY
Serves 4

When searching for ideas for using up left-over turkey, try this unusual recipe. It is equally good served as a main course or in individual shells as a starter.

375 g/14 oz cooked turkey, diced
50 g/2 oz butter
200 g/8 oz button mushrooms
100 g/4 oz frozen peas
250 ml/½ pt poultry stock
125 ml/¼ pt dry sherry
2 tablespoons soy sauce
Salt, pepper
25 g/1 oz cornflour
125 ml/¼ pt single cream
1 can (400 g) artichoke hearts

+ + +

2 tablespoons fresh breadcrumbs
2 tablespoons grated cheese

1. Put the butter in a large bowl. Cook until melted, 1 minute.
2. Add the mushrooms and peas, cover and cook 6 minutes, stirring occasionally.
3. Add the stock, sherry and soy sauce, and season with salt and pepper. Cook 4 minutes.
4. Blend the cornflour with 4 tablespoons water and stir in. Bring back to the boil, stirring occasionally, about 2 minutes.
5. Stir in the cream.
6. Arrange the turkey meat in a shallow casserole, cover with the artichoke hearts and pour the sauce over the top.

To serve without freezing
At step 6, reheat the turkey and artichoke hearts in the microwave oven for 5 minutes before cooking with the sauce. Sprinkle with breadcrumbs and

grated cheese, and brown under the grill.

To freeze At step 6 line the casserole with foil before putting in the turkey and artichokes. Cover with freezer foil and leave to cool, then overwrap with freezer foil. When the dish is frozen, remove the foil package and replace in the freezer.

To serve from the freezer
Remove foil wrappings and replace in the original casserole. To thaw by microwave, cover and switch on for 8 minutes, giving the casserole a $\frac{1}{4}$ turn every 2 minutes. Leave to rest for 5 minutes, then continue cooking until thoroughly reheated. Sprinkle with breadcrumbs and grated cheese and brown under the grill.

PHEASANT AUBERGE
Serves 2

The season for pheasant is from October to January. The younger the bird, the more moist and tender it will be, but all pheasants should be well hung before cooking.

1 pheasant, about 1 kg/2¼ lb
   dressed weight
Salt, pepper
1 large cooking apple, peeled,
   cored and sliced
1 medium onion, sliced
1 tablespoon cornflour
125 ml/¼ pt cider

1. Cut the pheasant in half through the backbone. Season with salt and pepper, and lay skin side down in a casserole.
2. Cover with the apple and onion slices.
3. Blend the cornflour with the

cider and pour over the pheasant.
4. Cover with a lid and cook 20 minutes, turning the dish once during cooking.

To serve without freezing
Leave to rest for 5 minutes before serving.

To freeze Cool rapidly, put in a shallow freezer container, seal and overwrap with foil.

To serve from the freezer
Remove wrappings and place pheasant in a serving dish. To thaw by microwave, cover and switch on for 2 minutes. Leave to rest for 5 minutes, then continue cooking until thoroughly reheated, 5 to 8 minutes.

SOMERSET RABBIT
Serves 4

One whole rabbit will serve 4 to 5, but if purchased in pieces 450 g/1 lb will serve 3 to 4.

1 rabbit, cut into pieces
25 g/1 oz butter
1 onion, finely chopped
1 carrot, finely chopped
1 cooking apple, peeled, cored
   and chopped
2 bay leaves, crumbled
Salt, pepper
375 ml/¾ pt dry cider
1 tablespoon cornflour

1. Preheat the browning skillet for 5 minutes.
2. Add the butter and toss in the rabbit pieces, stirring quickly to seal them.
3. Add the onion and cook 5 minutes.
4. Stir in the carrot, apple and bay leaves, and season with salt and pepper.

5. Pour the cider over the top, cover and cook 20 minutes, stirring occasionally.
6. Blend the cornflour with a little water. Stir into the sauce and continue cooking for 10 minutes.

To serve without freezing
Stir thoroughly so that all the pieces are coated with sauce. Serve straight from the skillet or turn into a heated casserole.

To freeze Cool rapidly and turn into a shallow freezer container. Seal.

To serve from the freezer
Remove from container and place rabbit in a serving dish. To thaw by microwave, cover and switch on for 5 minutes. Stir. Leave to rest for 5 minutes. Stir. Continue cooking until thoroughly reheated.

VENISON CUTLETS
Serves 4

The meat from a young deer will be tender and sweet, but an older animal will produce tough meat which must be marinated in oil and lemon juice to tenderise it before cooking.

4 venison cutlets
Salt
50 g/2 oz butter
4 tablespoons whisky
2 tablespoons Cranberry sauce
   (page 145)
Juice of 1 orange

1. Trim the venison cutlets and beat them with a meat hammer or the side of a cleaver to flatten them. Rub with salt.
2. Preheat the browning skillet for 5 minutes. Add the butter

and quickly brown the cutlets on
both sides.

3. Add the whisky, cranberry
sauce and orange juice. Cover
and cook 15 minutes, giving the
dish a ¼ turn every 4 minutes.

To serve without freezing
Arrange the cutlets on a heated
platter, and coat with the sauce.

To freeze Cool rapidly.
Transfer to a shallow freezer
container. Seal.

To serve from the freezer
Turn out on a serving dish. To
thaw by microwave, cover and
switch on for 5 minutes, giving
the dish a ¼ turn every minute.
Leave to rest for 5 minutes, then
continue cooking until
thoroughly reheated.

9 Vegetables

Vegetables

Microwave vegetable cookery is superior: it retains more vitamins than any other method, vegetables maintain their true colour, and their textures are improved. Crisp, crunchy shredded cabbage, carrots and leeks with each slice separate, and whole courgettes softened until just tender are a few examples. Unpeeled beetroots wrapped in paper or plastic film do not bleed and take only 5 to 10 minutes, compared with 1 or 2 hours when boiled conventionally.

Vegetables which are normally cooked in water should be covered to prevent them drying out. Salt the cooking water before adding the vegetables. Salt should never be sprinkled directly on to them because it draws out the natural juices, which are then drained off with the water. If possible, stir the vegetables occasionally as they cook.

Vegetables with shiny skins which are cooked unpeeled should first be pricked with a fork to prevent them bursting. The skins keep the heat in so there is no need to cover them.

Potatoes baked in their jackets should be of uniform size and well spaced out on the trays of the oven. It helps to turn them over halfway through cooking. Tomatoes cook very quickly indeed and become flat and mushy if too much time is allowed.

Vegetables which have similar cooking times may be cooked together. The dishes should be turned during cooking. As they continue cooking after the oven has been switched off, care must be taken not to overcook them, which would destroy their texture.

Although instructions for cooking cauliflower have been included in this book, there is a tendency for the flower to become mushy before the stem is soft. Because of this, you may prefer to use frozen cauliflower florettes for microwave cooking.

Cooked vegetables can all be reheated by microwave. Unlike meat and fish, vegetables are not subject to the multiplication of bacteria, so no special precautions have to be taken.

JUST AUBERGINES
Serves 4

Aubergines have a special flavour. Although usually stuffed, they are equally delicious unembellished.

2 large or 4 small aubergines
Salt
25 g/1 oz butter
Freshly ground black pepper

1. Cut the aubergines in half lengthways. Score the open flesh with a sharp knife and sprinkle with salt. Leave to drain in a colander for 1 hour. Rinse in cold water and shake off surplus water.
2. Place the aubergines in a shallow dish. Cover with plastic film and cook 8 to 12 minutes, giving the dish a $\frac{1}{4}$ turn every 2 minutes.
3. Scoop the flesh out of the shells, chop and mix with butter and pepper. Spoon back into the shells.

To serve without freezing
Serve hot as a starter or as an accompaniment for a main dish such as Meat Balls with Egg and Lemon Sauce (page 71).

To freeze Wrap aubergine halves individually in freezer film, taking care not to crush them. Leave until cold, then clamp the two halves together so that the skin is on the outside, and overwrap with freezer foil. Seal.

To serve from the freezer
Remove foil wrappings and thaw aubergine halves by microwave in the freezer film. Allow 1 minute for each half, but cut the total time to $3\frac{1}{2}$ minutes if thawing all the pieces together.

MUSHROOMS SMETANA
Serves 4

Mushrooms are very low in calories, but as cream and brandy are included in this recipe, slimmers should eat small portions only. If sour cream is not obtainable, substitute fresh double cream mixed with lemon juice.

25 g/1 oz butter
1 onion, finely chopped
1 garlic clove, crushed
450 g/1 lb mushrooms, sliced
125 ml/¼ pt sour cream
2 teaspoons brandy
Salt

1. Put the butter, onion and garlic in a dish or a browning skillet which has been preheated for 5 minutes. Cook until soft, 3 to 4 minutes.
2. Add the mushrooms and cook for 3 minutes. Stir.
3. Stir in the cream and brandy, and season with salt.

To serve without freezing
Cook in the microwave oven for 1 minute. Serve on a bed of boiled rice or spread on buttered toast.

To freeze Cool rapidly. Turn into a freezer container and seal.

To serve from the freezer
To thaw by microwave, switch on for 2 minutes, then leave to rest for 5 minutes. Separate the pieces with a fork and continue to cook until the mixture just boils. Serve as above.

APPROXIMATE MICROWAVE COOKING TIMES FOR FRESH VEGETABLES

Type	2 Servings (in minutes)	4 Servings (in minutes)	Addition of water (in tablespoons)
Artichokes, globe	8	12	see recipe
Jerusalem	10	14	4
Asparagus	6	10	4
Aubergine	8	13	see recipe
Beans, broad	8	12	8
French	7	10	8
runner	8	12	8
Beetroot, whole	10	14	8
Broccoli	7	9	see recipe
Brussels sprouts	5	7	4
Cabbage, shredded	5	10	8
Carrots, sliced	6	10	4
whole	8	14	6
Cauliflower, florettes	3	5	2
whole	6	10	4
Celery, whole/sliced	12	16	4
Chicory, whole	4	6	4
Corn on the cob, whole	4	8	none
kernels	5	8	4
Courgettes	4	7	none
Leeks, sliced	8	12	4
Marrow	6	9	none
Mushrooms	5	9	see recipe
Onions, whole/sliced	5	7	see recipe
Parsnips	8	14	8
Peas, shelled	6	8	8
Potatoes, peeled and quartered	8	14	4
baked (depending on size)	8	12	see recipe
Spinach	4	6	none
Tomatoes halved	1	1½	none
Turnips, diced	12	16	8

Vegetables

BLANCHING VEGETABLES FOR THE FREEZER

Vegetables must be blanched before freezing to halt enzyme action and prevent deterioration.

When blanching conventionally, you will need a large saucepan and a blanching basket. Fill the pan with water and bring to the boil. Put 450 g/1 lb prepared vegetables in the basket and plunge it into boiling water, making sure the vegetables are completely covered. Quickly bring the water back to the boil and calculate the blanching time from the moment the water starts boiling again (see table). Cool the vegetables rapidly under cold running water, then drain and dry before packing.

Blanching by microwave is much simpler. Put the prepared vegetables, 450 g/1 lb at a time, in a large casserole. Cover and place in the microwave oven without adding water. Switch on for a few minutes (see table), stirring occasionally.

Cool one batch in a colander under cold running water while the next batch is blanching. Drain, dry and pack.

BLANCHING TIMES FOR 450 g/1 lb FRESH VEGETABLES (WASHED AND PREPARED)

	Conventional (minutes in boiling water)	Microwave (minutes from cold)
Asparagus	4	3
Beans, broad	3	4
French	3	4
runner	2	4
Broccoli	3	3
Brussels sprouts	3	3
Cabbage	2	3
Carrots	3	4
Cauliflower	3	2
Celery	3	4
Corn on the cob	6	3
Marrow	3	2
Parsnips	2	5
Peas	1	4 (add 3 table-spoons water)
Peppers	3	4
Potatoes	3	4
Spinach	2	4

CARROTTY PUDDING
Serves 4

Serve this dish as a vegetable or top portions with a hamburger for a quick supper dish.

200 g/8 oz carrots, sliced
50 g/2 oz butter
15 g/$\frac{1}{2}$ oz brown sugar
1 egg, separated
75 g/3 oz plain flour
1 teaspoon baking powder
$\frac{1}{2}$ teaspoon salt
1 tablespoon lemon juice

1. Cover the carrots with boiling water in a casserole. Cover and cook 12 minutes, stirring occasionally. Drain and mash.
2. Cream the butter and sugar. Add the beaten egg yolk and the flour sifted with baking powder and salt. Beat in the lemon juice.
3. Combine the carrots with the pudding batter.
4. Stiffly beat the egg white and fold it into the pudding.
5. Spoon mixture into a lined, 25-cm/10-inch cake dish. Cook 4 minutes, giving the dish a $\frac{1}{4}$ turn every 1$\frac{1}{2}$ minutes.

To serve without freezing
Leave to rest for 2 to 3 minutes before cutting into wedges.

To freeze Open-freeze. Turn out on to a double thickness of foil and wrap tightly.

To serve from the freezer
Remove foil wrappings and replace the pudding in the original dish. To thaw by microwave, switch on for 2 minutes. Cut into wedges and continue to cook for 4 minutes until thoroughly reheated, turning the dish frequently.

CELERY À LA GRÈCQUE

Serves 4

Other vegetables may be cooked in the same way.

1 head of celery
2 tablespoons vegetable oil
1 tablespoon lemon juice
1 bay leaf
10 black peppercorns
$\frac{1}{4}$ teaspoon coriander seeds
$\frac{1}{2}$ teaspoon salt

1.　Separate celery stalks, wash them, remove the strings and cut the stalks into 2½-cm/1-inch pieces.
2.　Put celery in a bowl. Add all other ingredients and 125 ml/¼ pt water. Cover and cook 10 minutes, stirring occasionally.
3.　Remove the cover and continue cooking for a further 10 to 15 minutes, stirring frequently.

To serve without freezing
Leave to cool. Serve each portion with a spoonful of the cooking liquor.

To freeze　Cool. Pour the celery in its liquor into a freezer container. Seal.

To serve from the freezer
Turn the block of celery out in to a serving dish, ice side up. To thaw by microwave, cover and switch on for 10 minutes. Separate the pieces with a fork, then leave at room temperature until completely thawed. Serve cold in the liquor.

BLANCHING FRUIT FOR THE FREEZER

With the exception of apples, pears and rhubarb, fruit may be frozen without blanching. Whole fruit is usually packed dry. Soft berries should be spread on trays for open-freezing before packing. Alternatively, fruits may be puréed either cooked or raw. These take up less space in the freezer, but cannot be served in a fruit salad. Prepared fruit is packed either with dry sugar in the proportion of one quarter to the weight of the fruit, or in a syrup made up of 50 g/2 oz sugar and 500 ml/1 pt water for a thin syrup or 450 g/1 lb sugar to 500 ml/1 pt water for a thick syrup. A sprinkling of ascorbic acid crystals or a squeeze of lemon juice added to the hot syrup will prevent discolouration of the fruit. Sugar syrups must be cold before using.

Apples, pears and rhubarb require a blanching time of 1 minute per 450 g/1 lb. Microwave blanching times are: apples and pears, 2 minutes, stirring after 1 minute; rhubarb 3 minutes, stirring after 1½ minutes.

COOKING FROZEN VEGETABLES BY MICROWAVE

Frozen vegetables packed in cardboard cartons may be thawed and cooked by microwave in their wrappings, as can small plastic packs, provided they are pierced or opened. Frozen blocks should be placed in the oven ice side up so that the heat generated in the block will rise and speed thawing. Large quantities of cabbage, Brussels sprouts, broccoli and turnips or swedes have to be stirred during cooking, so for these a casserole with a lid should be used. All vegetables that are actually cooked in water must also be covered, and any salt should be dissolved in the water before the vegetables are added.

When cooking soft vegetables, or small quantities which will not need stirring, the dish may be sealed with plastic film. This causes greater heat to develop in the dish, thereby shortening the cooking time. When the vegetables are cooked, they can be drained through a hole pierced in the film, doing away with the need for a colander.

Vegetables which have similar cooking times can be cooked together or stacked in separate dishes but remember to increase the cooking time according to the total quantity.

Allow 75 g/3 oz frozen or cooked fresh vegetables per portion when more than one kind is being served. Two portions can be cooked in a ½-litre/1-pt dish. All vegetables should be stirred when they are taken out of the oven and left to stand for a few minutes before serving. During this time, cooking continues, promoting even tenderness and temperatures throughout.

Vegetables

APPROXIMATE MICROWAVE COOKING TIMES FOR FROZEN VEGETABLES

Type	2 Servings (in minutes)	4 servings (in minutes)	Additional water (in table-spoons)
Artichoke hearts	4	6	2
Asparagus	6	10	4
Beans, broad	7	10	8
green, whole			
or sliced	7	10	8
Broccoli	6	9	8
Brussel sprouts	6	10	8
Cabbage, shredded	6	10	8
Carrots, sliced			
or diced	6	9	4
whole	8	10	4
Cauliflower,			
florettes	4	6	None
Corn on the cob	8	12	2 tbsps butter
Corn kernels	4	7	4
Courgettes	4	6	none
Marrow	4	6	none
Mushrooms	4	6	none
Onions, rings			
or slices	4	6	none
Peas	4	6	8
Peppers, diced	4	6	4
quartered			
or whole	4	6	none
Potatoes, new	5	8	4
Spinach, chopped	4	6	none
leaf	4	6	2
Stewpack	7	10	4
Swedes, diced	7	10	4
Turnips, diced	7	10	4
Vegetables,			
mixed, diced	5	7	8

Note: Times can only be approximate as the depth of freezing will vary the time required.

BEETROOT À LA CRÈME
Serves 3–4

Beetroot belongs to the same family as chard and silver beet. It bleeds readily when the skin is pierced. When cooked, the skin should peel away easily.

8 small, even-sized raw beetroots
Salt
1 small onion, finely chopped
25 g/1 oz butter
25 g/1 oz cornflour
250 ml/½ pt vegetable stock
Pepper

+ + +

125 ml/¼ pt sour cream

1. Put the beetroots in a casserole with ¼ teaspoon salt. Add 250 ml/½ pt water.
2. Cover tightly and cook 15 to 20 minutes, turning the beetroots over once during cooking.
3. Drain, cool and peel the beetroots.
4. Rinse and dry the casserole. Add the onion and butter. Cook 2 minutes.
5. Blend in the cornflour. Cook uncovered ½ minute.
6. Gradually stir in the stock. Cook 3 minutes, stirring occasionally.
7. Season with salt and pepper.

To serve without freezing
Remove the beetroots from the casserole. Stir the sour cream into the sauce and replace the beetroots. Spoon the sauce over the beetroots just before serving.

To freeze Pack the beetroots into a freezer bag. Seal. Freeze the sauce separately in a freezer bag or container.

To serve from the freezer
Thaw beetroots and sauce
separately by microwave. Put
the beetroots in a serving dish.
Cover and switch on for 5
minutes. Leave to rest while
reheating the sauce. Cook the
sauce, covered, for 5 minutes.
Leave to rest for 5 minutes. Stir,
then continue cooking until
thoroughly reheated. Stir the
sour cream into the sauce,
reheat the beetroots if necessary
and coat with the sauce.

HARICOTS VERTS VERHALLE
Serves 3

Use fresh or frozen French
beans, but cut microwave
cooking time by half for frozen
vegetables.

350 g/12 oz French beans,
topped and tailed
15 g/½ oz butter
1 onion, chopped
½ teaspoon fennel seeds
Salt, pepper

1. Put the butter in a casserole
and cook until melted, ½ minute.
2. Add the onion and fennel
seeds, stir and cook 2 minutes.
3. Season with salt and
pepper.
4. Add the beans to the
casserole together with 8
tablespoons water. Cover and
cook 8 minutes, stirring
occasionally.

To serve without freezing
Drain beans, then return them
to the casserole and serve
immediately.

To freeze Leave beans to cool
in their liquor. Then drain and
place in container. Seal.

To serve from the freezer
To thaw by microwave, place
the block ice side up in a serving
dish and switch on for 3
minutes. Leave to rest for 5
minutes, then loosen the lumps
with a fork and continue
cooking until thoroughly
reheated. Drain if necessary.

BAKED TOMATOES

450 g/1 lb (4 large) tomatoes
Salt, pepper
25 g/1 oz butter

1. Cut the tomatoes in half
crossways.
2. Arrange them in a dish, cut
sides uppermost.
3. Season with salt and
pepper, and place a dab of
butter on each half.
4. Cover with greaseproof
paper and cook for 3 to 4
minutes, giving the dish a ¼ turn
every minute. Some tomatoes
may become cooked before
others. Remove these as soon as
they are soft and keep warm.

Baked tomatoes are not suitable
for freezing.

BUTTERED BROCCOLI
Serves 4

Sprinkle cooked broccoli with
grated cheese, chopped
hard-boiled egg, or toss in sour
cream. If the broccoli is to be
deep frozen, cook for only 6
minutes.

450 g/1 lb fresh broccoli

+ + +

25 g/1 oz butter
Salt, pepper

1. Discard the tough ends of
the broccoli stalks and leaves.
Split the stalk lengthways.
2. Arrange the broccoli in a
serving dish with the tops in the
middle and the stalks towards
the outside. Add 4 to 8
tablespoons water.
3. Cover and cook 8 minutes.
Leave to rest for 5 minutes.
Drain.

To serve without freezing
Add the butter and season with
salt and pepper. Turn the
broccoli with a fork. Cover and
cook 2 to 3 minutes longer until
the broccoli is tender.

To freeze To freeze for a short
storage time only, drain broccoli
in a colander and cool under
cold running water. Drain
thoroughly and pack in freezer
bags in convenient-sized
portions. Home-grown broccoli
should be blanched (page 92)
before freezing.

To serve from the freezer
Remove from bags. Place the
uncooked frozen broccoli in a
serving dish, ice side up. Cover
and switch on for 2 minutes.
Separate the broccoli spears.
Add 8 tablespoons hot water,
then continue cooking for 6 to 8
minutes until thoroughly
reheated. Drain, then mix in the
butter and season with salt and
pepper. Cover and cook for a
further 2 minutes. Single
previously-cooked portions
should be thawed in the
microwave oven in a small dish.
Cover and switch on for 2
minutes. Separate the pieces
and add a knob of butter.
Season with salt and pepper.
Replace the cover and cook for a
further 2 minutes, or until
thoroughly reheated.

STUFFED VEGETABLE MARROW
Serves 4

1 vegetable marrow, about
    675 g/1½ lb
50 g/2 oz fresh breadcrumbs
50 g/2 oz butter, softened
Salt, pepper
Pinch of dried thyme
2 tablespoons grated Cheddar
    cheese

+ + +

2 tablespoons grated Cheddar
    cheese

1. Peel the marrow and cut
into slices 3½ to 4 cm/1½ inches
thick. Remove the seeds.
2. Lay the marrow slices in a
dish. Cover and cook 6 minutes,
stirring frequently.
3. Remove the cover and drain
off surplus liquid, reserving 1 or
2 tablespoons to mix with the
stuffing.
4. Mix the breadcrumbs,
butter, salt, pepper, thyme and
cheese together. Moisten with a
little liquid from the marrow.
5. Fill the marrow rings with
the stuffing. Cook, covered, for
4 minutes, giving the dish a ¼
turn every minute.

To serve without freezing
Sprinkle the marrow with grated
cheese and brown under the
grill.

To freeze Leave marrow in the
covered casserole until cold,
then transfer slices carefully to a
shallow freezer container. Seal.

To serve from the freezer
To thaw by microwave, remove
the wrappings and arrange the
marrow slices in a heatproof
dish. Switch on for 2 minutes,
giving the dish a ½ turn after 1
minute. Sprinkle with grated

cheese and brown under the
grill.

SAVOURY LEEKS AND BACON
Serves 2

450 g/1 lb (4) leeks, washed and
    thinly sliced
4 bacon rashers

1. Lay the bacon rashers in a
dish and cook 2 minutes.
2. Remove the bacon from the
dish and drain on absorbent
paper. Trim off and discard the
rind. Chop the bacon into small
pieces with scissors and put it
aside.
3. Drain off most of the bacon
fat in the dish, then add the
leeks. Cover with plastic film
and cook 10 minutes. *Do not
overcook.*
4. Drain leeks and stir in the
bacon.

To serve without freezing
Reheat for 1 to 2 minutes before
serving.

To freeze Cool rapidly. Seal in
a freezer container.

To serve from the freezer
Turn block out into a serving
dish. Cover with greaseproof
paper. To thaw by microwave,
switch on for 3 minutes, stirring
occasionally. Leave to rest for 2
minutes, then continue cooking
until thoroughly reheated.

OKRA
Serves 4

Okra, ladies' fingers, bhindi,
bamia and gumbo are all names
for the same vegetable. Shaped
like small carrots and coloured

green, they have furry skins and
contain seeds.

450 g/1 lb small fresh okra
Salt
25 g/1 oz butter

1. Trim away the stems from
the okra, wash in cold water and
drain in a colander.
2. Sprinkle with salt and leave
in the colander for 30 minutes.
3. Wash and drain once more.
4. Place the okra in a casserole
with the butter and 4
tablespoons water. Cover and
cook 7 minutes, stirring
occasionally. Drain.

To serve without freezing
Serve with Hollandaise sauce
(page 145), handed separately.

To freeze Leave okra to cool,
then transfer to freezer
containers in the portions
required. Seal.

To serve from the freezer
Put the okra in a serving dish.
To thaw by microwave, cover
and switch on for 2 minutes for 1
portion, 4 minutes for 4
portions. Separate the pieces
with a fork. Continue cooking
until thoroughly reheated. Serve
as above.

FRIED ONIONS

Serve fried onions with meats
and fish, and use them as a
garnish for gratins.

225 g/8 oz fresh or frozen
    onions, sliced
2 tablespoons vegetable oil

1. If using *fresh* onions, put
them in a dish with the oil. Cook
7 to 8 minutes, stirring
occasionally.

2. Place *frozen* onions in a dish in the microwave oven. Switch on for 4 minutes, drain. Dry on absorbent paper, then return them to the dish with the oil, and cook for 5 minutes or until brown, stirring occasionally.

To serve without freezing
Drain on absorbent paper and use as necessary.

To freeze Freeze fresh fried onions in a freezer bag. Seal.

To serve from the freezer
Remove onion slices from bag and place them in a dish. To thaw by microwave, switch on for 2 to 4 minutes depending on the quantity, stirring occasionally.

SAUTÉED ONIONS
Serves 2

Rub your hands with lemon juice and rinse in cold water to remove the smell of onions. Cooking times depend on the size of the onions. Very small Breton onions will only take 2 minutes to cook.

**450 g/1 lb (4) medium-sized
 onions, peeled
25 g/1 oz butter
Salt, pepper**
+ + +

**250 ml/½ pt Basic White sauce
 (page 140)**

1. Put the butter in a dish and cook until melted, 1 minute.
2. Add the onions and turn them to coat with butter.
3. Cover the dish with greaseproof paper and cook about 6 minutes, turning the onions over once during

cooking. Season with salt and pepper.

To serve without freezing
Leave the onions to continue cooking in the residual heat, while reheating the sauce in the microwave oven for 3 to 4 minutes.

To freeze Leave the onions to cool. Drain and wrap each one individually in freezer film. Overwrap with foil.

To serve from the freezer
Remove wrappings. Place the onions side by side in a dish. To thaw by microwave, switch on for 3 minutes, giving the dish a ½ turn halfway through. Coat with the sauce and reheat for 2 minutes. If frozen sauce is used, it should first be thawed for about 5 minutes.

LEMON PARSNIPS
Serves 4

If preferred, cook young parsnips whole, but allow 14 minutes cooking time.

**350 g/12 oz parsnips
½ lemon
Salt, pepper
15 g/½ oz butter**

1. Top, tail and peel the parsnips. Cut into quarters lengthways and remove cores if necessary. Cut parsnips into chunks.
2. Put parsnip chunks in a casserole with 8 tablespoons water, the juice of ½ lemon, the lemon shell, salt, pepper and the butter. Cover with the lid and cook 6 to 8 minutes, stirring occasionally.
3. Leave the lid on for 5

minutes before draining. Discard the lemon shell.

To serve without freezing
Serve hot.

To freeze Cook 6 minutes, drain immediately and leave to cool, uncovered. Freeze in a sealed freezer bag.

To serve from the freezer
Turn parsnip chunks into a serving dish. To thaw by microwave, cover and switch on for 5 minutes. Stir, then continue cooking until thoroughly reheated. Leave to stand in the covered dish for 5 minutes before serving.

PETITS POIS À LA CRÈME
Serves 4

Peas are the most widely used of frozen vegetables. Young small peas (petits pois) are more expensive than mature ones, but have a much sweeter flavour.

**200 g/8 oz frozen petits pois
1 small onion, minced
25 g/1 oz butter
1 teaspoon finely chopped fresh
 mint
Salt, pepper**
+ + +

**125 ml/¼ pt single cream
1 small red pepper, seeded,
 cored and cut into rings**

1. Mix the onion and butter in a bowl. Cook 2 minutes, stirring occasionally.
2. Put the peas in a serving dish and add water just to cover. Cover dish with plastic film. Cook 4 minutes. Drain.
3. Combine the peas, sautéed onion, mint, salt and pepper in

the serving dish. Cook 1 minute.

To serve without freezing
Stir in the cream and reheat for ½
minute. Serve garnished with
red pepper rings.

To freeze Omit Step 2. Leave
to cool, then pack in freezer bags
in the quantities required.

To serve from the freezer
Empty the petits pois into a
suitable serving dish. To thaw
by microwave, switch on for 4
minutes. Break up the lumps
with a fork, then continue
cooking for 2 to 3 minutes longer
until thoroughly cooked. Stir in
the cream and garnish with
pepper rings.

DUCHESSE POTATOES
Serves 4

550 g/1¼ lb potatoes
25 g/1 oz butter or margarine
Salt, white pepper
1 egg, beaten
1–2 tablespoons creamy milk

1. Scrub and peel the potatoes,
and cut them into small chunks.
2. Put the potatoes in a bowl
and add 4 tablespoons water.
Cover and cook 14 minutes,
stirring occasionally.
3. Drain thoroughly. Rub
potatoes through a sieve or
mouli-légumes and return to the
microwave oven for 2 minutes.
4. Beat in the butter, season
with salt and pepper, then add
the egg and beat thoroughly.
5. Beat in enough milk to give
purée a soft consistency.
6. Turn the mixture into a
forcing bag fitted with a
1-cm/½-inch star nozzle and pipe
into rosettes, whirls or nests on a
greased baking tray.

To serve without freezing
Brown under the grill or bake in
a conventional oven at
200°C/400°F/Gas 6 for 15
minutes.

To freeze Leave potato
rosettes until quite cold, then
open-freeze on the baking trays.
Layer between sheets of
greaseproof paper in a freezer
container. Seal.

To serve from the freezer
Arrange the number of potato
rosettes required on a sheet of
non-stick paper. To thaw by
microwave, switch on for 2 to 3
minutes. Then transfer rosettes
to a greased baking tray and
brown under the grill or bake in
a 200°C/400°F/Gas 6 oven for 15
minutes.

BAKED POTATOES
(CHEESE FILLED)
Serves 4

Cooking times for baked (jacket)
potatoes vary depending on the
type and size. The following
guide, though approximate,
may be helpful.

1 potato	4 minutes
2 potatoes	7 minutes
3 potatoes	11 minutes
4 potatoes	14 minutes

4 large potatoes, about
   225 g/8 oz each
1 small egg, beaten
25 g/1 oz butter
8 tablespoons grated cheese
Salt, pepper

+ + +

Finely chopped parsley

1. Scrub the potatoes clean.
Dry them and prick thoroughly.
2. Arrange the potatoes in a

circle on a sheet of absorbent
paper, leaving 2½ cm/1 inch
space between each. Cook 14
minutes. Leave to stand for 5
minutes.
3. Cut the potatoes in half
lengthways. Scoop out the pulp
and beat with the egg, butter
and cheese. Season with salt
and pepper.
4. Pack back into the potato
shells.

To serve without freezing
Serve immediately, garnished
with parsley, or first brown tops
under the grill, then garnish
with parsley and serve.

To freeze Cook potatoes for
only 12 minutes at Step 2. Leave
them to cool, then wrap each
half separately in freezer film
and overwrap.

To serve from the freezer
Remove wrappings. To thaw by
microwave, switch on, allowing
2 minutes for a single half (4
minutes for 2 halves of potato).
Continue cooking as required
until thoroughly reheated,
changing the position of the
potatoes from time to time.
Garnish with chopped parsley.

SCALLOPED POTATO
LYONNAISE
Serves 3–4

This is a creamy, delicately
flavoured dish. The potatoes
must not be overcooked if they
are to be frozen before serving.

250 ml/½ pt milk
4 cloves
25 g/1 oz butter
1 bunch spring onions, thinly
   sliced
1 tablespoon cornflour

Salt, pepper
450 g/1 lb potatoes, peeled and
thinly sliced.

1. Heat the milk in a jug with
the cloves for 2 minutes. Leave
to infuse for 15 minutes.
2. Meanwhile, put the butter
in a shallow dish. Cook until
melted, 1 minute.
3. Add the onions, stirring to
coat them thoroughly with the
butter. Cook 2 minutes.
4. Mix the cornflour smoothly
with 2 tablespoons cold water
and stir into the onion mixture.
5. Strain the milk into the
onion mixture and stir
thoroughly. Cook 3 minutes,
stirring occasionally. Season
with salt and pepper.
6. In a deep dish, layer the
potatoes with the sauce,
finishing with a layer of sauce.
7. Cover the dish tightly and
cook for 12 to 15 minutes until
the potatoes feel soft when
pierced with a skewer, giving
the dish a ¼ turn every 3
minutes.

To serve without freezing
Leave to rest for 5 minutes
before serving.

To freeze Leave until cold,
then overwrap dish with freezer
foil or transfer to a freezer
container with a fish slice and
seal.

To serve from the freezer
Transfer potato mixture to a
suitable dish. To thaw by
microwave, cover and switch on
for 4 minutes, giving the dish ¼
turn every minute. Leave to rest
for 5 minutes, then continue
cooking if necessary until
thoroughly reheated.

PAPRIKA CHEESE POTATO FINGERS
Serves 2

Serve this potato dish as a
vegetable, or with a fried egg as
a supper dish.

450 g/1 lb potatoes, peeled and
chipped
Salt, pepper
1 teaspoon sweet paprika
25 g/1 oz butter

+ + +

4 tablespoons grated Edam
cheese

1. Dry the chipped potatoes
and toss them in salt, pepper
and paprika.
2. Heat the browning skillet for
5 minutes. Add butter at once.
3. Stir in the potatoes as
quickly as possible. Cook 4 to 5
minutes, stirring occasionally.
Do not overcook.
4. Tip the skillet and drain
away the surplus butter.

To serve without freezing
Sprinkle the cheese over the
potatoes. Cook 2 minutes and
serve immediately.

To freeze Cool potatoes
rapidly. Turn into a shallow
dish, cover with freezer film and
overwrap.

To serve from the freezer
To thaw by microwave, remove
wrappings and switch on for ½
minute, then give the dish a ¼
turn. Continue cooking and
turning until the potatoes are
thoroughly reheated.

RADISHES MORNAY
Serves 4

Radishes are rarely served as a
cooked vegetable, but blanched
radishes soften and lose their
bitter flavour. Choose large,
even-sized radishes for this
dish.

2 bunches radishes
Salt
Lemon juice

Sauce

15 g/½ oz butter
2 tablespoons flour
250 ml/½ pt milk
8 tablespoons grated Cheddar
cheese

+ + +

1 tablespoon flour
Milk

1. Top and tail the radishes,
but do not peel them. Put them
in a dish.
2. Cover with cold, salted
water and add a squeeze of
lemon juice.
3. Cover the dish tightly and
cook 3 minutes. Drain.
4. To make sauce: put the
butter in a large bowl. Cook
until melted, 1 minute.
5. Blend in flour. Cook ½
minute.
6. Slowly add half of the milk,
blending it in thoroughly. Cook
for 2 minutes. Stir.
7. Beat in the remaining milk.
Cook 1 minute.
8. Stir in the cheese.

To serve without freezing
Serve immediately.

To freeze Blend the remaining
tablespoon of flour smoothly
with a little cold milk and stir
into the cooled sauce. Add

radishes to the sauce. Cover with freezer film or put into a suitable container. Seal.

To serve from the freezer
Remove freezer wrappings. To thaw by microwave, switch on for 2 minutes. Leave to rest for 5 minutes. Stir.

RATATOUILLE PROVENÇALE
Serves 4

A mixture of colourful fresh vegetables cooked in olive oil until soft. The flavours then combine to produce a versatile dish which can be served hot with poultry or meat, or cold on its own as an hors d'oeuvre.

2 aubergines
Salt
1 red pepper
1 green pepper
450 g/1 lb tomatoes
450 g/1 lb onions
1 garlic clove, crushed
2 tablespoons olive oil
Black pepper
1 tablespoon dry red wine

1. Top and tail the aubergines, slice thinly and put into a colander. Sprinkle with salt and set aside for 1 hour.
2. Seed, core and slice the peppers thinly. Skin and chop the tomatoes, and slice the onions thinly.
3. Put the onions and garlic in a casserole with the oil. Cover and cook 3 minutes.
4. Drain, rinse and dry the aubergines with kitchen paper. Add to the casserole with the peppers. Cook 4 minutes.
5. Stir in the tomatoes, add a few shakes of pepper, a little salt

and a tablespoon red wine.
6. Cover the casserole with a lid and cook 4 minutes. Then remove the lid and cook for a further 4 minutes.

To serve without freezing
Taste and add more seasoning if required. Cook for 3 minutes longer.

To freeze Leave to cool, then turn into freezer containers in the quantities required. Seal.

To serve from the freezer
Empty into a serving dish. To thaw by microwave, cover and switch on for 5 minutes. Break up any lumps with a fork and leave to rest 5 minutes, then continue cooking 6 to 8 minutes longer until vegetables are thoroughly cooked and tender.

CREAMED SWEDES
Serves 4

1 swede, about 450 g/1 lb
Salt, pepper
15 g/$\frac{1}{2}$ oz butter
Lemon juice

1. Peel the swede and chop it into small cubes.
2. Put cubes in a large casserole with 125 ml/$\frac{1}{4}$ pt water. Cover and cook 15 minutes, stirring occasionally. Leave to rest for 5 minutes.
3. Drain, mash with a fork and add salt, pepper, butter and a squeeze of lemon juice.

To serve without freezing
Serve hot.

To freeze Leave to cool. Turn into a freezer container. Seal.

To serve from the freezer
To thaw by microwave, turn into a serving dish and switch on for 5 minutes, stirring occasionally.

SWEET POTATO CAFFERTY
Serves 4

Sweet potatoes are popular in the USA and are known as Kumara in New Zealand. This recipe can also be made with yams, which are less sweet.

450 g/1 lb sweet potatoes
1 small can (200 g) pineapple rings, drained
4 tablespoons clear honey

1. Scrub the sweet potatoes clean and prick them all over with a fork. Arrange them on a piece of absorbent paper, well spaced out, in the microwave oven. Cook 8 to 10 minutes, turning the potatoes after 5 minutes.
2. Peel the sweet potatoes and cut them into thin slices.
3. Mix the honey with 4 tablespoons water and pour half into a shallow dish.
4. Arrange the potato slices in the dish, lay the pineapple rings on top and sprinkle with the remaining honey mixture.
5. Cover with plastic film and cook 4 minutes.

To serve without freezing
Leave to rest for 5 minutes before carefully removing the plastic film.

To freeze Leave to cool, then cover dish with freezer foil.

To serve from the freezer
Remove foil, but leave the plastic film intact. To thaw by

microwave, switch on for 5 minutes, giving the dish a ¼ turn every minute. Leave to rest for 5 minutes, then continue cooking until thoroughly reheated.

DRY VEGETABLE CURRY
Serves 4

The 'hotness' of a curry is determined by the quantity of chilli powder used. Curries are always improved if left for several hours after cooking for the flavour of the spices to develop.

75 g/3 oz frozen sliced onions
2 tablespoons vegetable oil
450 g/1 lb mixed frozen
   vegetables: peppers, butter
   beans, French beans,
   mushrooms, cauliflower,
   peas, okra, carrots

Curry

2 teaspoons ground coriander
2 teaspoons turmeric
1 teaspoon compound chilli
   powder
1 teaspoon dried parsley flakes
1 tablespoon salt
2 teaspoons brown sugar
       + + +

2 teaspoons curry powder

1.   Put the onions and oil in a large bowl, and cook 8 minutes, or until soft and golden, stirring occasionally.
2.   Mix the curry ingredients with 5 tablespoons water.
3.   Stir the curry mixture into the onions, then add the vegetables and mix well. Cover and cook 5 minutes, stirring occasionally. Leave to rest for at least 2 hours before serving.

To serve without freezing
Stir in the curry powder and reheat in a covered dish for 8 to 10 minutes, stirring occasionally.

To freeze   Stir in the curry powder and turn into a polythene bag resting inside a bowl. Seal. When frozen, remove the bowl and overwrap the bag with freezer foil.

To serve from the freezer
Remove wrappings. Turn the contents of the bag into a serving dish. To thaw by microwave, switch on for 3 minutes. Leave to rest for 5 minutes, then continue cooking until thoroughly reheated.

VEGETABLE MAIN COURSE
Serves 6

This dish may be sprinkled with chopped hard-boiled egg to provide additional protein.

50 g/2 oz soft margarine
2 large onions, thinly sliced
150 g/6 oz brown rice
450 g/1 lb courgettes, sliced
1 green pepper, seeded, cored
   and sliced into rings
100 g/4 oz green beans, topped,
   tailed and sliced crossways
100 g/4 oz peas
Salt, pepper
1 can (200 g) tomatoes
375 ml/¾ pt vegetable stock
       + + +

1 tablespoon finely chopped
   parsley
4 tablespoons grated Cheddar
   cheese

1.   Put the margarine in a large dish. Cook until melted, 1 minute.
2.   Mix in the onions and the rice, and cook 5 minutes. Stir.
3.   Cover the mixture with layers of courgettes, green pepper, beans and peas, seasoning each layer with salt and pepper.
4.   Add the tomatoes and their liquor, and pour in the vegetable stock. Cover the dish tightly and cook 20 minutes, giving the dish a ¼ turn every 5 minutes and removing the plastic film after 15 minutes.

To serve without freezing
Leave dish to rest, covered, for 5 minutes before serving garnished with chopped parsley and grated cheese.

To freeze   Leave to cool, then cover the dish with freezer foil or transfer with a fish slice to a freezer container lined with foil. When the dish is frozen, turn out on to a large piece of freezer foil, wrap and return to the freezer.

To serve from the freezer
Remove wrappings and place block on a suitable dish. To thaw by microwave, switch on for 5 minutes. Leave to rest for 5 minutes, then continue cooking until thoroughly reheated, giving the dish a ¼ turn occasionally. Sprinkle with cheese and chopped parsley.

VEGETARIAN JAMBALAYA
Serves 4

If desired, add 200 g/8 oz cooked chicken or sliced salami, or 100 g/4 oz cooked shellfish to the jambalaya while it is reheating.

200 g/8 oz long-grain rice, washed and drained
25 g/1 oz butter
1 green pepper, seeded, cored and diced
1 onion, finely chopped
1 stalk celery, thinly sliced
200 g/8 oz mushrooms, sliced
1 small can (200 g) pimientos, drained and sliced
Salt, pepper
1 tablespoon Worcestershire sauce

+ + +

25 g/1 oz butter
1 tablespoon finely chopped chives

1. Put the butter in a large casserole. Cook until melted, 1 minute.
2. Stir in the pepper, onion and celery. Cook 4 minutes, stirring occasionally.
3. Add mushrooms and pimientos, and season with salt and pepper. Cover and cook 3 minutes.
4. Stir in the rice, 500 ml/1 pt boiling water and the Worcestershire sauce. Cook 12 minutes, stirring occasionally.

To serve without freezing
Cover the casserole and leave for 10 minutes. Add chicken, salami or prawns, if used. Reheat for 5 minutes. Stir in the butter and garnish with chopped chives.

To freeze   Cover and leave to cool. Turn into a freezer bag in the portions required. Seal.

To serve from the freezer
Put the contents of the bag in a serving dish. To thaw by microwave, cover and switch on for 5 minutes. Break up the lumps with a fork. Leave to rest for 5 minutes, then continue cooking until the mixture is thawed. Stir in any additions and cook for 5 minutes longer. Stir in the butter and garnish with chopped chives.

10 Pasta, Rice and Pulses

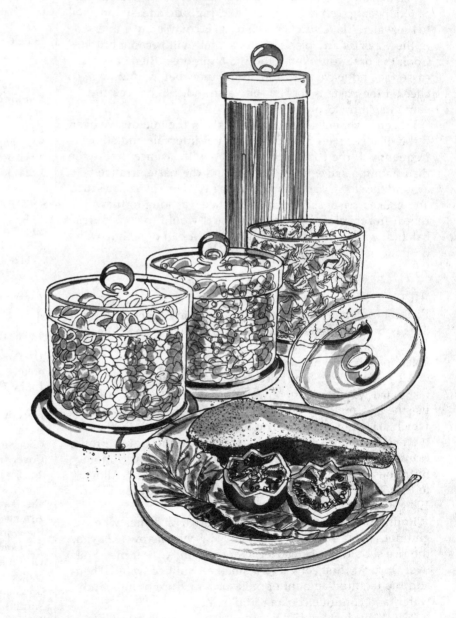

Pasta, Rice and Pulses

PASTA

The maximum quantity of pasta recommended for cooking in the microwave oven at one time is 200 g/8 oz. Allow 75 to 100 g/3 to 4 oz per person if serving it as a main course, 50 g/2 oz if it is to be an accompaniment instead of potatoes or rice.

Pasta should be cooked in a large casserole half-filled with salted, boiling water. To prevent sticking, add a teaspoon of oil to the water. Make sure that the pasta is completely immersed in the water as any pieces that stick out will become brittle. Cook the pasta uncovered for 5 to 6 minutes, then cover the casserole and leave to rest for 10 minutes before draining. To check if the pasta is cooked, bite a strand. Slight pressure should split it cleanly.

Frozen pasta will thaw more quickly in the microwave oven if the dish is covered. Turn the dish at intervals and stir frequently. If the pasta is to be served with a sauce, freeze the dish with the sauce in the middle and the pasta arranged around the sides. Time would not be saved by freezing a sauce and cooked pasta separately, for it takes as long to thaw and reheat frozen pasta by microwave as it would to cook a fresh batch. It will, of course, thaw rapidly in a pan of boiling water on the conventional hob.

RICE

Rice cooks better by microwave than by any other method. This is true for prime cooking and for thawing and reheating after freezing. Conventional methods of reheating are unreliable, and I would not recommend them.

All kinds of long-grain rice may be boiled in the old-fashioned way in plenty of water (see page 108). Or you can use the 1:2:1 method (1 cup rice, 2 cups water, 1 teaspoon salt) which, it is claimed, retains more of the B vitamins. By the time the rice is cooked, it will have absorbed all the water. Brown rice will take a minute or two longer to cook but it is more nutritious than white rice and has a delicious flavour. Allow 50 to 65 g/2 to $2\frac{1}{2}$ oz raw rice per person. This produces 150 to 190 g/6 to $7\frac{1}{2}$ oz cooked rice.

Round rice is used mainly for puddings or dishes where a glutinous mass is required. When using the microwave oven, the rice should not be cooked wholly in milk, or it may boil over. Instead, first cook it in a small amount of water. Then add the required amount of milk, or a mixture of milk and water, and continue cooking until ready.

'Quick' or 'instant' rice is rice which has been partially cooked and dehydrated. It cooks in about a quarter of the time necessary for untreated rice. Use the amount of water recom-

LASAGNE AL FORNO
Serves 3–4

This dish may be prepared with plain lasagne, but green lasagne, which is flavoured and coloured with spinach, makes it both tastier and more attractive.

150 g/6 oz (8 sheets) green lasagne
1 teaspoon salt
Vegetable oil
1 onion, chopped
200 g/8 oz minced lean beef
1 can (400 g) tomatoes
Salt, pepper
2 teaspoons cornflour
1 teaspoon concentrated meat extract
$\frac{1}{4}$ teaspoon dried oregano
50 g/2 oz butter
50 g/2 oz flour
625 ml/1$\frac{1}{4}$ pt Herbed milk (page 142)

+ + +

1 teaspoon flour

+ + +

4 to 6 tablespoons grated cheese

1. Put the lasagne in a deep, oblong dish measuring 22$\frac{1}{2}$ by 12$\frac{1}{2}$ by 7$\frac{1}{2}$ cm/9 by 4$\frac{1}{2}$ by 3 inches. Cover with boiling water to reach halfway up the dish. Add the salt and 1 teaspoon oil. Cook, uncovered, 6 minutes. Cover and leave for 10 minutes.
2. Drain the lasagne and pour cold water through it until the sheets are cold and separated. Arrange the sheets separately on the working surface.
3. Combine 2 tablespoons oil with the onion and meat, and cook 6 minutes, stirring occasionally. Spoon away any surplus fat.
4. Drain the tomatoes, reserving the liquor for use in other recipes. Chop the

tomatoes and add them to the meat. Season with salt and pepper. Cover and cook 5 minutes.

5. Blend cornflour with the beef extract and a little cold water, and stir into the sauce together with the oregano. Cook 2 minutes.

6. Put the butter in a large bowl. Cook until melted, 1 minute.

7. Blend in the flour. Cook $\frac{1}{2}$ minute.

8. Gradually add half of the herbed milk, stirring vigorously. Cook 2 minutes, stirring occasionally.

9. Stir in the remaining milk and cook for a further 4 minutes, stirring frequently.

To serve without freezing
Arrange layers of meat sauce, lasagne and white sauce in a serving dish. Reheat in the microwave oven for 2 minutes, giving the dish $\frac{1}{4}$ turn every $\frac{1}{2}$ minute. Sprinkle with the cheese and brown under the grill.

To freeze Stir 1 teaspoon flour into white sauce. Line a serving dish with plastic film and fill with layers of meat sauce, lasagne and white sauce. Open-freeze and then remove from the dish and put in a freezer bag. Seal.

To serve from the freezer
Transfer lasagne to a suitable serving dish. To thaw by microwave, switch on for 5 minutes. Leave to rest for 5 minutes, then continue cooking until thoroughly reheated, turning the dish occasionally. Total reheating time may be as much as 25 minutes. Sprinkle with cheese and brown under the grill.

mended on the packet. At the end of the cooking time, cover the dish and leave it to stand for a few minutes before serving.

'Prefluffed' or 'easy-cook' rice cooks well in the microwave oven. It absorbs more water than ordinary long-grain rice and produces 25 per cent more cooked rice. Use the amount of water recommended on the packet and allow 1 or 2 minutes more of microwave energy than for ordinary (untreated) rice.

Cooked rice will keep for 3 or 4 days in a covered (not airtight) container in the refrigerator. In the freezer, it may be stored for up to 2 months. Thawing by microwave is quick and easy: put the frozen rice in the oven in an uncovered dish and switch on for 1 or 2 minutes. Break up the lumps with a fork and continue cooking for a further 1 or 2 minutes until thoroughly hot.

PULSES

Pulses, the dried seeds of leguminous plants, require lengthy soaking before cooking conventionally or by microwave. They may either be soaked overnight in plenty of cold water, or put in a pan of water, brought slowly to the boil, simmered for 2 minutes, then covered and put aside for at least an hour to swell and soften.

Boiled conventionally, pulses take $1\frac{1}{2}$ to 2 hours to cook. A pressure cooker will shorten this cooking time considerably but the microwave oven has the added advantage that there is no cumbersome pan to wash up afterwards.

Lentils cook the quickest of all, taking 15 to 20 minutes in the microwave oven if they have first been soaked, 35 to 40 minutes if cooked straight from the packet in plenty of water. Larger pulses, which must be soaked first, take 30 to 40 minutes.

CANNELLONI

Serves 3–4

If cannelloni tubes are not available, substitute large squares of flat pasta, filled and rolled after boiling.

150 g/6 oz (12 tubes) cannelloni
1 teaspoon vegetable oil
Salt
200 g/8 oz minced cooked beef
150 g/6 oz frozen chopped leaf
    spinach, thawed
2 tablespoons tomato purée
1 teaspoon Worcestershire sauce
Freshly ground black pepper
25 g/1 oz butter
25 g/1 oz flour
250 ml/½ pt milk
2 tablespoons grated Parmesan
    cheese

+ + +

2 tablespoons grated Parmesan
    cheese

+ + +

1 teaspoon flour

1.   Put the cannelloni into a deep casserole and cover with 1 litre/1¼ pt boiling water. Add the oil and 1 teaspoon salt. Cook, uncovered, for 6 minutes. Cover the casserole and put aside for 10 minutes. Drain.
2.   Combine the meat, spinach, tomato purée and Worcestershire sauce, and season with salt and pepper.
3.   Fill the cannelloni tubes with the mixture and arrange them side by side in a shallow dish.
4.   Put the butter in a bowl and cook until melted, 1 minute.
5.   Blend in the flour. Cook ½ minute.
6.   Gradually stir in the milk. Cook 3 minutes, stirring occasionally.

7.   Add 2 tablespoons grated Parmesan cheese and season with salt and pepper.

To serve without freezing
Pour the sauce over the cannelloni and reheat in the microwave oven for 2 minutes, giving the dish a ¼ turn every ½ minute. Sprinkle with the remaining Parmesan cheese and brown under the grill.

To freeze   Blend 1 teaspoon flour with 2 tablespoons cold water. Stir into the sauce. Arrange side by side in a shallow dish and pour the sauce over. Open-freeze, then lift out the frozen block and pack in a freezer bag. Seal.

To serve from the freezer
Remove cannelloni from bag and transfer to a serving dish. To thaw by microwave, cover and switch on for 2 minutes. Leave to rest for 5 minutes. Separate the cannelloni and rearrange them in the dish so that those outside are placed in the middle. Reheat for 5 minutes, rest for 5 minutes, then continue cooking until thoroughly reheated. Sprinkle with remaining Parmesan and brown under the grill if desired.

MACARONI CHEESE WITH HAM

Serves 4

200 g/8 oz macaroni
Salt
1 teaspoon vegetable oil
25 g/1 oz butter
25 g/1 oz flour
500 ml/1 pt milk
White pepper

½ teaspoon dry mustard
150 g/6 oz grated Cheddar
    cheese
100 g/4 oz (2 slices) ham, diced

+ + +

1 teaspoon cornflour

1.   Put the macaroni in a large casserole, add 2 teaspoons salt and the oil, and cover with 1 litre/1¾ pt boiling water. Cook 6 minutes. Cover and leave to stand for 10 minutes. Drain macaroni in a colander and rinse under cold running water.
2.   Put butter in a large bowl. Cook until melted, 1 minute.
3.   Blend in the flour. Cook ½ minute.
4.   Gradually stir in the milk. Cook 3 minutes, stirring frequently.
5.   Season with salt, pepper and mustard. Stir in the cheese and ham.

To serve without freezing
Mix the macaroni with the sauce and serve hot with a green salad.

To freeze   Blend cornflour with 2 tablespoons water. Stir into the sauce. Pour the sauce into a freezer container. Seal. Freeze the macaroni separately in a suitable container.

To serve from the freezer
Transfer the sauce to a serving dish large enough to hold the macaroni. To thaw by microwave, cover and switch on for 5 minutes. Stir thoroughly. Continue cooking until the sauce bubbles. Put the macaroni in a large bowl and cover with boiling water. Place in the microwave oven until the water returns to boiling point. Drain. Thoroughly mix the macaroni into the sauce and reheat for 2 minutes.

NOODLES NIÇOISE

Serves 3–4

If preferred, freeze cooked noodles and sauce separately. Combine and garnish before serving.

150 g/6 oz noodles
1 teaspoon salt
1 teaspoon vegetable oil
1 onion, finely chopped
½ garlic clove, crushed
25 g/1 oz margarine
4 tablespoons Tomato concassé
  (page 144)
Freshly ground black pepper

+ + +

12 anchovy fillets
4 black olives, pitted and sliced

1. Put the noodles in a large bowl. Cover with boiling water to reach halfway up the bowl. Add the salt and oil, and stir. Cook 6 minutes.
2. Cover bowl and leave to rest for 8 minutes. Drain noodles in a colander, then rinse under cold running water until they separate.
3. Combine the onion, garlic and margarine in a serving dish. Cook 3 minutes, stirring occasionally.
4. Add the tomato concassé and pepper. Cook 1 minute.
5. Add noodles and toss until thoroughly coated with sauce.

To serve without freezing
Reheat in the microwave oven for 3 minutes, then garnish with a lattice of anchovy fillets filled with olive slices.

To freeze Line a suitable serving dish with plastic film and fill with the noodles. Open-freeze, then remove from the dish and pack in a freezer bag. Seal.

To serve from the freezer
Return the block of noodles to the serving dish. To thaw by microwave, switch on for 8 minutes, stirring occasionally. Leave to rest for 5 minutes, then continue cooking until thoroughly reheated. Decorate with the anchovy fillets and olives, and serve immediately.

RAVIOLI FILLED WITH CREAM CHEESE

Serves 4

Ravioli can be bought ready for cooking, but if you make your own, you can select your own filling. Serve this dish with Asparagus or Tomato sauce (pages 143, 144)

Ravioli Dough

225 g/9 oz strong flour
1 teaspoon salt
2 large eggs, beaten
2 teaspoons vegetable oil
Beaten egg, to glaze

Filling

75 g/3 oz cream cheese
15 g/½ oz butter
25 g/1 oz Parmesan cheese,
  grated
½ teaspoon finely chopped
  parsley
Freshly ground black pepper
Freshly grated nutmeg

+ + +

1 teaspoon salt
125 g/¼ pt Asparagus or Tomato
  sauce (pages 143, 144)
Grated Parmesan cheese

1. Sift the flour and salt into a bowl, and make a well in the middle. Add the beaten eggs and work in the flour until half is incorporated.
2. Mix in the oil and 2 tablespoons water, and knead to a stiff, pliable dough.
3. Roll the dough into a ball. Cover with the bowl and leave to rest for at least 10 minutes.
4. Roll out half of the dough into a thin rectangle, about 30½ by 25½ cm/12 by 10 inches.
5. Combine all the filling ingredients smoothly, adding pepper and nutmeg to taste.
6. Place tiny spoonfuls of filling evenly spaced 2½ cm/1 inch apart on the dough. Brush round the mounds of filling with beaten egg.
7. Roll out the remaining dough into a sheet slightly larger than the first and carefully place it loosely on top, keeping the edges level. Press round each mound of filling to seal it.
8. Cut out the squares with a sharp knife or a pastry wheel.
9. Leave ravioli covered with a dry floured teacloth, until the pastry dries out, 3 to 4 hours.

To serve without freezing
Pour 1½ litres/2¾ pt boiling water into a large bowl. Add 1 teaspoon salt and stir in the ravioli. Cook 6 minutes. Cover bowl and leave to rest for 10 minutes. Drain. Rinse ravioli with hot water. Turn into a warm serving dish and coat with the sauce. Hand a bowl of grated Parmesan cheese separately.

To freeze Pack ravioli (without sauce) into a freezer container and freeze.

To serve from the freezer
Thaw and cook ravioli by microwave. Pour 1½ litres/2¾ pt boiling water into a large bowl. Add salt. Stir in the ravioli and switch on for 2 or 3 minutes, until the water returns to boiling

Pasta, Rice and Pulses

point. Stir, then cover and
continue cooking for a further 5
minutes. Leave to rest for 10
minutes. Drain, rinse with hot
water to separate the ravioli and
serve coated with the sauce.
Hand a bowl of grated Parmesan
cheese separately.

SPAGHETTI NAPOLITANA
Serves 4

100 g/4 oz spaghetti
Salt
1 onion, finely chopped
1 garlic clove, crushed
2 tablespoons vegetable oil
1 large can (400 g) tomatoes
1 bay leaf, crumbled
1 teaspoon ground pine nuts
1 teaspoon dried basil
1 teaspoon grated Parmesan
   cheese
Pepper

+ + +

Grated Parmesan cheese

1. Pour 500 ml/1 pt boiling
water into a large bowl. Add ½
teaspoon salt and lower in the
spaghetti. Cook 6 minutes.
Cover bowl and leave to rest for
10 minutes.
2. Put the onion, garlic and oil
in a dish. Cook 2 minutes.
3. Drain tomatoes, reserving
the liquor, and stir them in. Add
the bay leaf, pine nuts, basil and
cheese. Cover and cook 3
minutes.
4. Mash tomato mixture, then
add enough of the reserved
tomato liquor to form a coating
sauce. Season with salt and
pepper.

To serve without freezing
Drain the spaghetti and pile on a
heated serving dish. Pour the

sauce over the top. Reheat in the
microwave oven for 2 minutes.
Hand Parmesan cheese
separately.

To freeze Drain the spaghetti
and place in a freezer container.
Pour the sauce around the outer
edge of the spaghetti. Seal.

To serve from the freezer
Turn out in a serving dish.
Cover with plastic film and thaw
by microwave. Switch on for 4
minutes. Stir, then continue
cooking for a further 5 minutes,
or until thoroughly reheated.
Sprinkle individual portions
with more grated Parmesan
cheese.

BOILED RICE (LONG-GRAIN)

Boiling rice in the old-fashioned
way but using the most
up-to-date appliance gives the
cook the best of both worlds. If
the rice is to be frozen,
undercook it slightly to allow for
thawing and reheating.

50 g/2 oz rice
½ teaspoon salt
250 ml/½ pt boiling water
(Cook for 10 minutes)

100 g/4 oz rice
1 teaspoon salt
500 ml/1 pt boiling water
(Cook for 12 minutes)

200 g/8 oz rice
2 teaspoons salt
750 ml/1½ pt boiling water
(Cook for 15 minutes)

1. Wash and drain the rice,
and put it in a large uncovered
casserole with the salt and the
boiling water. Stir.
2. Cook for the specified time,
stirring once.

3. Tip the rice into a colander
and pour cold water through
until the grains separate.
4. Make holes in the rice with
the handle of a wooden spoon
and leave in the colander to
drain completely.

To serve without freezing
Put the required amount of
cooked rice in a serving dish and
reheat for 1 to 2 minutes in the
microwave oven, stirring
occasionally.

To freeze Pack the rice in
freezer bags in the quantities
required. Seal.

To serve from the freezer
Put the rice in a serving dish. To
thaw by microwave, switch on
for 5 minutes. Stir, then
continue cooking until
thoroughly reheated.

MEXICAN RICE
Serves 3

An impressive tomato-flavoured
rice dish which is very easy to
prepare. Use stock cubes and
water when no fresh chicken
stock is available.

100 g/4 oz long-grain rice
4 tablespoons vegetable oil
½ onion
1 small can (200 g) tomatoes
1 garlic clove
250 ml/½ pt chicken stock
Salt

1. Put the rice in a large
casserole and cover with boiling
water. Leave to soak for 25
minutes.
2. Pour off the water, rinse the
rice in cold water and drain
thoroughly.
3. Replace the rice in the
casserole and add the oil. Mix

well and cook 5 minutes until the rice starts to turn brown, stirring frequently.

4. Break up the rice with a spoon as it will have become crispy.

5. Purée the onion, tomatoes (including their liquor) and garlic in an electric blender, or chop finely. Add to the rice and mix well. Cook 1 or 2 minutes. Stir.

6. Stir in the stock and salt to taste. Cook, covered lightly with a piece of greaseproof paper, until all the liquid is absorbed, 6 to 8 minutes.

7. Leave to stand, covered, for 30 minutes, during which time the rice will continue to cook.

To serve without freezing
Reheat rice in the microwave oven for 2 to 3 minutes before serving.

To freeze Dip the base of the dish in ice-cold water to cool it as quickly as possible. Pack in freezer bags in individual or small portions, as blocks of frozen rice are difficult to divide. Seal.

To serve from the freezer
Transfer the rice to a suitable dish. To thaw by microwave, switch on for 3 minutes. Break up the rice with a fork. Continue cooking until the rice is thoroughly hot, 1 to 5 minutes, depending on the size of the portion.

RIZ d'ESPAGNE
Serves 3

300 g/12 oz minced lean beef
1 medium onion, sliced
2 green peppers, seeded, cored
  and diced

150 g/6 oz long-grain rice
Garlic powder, a shake
2 teaspoons ground turmeric
Salt, pepper
375 ml/$\frac{3}{4}$ pt beef stock

1. Put the minced beef in a dish and cook 3 minutes, stirring once during cooking.
2. Add the onion and peppers. Cook 2 minutes.
3. Stir in the rice and cook 2 minutes.
4. Add garlic powder and turmeric, and season with salt and pepper.
5. Pour over boiling stock and cook 15 minutes, stirring during cooking.

To serve without freezing
Cover and leave to rest for 5 minutes. Stir and serve immediately.

To freeze Cool rapidly. Pack in a freezer bag. Seal.

To serve from the freezer
To thaw by microwave, remove the seal from the bag, place in the oven and switch on for 2 minutes. Turn the contents of the bag into a serving dish, cover loosely and switch on for 4 minutes, or until thoroughly reheated, stirring once halfway through cooking.

VEAL, PISTACHIO AND PINE NUT PILAU
Serves 3

A trifle expensive, but the flecks of green from the pistachios and the flavour of pine nuts combine to produce a tasty and attractive rice dish for a party.

200 g/8 oz (4 thin slices) veal
Salt, pepper
375 ml/$\frac{3}{4}$ pt chicken stock
25 g/1 oz shelled pistachio nuts
100 g/4 oz long-grain rice
25 g/1 oz pine nuts
25 g/1 oz butter
$\frac{1}{2}$ teaspoon grated nutmeg

1. Put the slices of veal in a dish. Season with salt and pepper, and add 2 tablespoons of the chicken stock. Cover and cook 5 minutes. Leave for 5 minutes, then cut into thin strips.
2. Cover the pistachios with boiling water. Leave for 5 minutes, then remove their skins.
3. Wash and drain the rice, and put it in a large bowl. Add the remaining hot stock. Cover and cook 12 minutes. Leave to stand for 5 minutes.
4. Chop the pistachio and pine nuts roughly and put them in a large bowl with the butter. Cook 2 minutes.
5. Mix in the rice and veal, and add the grated nutmeg.

To serve without freezing
Reheat in the microwave oven for 3 minutes. Serve immediately.

To freeze Cool rapidly. Turn into a freezer container and seal.

To serve from the freezer
Put the block of pilau in a serving dish and cover. To thaw by microwave, switch on for 5 minutes, then turn the block over. Cook for a further 3 minutes. Separate any lumps with a fork. Turn the block again and cook until thoroughly reheated.

Pasta, Rice and Pulses

LENTIL CROQUETTES
Makes 8–10

There are many kinds of lentils and all are suitable in this recipe, but cooking times may vary slightly.

200 g/8 oz yellow or red lentils
1 teaspoon salt
2 bay leaves
2 tablespoons vegetable oil
1 small onion, finely chopped
2 teaspoons curry powder
2 teaspoons ground coriander
½ teaspoon compound chilli
powder
½ teaspoon cayenne pepper
½ teaspoon ground ginger
1 tablespoon natural yoghurt
6 to 8 tablespoons flour

+ + +

4 tablespoons vegetable oil

1. Wash and drain the lentils. Put them in a large casserole.
2. Add 1 litre/1¾ pt boiling water, the salt and bay leaves. Stir. Cook 15 minutes, stirring occasionally.
3. Drain the lentils and remove the bay leaves. Mash the lentils with a fork or potato masher.
4. Preheat the browning skillet for 5 minutes.
5. Add 2 tablespoons oil and quickly stir in the onion and spices. Cook 2 minutes.
6. Mix the spices into the mashed lentils, followed by the yoghurt. Bind with the flour.
7. Shape into croquettes on a floured surface.

To serve without freezing
Preheat the browning skillet for 5 minutes. Add 4 tablespoons oil and cook the cutlets 4 at a time for 6 minutes, turning them over halfway through the cooking time. Drain on absorbent paper.

The browning skillet must be reheated for a further 3 minutes before cooking the next batch.

To freeze Open-freeze croquettes, then layer them between sheets of non-stick paper and pack them in a freezer container. Seal.

To serve from the freezer
Unwrap croquettes. Preheat the browning skillet for 5 minutes. Add 4 tablespoons oil and cook the croquettes 4 at a time for 8 minutes, turning them over halfway through the cooking time. Drain on absorbent paper. The browning skillet must be reheated for a further 3 minutes before cooking the next batch.

SOUTH AMERICAN CHICK PEAS
Serves 4

250 g/10 oz dry or canned chick
peas
Salt
1 medium onion, minced
1 garlic clove, crushed
1 sweet red pepper, seeded,
cored and thinly sliced
2 tablespoons olive oil
1 can (400 g) tomatoes
2 tablespoons tomato purée
Pepper

+ + +

½ green pepper, seeded, cored
and sliced into rings

1. If using dried chick peas, first soak them in cold water for 8 to 12 hours. Drain.
2. Put them in a bowl. Cover with 1 litre/1¾ pt boiling water. Stir in 1 teaspoon salt and cook 10 minutes, stirring occasionally.
3. Add the onion, garlic, sliced red pepper and oil. Mix well and

cook for 15 minutes if using dried chick peas or 6 minutes if using canned, stirring occasionally.
4. Mix in the tomatoes and tomato purée, and season with salt and pepper. Cook 5 minutes.

To serve without freezing
Turn into a heated serving dish and garnish with rings of green pepper.

To freeze Transfer to a freezer container. Seal.

To serve from the freezer
Turn chick peas out into a serving dish. To thaw by microwave, cover and switch on for 5 minutes. Stir. Continue cooking until thoroughly reheated. Garnish with rings of green pepper.

11 Sweets, Puddings and Pastries

Sweets, Puddings and Pastries

A large variety of light sweets, substantial puddings and pastries can be cooked successfully by microwave and stored in the freezer until needed, then thawed by microwave and served.

SWEETS AND PUDDINGS

All kinds of egg custard are suitable for cooking in a microwave oven. A proportion of 4 eggs or 8 egg yolks to 500 ml/1 pt milk produces a firm but creamy result. A small portion takes about 1 minute to cook by microwave, a large one 3½ to 4 minutes. This compares very favourably with cooking times of up to 45 minutes in a water bath in a conventional oven. Stop cooking as soon as the custard begins to bubble. Further cooking takes place after the oven has been switched off. Undercooking is easily rectified, but overcooking will cause the custard to toughen or curdle.

Crème brûlée is chilled after cooking (in a heatproof dish), then covered with brown sugar and grilled under fierce heat until the sugar melts and caramelises. It should be frozen uncooked, then lightly thawed before cooking by microwave.

Blancmanges and cornflour custards cooked by microwave will have no lumps. Mousses and cold soufflés can be partially prepared by microwave up to the stage when beaten egg whites are folded in. Jellies can also be partially prepared by microwave, but they should not be frozen.

Milk puddings containing small grains such as tapioca, semolina and sago, cook quickly in the microwave oven, provided the bowl is large enough to ensure that the milk does not boil over. There is no advantage in freezing this type of pudding as thawing and reheating would take as long as cooking it from scratch.

Large grains such as rice must first be cooked in water. Then add the milk and continue cooking until the grains are quite soft. If the pudding is to be frozen, use homogenised or skimmed milk.

Fresh and frozen fruit cooks quickly in the microwave oven. If fruit is stewed on the hob, water must be added to prevent the fruit sticking to the bottom of the pan. This dilutes the juices and tends to make the flavour insipid. However, no water is needed when cooking by microwave. Easy sweets can be made by thawing out prepared frozen fruit or by using a combination of defrosted or cooked fruit and custard for a fruit fool. Although it is preferable to soak dried fruit before stewing it, you can also obtain satisfactory results by covering the fruit with cold water and cooking it in the microwave oven for 10 to 15 minutes.

APPLE AND ORANGE CRUMBLE
Serves 6

The orange segments used in this crumble may be fresh or frozen. Serve custard sauce or whipped cream to complete the dish.

450 g/1 lb frozen apple slices
2 oranges, peeled and segmented
225 g/8 oz frozen Sweet crumble mix (page 121)
75 g/3 oz demerara sugar

1. Line a dish with apple slices and cover with the orange segments.
2. Sprinkle with half the sugar and cover with crumble mix.
3. Cook 10 to 12 minutes, until the apples are soft and the paste begins to stick together. Give the dish a ½ turn once during cooking.
4. Sprinkle the remaining sugar evenly over the crumble and brown under a very hot grill.

To serve without freezing
Leave the crumble to rest for 5 minutes before eating. Serve hot or cold. Any left-over crumble should be stored in the refrigerator. It can be quickly reheated in the microwave oven when required by switching on for 2 or 3 minutes.

CHEESE CAKE

To crush biscuits easily, put into a large polythene bag and press with a rolling pin,

100 g/4 oz butter
200 g/8 oz digestive biscuits,
    crushed
½ teaspoon ground cinnamon
2 large eggs, separated
100 g/4 oz castor sugar
375 g/14 oz curd cheese
2 teaspoons flour
2 teaspoons semolina
Grated rind and juice of 1
    lemon
4 tablespoons sour cream
1 tablespoon sultanas

+ + +

Whipped double cream

1.   Put the butter in a dish and
cook until melted, 1 minute. Mix
in crushed biscuits and
cinnamon.
2.   Line the base of a round
dish 25 cm/10 inches in diameter
with non-stick paper.
3.   Press biscuits into dish.
4.   Beat egg yolks and sugar
together. Add the cheese, flour,
semolina, lemon rind, juice, and
sour cream. Mix well.
5.   Beat the egg whites until
stiff and snowy. Fold into the
cheese mixture with sultanas.
6.   Spoon cheese mixture on to
biscuit base. Cook 5 to 6
minutes, giving the dish a ¼ turn
every 1½ minutes, until the filling
is just set on the outside, but is
still damp in the middle.

To serve without freezing
Allow to cool, then decorate
with rosettes of whipped cream.

To freeze   Leave cheese cake
until cold. Open-freeze. Turn
out on to a double sheet of foil
and overwrap with freezer foil.

To serve from the freezer
Remove wrappings and thaw
cheese cake at room
temperature. Decorate with
whipped cream.

SUBSTANTIAL PUDDINGS

For puddings made with creamed or rubbed-in mixtures the
same rules apply as for cakes cooked by microwave (see pages
125–127). Hot sponge puddings cooked in pudding basins with
or without jam or fruit should not be confused with suet
puddings, where the fruit is encased in a suet dough. The
latter are inclined to dry out and toughen if cooked by
microwave, so no recipes for them have been given. However,
when the suet is included in a fruit mixture (see the recipe for
Christmas Pudding on page 115), the results are extremely
successful.
   Yeast mixtures which contain a good proportion of egg
require the same attention as bread (see page 124) and turn out
as light as air.

SHORTCRUST PASTRY

Microwave shortcrust should be made with milk, not water,
and I find that soft margarine gives better results than butter.
The pastry does not have to be chilled before rolling out and
baking by microwave, but it is easier to manage if it is wrapped
in plastic film or foil and allowed to rest and firm up in the
refrigerator for a ½ hour before use.
   For a one-crust pie or tart that is to be cooked, frozen and
served from the same dish, fit the pastry into the dish and
pinch around the edges for decoration. This crust should be
cooked before the filling is added to it, as should the bottom
crust of a covered pie. Then cook the top crust and the filling at
the same time. Freeze, thaw and reheat by microwave in the
same dish. Finally, the pie may be browned under the grill or
finished off for 5 minutes in a 230°C/450°F/Gas 8 oven.
   Not everyone can spare dishes for storing in the freezer, and
in any case, metal must not be used when cooking by microwave. There are two alternatives. Either cook and freeze in
paper plates, or use a suitable dish lined with plastic film. After
cooking, open-freeze, then lift the pie out of the dish, together
with the plastic film, overwrap with foil and return to the
freezer. To thaw by microwave, remove the wrappings, including the plastic film, and place the pie on a serving dish.
   If you wish to freeze an uncooked pastry case, fit the pastry
into a dish lined with plastic film, open-freeze and wrap as
above. The pastry case can then be thawed and cooked by
microwave without removing the plastic lining. (It does,
however, have to be taken off before the pastry is browned
under the grill or in a conventional oven.)
   When using a frozen, uncooked pastry case, extra cooking
time must be given before adding the filling. For even results,

Sweets, Puddings and Pastries

give the dish a ¼ turn a quarter through the cooking time and repeat until the pastry is ready. Fresh or frozen fillings may then be added and cooked for the time specified. If the filling requires more than 2 minutes reheating or cooking, the exposed edges of the pastry will have to be covered carefully with crumpled foil to prevent them becoming overcrisp. To avoid this hazard, shape the pastry case so that it does not have a protruding pastry 'lip'.

Flan pastry containing a little icing sugar and bound with egg is often used for sweet pies and tarts. This should be watched carefully when thawing by microwave in case it burns, but otherwise the general rules for freezing and thawing shortcrust pastry apply.

PUFF PASTRY

Puff pastry should be pricked thoroughly before cooking by microwave, then cooked on the base of the oven. It rises from six to 12 times its original thickness and so is inclined to topple over. Whenever possible, small pieces, which are more likely to keep their shape, should be used. However, if larger rectangles, squares or rounds are required, cook them in deep dishes which will help them to stay upright as they rise. Puff pastry is ready as soon as it stays in its risen position when the oven is switched off. If it flops, it just needs more cooking.

Commercial puff pastry rises more evenly than home-made pastry but flaky pastry (two-thirds the weight of fat to flour) rises less, so uneven rolling in the preparation is not so noticeable. Frozen puff pastry should be thawed at room temperature until pliable before it is rolled out.

Puff and flaky pastry cannot be cooked by microwave if it already contains a filling (e.g. sausage rolls) as the weight of the filling would prevent the pastry rising.

Cooked puff pastry is inclined to toughen in the freezer and whether it can be 'refreshed' in a conventional oven will depend on the type of filling it has. Since it cooks so quickly by microwave, I prefer to use fresh or frozen uncooked pastry every time.

Oven-browning is unnecessary for puff pastry. A quick flash under the grill is all that it will need.

DECORATIONS

Most desserts are enhanced by decorations. These should be put on just before serving. Decorations are particularly useful when cooking by microwave as they can be used to conceal any lack of browning, thus making the oven suitable for a very wide range of sweets, puddings and pastries.

114

CARROT HALWA
Serves 4

A delicious Indian sweetmeat that is served as a dessert. Silver leaf is becoming more difficult to obtain as it is not always sufficiently pure, but it is obtainable by post from Patak Ltd., Drummond St., London NW1.

800 g/1¾ lb carrots, finely grated
125 ml/¼ pt milk
50 g/2 oz soft brown sugar
25 g/1 oz butter
6 white cardamom pods
1 teaspoon rose water

+ + +

1 sheet silver leaf

1. Combine carrots and milk in a bowl. Cover bowl and cook 10 minutes. Stir.
2. Remove cover and cook 5 minutes, stirring occasionally.
3. Add sugar and cook 10 minutes, stirring occasionally.
4. Stir in the butter.
5. Crush cardomon pods. Discard papery shells and mix seeds into carrots.
6. Add rose water. Cook 5 minutes, stirring occasionally.
7. Press the mixture into a mould.

To serve without freezing
Place silver leaf over the warm Halwa and leave to cool.

To freeze At Step 7, press the Halwa into a freezer container. Seal.

To serve from the freezer
Leave to thaw in a warm atmosphere for 1 hour. Heat in the microwave oven for 1 minute, then cover with silver leaf.

CHESTNUT ICE CREAM
Serves 4–6

A combination of chestnut purée, egg custard and whipped cream. The microwave oven timing for making the custard is critical and care must be taken not to overcook it, which would result in the mixture curdling.

125 ml/¼ pt milk
25 g/1 oz sugar
2 egg yolks
Few drops of vanilla essence
1 small can (225 g) sweetened
   chestnut purée
250 ml/½ pt double cream

+ + +

2 tablespoons grated chocolate
Whipped cream

1. Put the milk and sugar in a wide-mouthed jug. Cook to heat and dissolve the sugar, 1 minute.
2. Beat egg yolks with the vanilla essence and stir into the milk. Cook ½ minute. Stir. Cook for a further ½ minute. Stir again. The custard should be very thin.
3. Beat in the chestnut purée. Leave to cool.
4. Half-whip the cream until soft peaks form and fold it into the custard.
5. Pour into individual soufflé dishes.

To serve immediately
Open-freeze until the ice cream is firm, then decorate with grated chocolate and rosettes of whipped cream.

To freeze Open-freeze until the ice cream is firm. Overwrap soufflé dish with freezer foil.

To serve from the freezer
Remove wrappings and leave to thaw at room temperature, then decorate with grated chocolate and rosettes of whipped cream.

CHRISTMAS PUDDING
Serves 4–6

Conventionally-cooked Christmas pudding cannot be overcooked, but excess microwave cooking will burn the pudding.

100 g/4 oz stoned raisins
25 g/1 oz mixed peel
50 g/2 oz currants
50 g/2 oz sultanas
25 g/1 oz flaked almonds
1 teaspoon mixed spice
1 teaspoon grated nutmeg
½ teaspoon ground cinnamon
25 g/1 oz ground almonds
25 g/1 oz plain flour
100 g/4 oz shredded suet
50 g/2 oz fresh white
   breadcrumbs
25 g/1 oz soft brown sugar
2 large eggs, lightly beaten
2 tablespoons brandy
1 tablespoon black treacle
1 tablespoon gravy browning
Milk, if required

1. Chop raisins, peel, currants, sultanas and flaked almonds. Put them in a large bowl and add barely enough boiling water to cover. Cover bowl and leave overnight.
2. Stir in spices, ground almonds, flour, suet, breadcrumbs and sugar. Mix well.
3. Add the lightly beaten eggs, brandy, treacle and gravy browning, and mix to a soft dropping consistency, adding a little milk if necessary.
4. Turn into a greased ½-kg/1-lb pudding basin. Cover loosely with plastic film. Cook 8 minutes.

To serve without freezing
Leave for a few hours for the flavour to develop, then reheat in the microwave oven for 2 to 3 minutes until the top of the pudding feels hot. Serve with brandy butter, cream or custard.

To freeze Turn out on to a double sheet of foil and wrap up tightly. Leave until cold before freezing.

To serve from the freezer
To thaw by microwave, unwrap pudding and put it on a serving dish. Switch on for 3 minutes, leave to rest for 5 minutes, then continue cooking until thoroughly reheated.

CITRON SORBET
Serves 4

A sorbet is not to be confused with a granita, which has a much coarser texture, but if you find that your sorbet is a little inclined this way call it 'Citron Granita'.

2 teaspoons powdered gelatine
150 g/6 oz sugar
250 ml/½ pt orange juice
Grated rind and juice of 1
   lemon
2 egg whites

+ + +

Fresh orange and lemon slices

1. Put the gelatine with 125 ml/¼ pt water in a large jug in the microwave oven. Stir, then cook 1 minute. Stir again.
2. Mix sugar with a further 125 ml/¼ pt water. Cook to boil, 1½ minutes, then boil for 1 minute longer.
3. Cool syrup for a few minutes, then mix in the

dissolved gelatine. Stir well. Leave to cool.

4.   Stir in orange juice, lemon juice and rind.

5.   Pour into a shallow container and put in the freezer until just set.

6.   Remove from freezer and mash lightly.

7.   Beat egg whites until stiff but not dry. Fold them into the fruit mixture and spoon into individual dishes.

8.   Quickly replace dishes in coldest part of freezer. When completely frozen, cover each dish with foil.

To serve   Remove foil. Allow dishes to stand at room temperature for 10 minutes, then serve decorated with twists of orange and lemon slices.

BAKED CUSTARD

Serves 2–3

Reheating a cold baked custard will take only $\frac{1}{2}$ minute in the microwave oven.

2 eggs
15 g/$\frac{1}{2}$ oz sugar
250 ml/$\frac{1}{2}$ pt milk
$\frac{1}{4}$ teaspoon vanilla essence

+ + +

Grated nutmeg

1.   Beat the eggs and sugar with 2 tablespoons of the milk.

2.   Heat the remaining milk in a jug in the microwave oven for 2 minutes until hot but not boiling.

3.   Stir into the egg mixture together with the vanilla essence.

4.   Strain into a baking dish.

To serve without freezing
Stand the dish in a larger dish

containing 250 ml/$\frac{1}{2}$ pt boiling water. Cook $3\frac{1}{2}$ to 4 minutes until the custard begins to bubble. Leave for 3 minutes, then switch on for $\frac{1}{2}$ minute, or until the custard is just set. Sprinkle with grated nutmeg and serve warm.

To freeze   At Step 3, line the baking dish with freezer film before straining in the custard. Open-freeze, then remove custard from the dish and wrap it in freezer film. Put it in a freezer bag. Seal.

To serve from the freezer
Remove wrappings and put the custard back in the original dish. To thaw by microwave, switch on for 1 minute, leave to rest for 2 minutes, then switch on for a further minute. Leave to rest until thawed. Then stand the dish in a larger dish containing 250 ml/$\frac{1}{2}$ pt boiling water. Switch on for $3\frac{1}{2}$ to 4 minutes, giving the dish $\frac{1}{4}$ turn every minute. The custard will be ready when the centre is still slightly moist.

CRÈME CARAMEL

Serves 4–6

A caramel syrup can be prepared in the microwave oven but it must be watched carefully to make sure it does not burn. It is easier to prepare this syrup on the hob.

150 g/6 oz castor sugar
500 ml/1 pt milk
4 eggs
$\frac{1}{2}$ teaspoon vanilla essence

1.   To make the caramel, dissolve 100 g/4 oz sugar in 125 ml/$\frac{1}{4}$ pt water over a low heat on the hob; bring to the boil

and cook until the syrup is golden brown.

2.   Dip the base of the pan in cold water and immediately pour the caramel into individual ovenproof glass or ceramic moulds. Swirl the syrup round the base and sides to coat them. Leave to set.

3.   Pour the milk into a jug and cook $3\frac{3}{4}$ minutes in the microwave oven until hot but not boiling.

4.   Beat the eggs, the remaining sugar and vanilla essence together until fluffy and lemon-coloured.

5.   Pour the milk into the egg mixture, mix well, and strain into the caramel-coated dishes.

To serve without freezing
Stand the moulds, well spaced out, in a square dish containing 250 ml/$\frac{1}{2}$ pt boiling water. Cook $4\frac{1}{2}$ to 5 minutes until the custards begin to bubble, turning moulds occasionally. Leave until quite cold before turning out.

To freeze   Open-freeze. Seal each dish with freezer foil.

To serve from the freezer
Remove wrappings. To thaw by microwave, place moulds, well spaced out, in the oven and switch on for 1 minute. Then leave to rest until completely thawed. To cook custards, stand the moulds, well spaced out, in a square dish containing 250 ml/$\frac{1}{2}$ pt boiling water. Cook $4\frac{1}{2}$ to 5 minutes until the custards begin to bubble, turning dishes occasionally. Leave until quite cold before turning out.

GINGER CREAM
Serves 4

Frozen creams are best cooked in the microwave oven 1 or 2 at a time. It may be necessary to turn the dishes during cooking if 4 are put in at once. Frozen creams may seem to be cooked on top when the mixture underneath is still liquid, so check that they are set all the way through.

3 eggs
25 g/1 oz castor sugar
375 ml/¾ pt milk
½ teaspoon vanilla essence
25 g/1 oz crystallised ginger, finely chopped

1. Beat the eggs with the sugar and a little of the milk. Add the vanilla essence.
2. Heat the remainder of the milk until hot but not boiling, 3 minutes.
3. Pour on to the egg mixture, stirring vigorously, then strain into a jug.
4. Divide the ginger between individual soufflé dishes and pour the custard mixture over it.

To serve without freezing
Pour 250 ml/½ pt boiling water in a suitable square dish. Arrange the dishes well spaced out in the receptacle. Cook 4½ to 5 minutes until the mixture begins to bubble, turning the dishes occasionally.

To freeze Open-freeze, then cover each dish with freezer film.

To serve from the freezer
Remove wrappings. To thaw creams, put them well spaced out in the microwave oven. Switch on for 1 minute. Leave to

rest until thawed. Then stand the dishes in a square receptacle containing 250 ml/½ pt boiling water and cook until the creams begin to bubble. A single dish will take approximately 2½ minutes, 2 dishes 3½ minutes, 4 dishes 5 minutes. Leave to cool before serving.

MARMALADE ROLL
Serves 2

Non-stick paper is washable and can be used several times provided it has not been scorched in a conventional oven.

100 g/4 oz plain flour
¼ teaspoon salt
50 g/2 oz soft margarine
5–6 teaspoons milk
2–4 tablespoons orange marmalade
125 ml/¼ pt cornflour custard (page 154)

1. Sift the flour and salt into a bowl, and rub in the margarine.
2. Add the milk all at once and mix to a soft dough.
3. Roll out to a rectangular shape about 23 by 18 cm/9 by 7 inches.
4. Moisten the edges with water.
5. Spread the marmalade along one long edge, leaving a 2½-cm/1-inch margin on either side.
6. Roll up into a sausage shape starting at the long edge and allowing the marmalade to spread over the pastry. Press the edges lightly to seal the roll.
7. Place the roll at one end of a sheet of non-stick paper and roll up. The roll of pastry should be 5 cm/2 inches narrower than the paper. Cook 2 minutes.

To serve without freezing
Leave to rest for 10 minutes, then test for cooking. Insert a cocktail stick into the pastry, which should be crisp. Do not overcook or the marmalade will burn.

To freeze Leave until cold. Remove the non-stick paper and wrap the roll in freezer film. Overwrap with freezer foil.

To serve from the freezer
Remove wrappings. To thaw and reheat by microwave, switch on for 3 minutes. Leave to rest for 5 minutes before serving.

MILLES FEUILLES
Serves 6

Puff pastry rises at an astonishing speed in the microwave oven, but will sink if the oven door is opened before the pastry is completely cooked. However, the pastry will rise once more and continue cooking as soon as the oven is switched on again.

1 packet (200 g) frozen puff pastry
4–6 tablespoons raspberry jam
250 ml/½ pt double cream, whipped
150 g/6 oz icing sugar, sifted
Red food colouring

1. Leave puff pastry to thaw at room temperature for 1 hour.
2. Cut the pastry in half. Roll each piece out and cut it into a 15 cm/6 inch round. Reserve trimmings. Prick each round well on both sides.
3. Cook each pastry round separately on a sheet of paper for 3 minutes, or until the pastry

stays risen when the oven is opened. Split each round in half horizontally, making 4 rounds in all, and leave to cool.

4. Cook all the pastry trimmings in the same way, then crush them and brown them under the grill.

5. Sandwich each 2 pastry halves with jam and a quarter of the cream. Spread the remaining cream round the outside. Press in the browned pastry trimmings.

6. Mix the icing sugar smoothly with enough warm water to give it a coating consistency.

7. Mix about 2 tablespoons of this icing with a few drops of red colouring.

8. Spread the remaining white icing over the pastries and immediately pipe thin lines of red icing 1 cm/½ inch apart on top of the pastries.

9. Quickly draw a skewer across these red lines in alternate directions for a feathered effect.

To serve without freezing
Cut each pastry into 3 wedges.

Freezing is not recommended for these pastries. Some of the crispness will be lost in the freezing process and the coloured icing may run when the pastries are thawed.

PALESTINE PUDDING
Serves 6–8

4 eggs
100 g/4 oz castor sugar
2 tablespoons grated orange rind
125 ml/¼ pt natural yoghurt
6 tablespoons vegetable oil

200 g/8 oz plain flour
2 teaspoons baking powder
Pinch of salt
250 ml/½ pt clear honey

+ + +

Whipped cream

1. Grease a 15-cm/6-inch soufflé dish and line the base with non-stick paper.

2. Beat the eggs and sugar together until thick and lemon-coloured.

3. Fold in the orange rind, yoghurt and vegetable oil.

4. Sift the flour, baking powder and salt together, and fold them into the mixture.

5. Pour the mixture into the prepared dish. Cook 6 minutes, giving the dish a ¼ turn every 1½ minutes.

6. Brown the top quickly under the grill and turn out on to a wire cooling rack.

7. Put the honey in a jug and cook until melted, ½ minute. Pour over the pudding.

To serve without freezing
To serve hot, turn out on to a heated dish before browning the top under the grill at Step 6. Pour over the warmed honey and leave for a few minutes for the honey to soak into the pudding. Serve with whipped cream.

To freeze Cover with freezer film and overwrap with freezer foil.

To serve from the freezer
Remove the foil but leave the film wrapping intact. To thaw by microwave, switch on for 1 minute. Leave to rest for 2 minutes. To serve hot, switch on for 1 or 2 minutes longer. Serve with whipped cream.

PETITS POTS DE CHOCOLAT
Serves 6

Chocolate is very easy to melt by microwave and there is no waste.

150 g/6 oz plain chocolate
4 eggs, separated
2 tablespoons single cream
½ teaspoon vanilla essence

+ + +

Whipped cream

1. Break up the chocolate and put it in a bowl. Cook until melted, 2 minutes. Stir until smooth.

2. Remove the strings from the egg yolks with a fork, then beat the yolks lightly and stir them into the melted chocolate.

3. Mix in the single cream and vanilla essence.

4. Beat the egg whites until stiff but not dry. Stir a spoonful of beaten egg white into the chocolate mixture, then fold in the remainder.

To serve without freezing
Spoon into individual soufflé dishes and refrigerate for 1 hour. Serve decorated with a rosette of cream.

To freeze Spoon into individual soufflé dishes and cover with freezer film.

To serve from the freezer
Remove freezer film and thaw by microwave. Put 4 dishes at a time in the microwave oven and switch on for ½ minute. Decorate with whipped cream and leave to complete thawing at room temperature.

PINEAPPLE DESSERT
Serves 4

Frozen pineapple rings revert to the flavour of fresh fruit. If the rings are frozen together in a block, thaw by microwave for ½ minute and separate them with the blade of a knife. Fresh pineapple may be used in this recipe, but canned pineapple rings are unsuitable because they are too sweet and likely to be too soft.

450 g/1 lb (8) frozen pineapple
  rings
4–6 tablespoons blackcurrant
  jam

+ + +

Whipped cream

1. Lay frozen pineapple rings in a shallow dish.
2. Spread jam on top, cover lightly with greaseproof paper and cook 4 minutes, giving the dish a ½ turn after 2 minutes.

To serve Serve in individual dishes, accompanied by a bowl of whipped cream.

QUICK WHIP RASPBERRY JELLY

1 packet Raspberry Jelly
150 g/6 oz frozen raspberries

1. Place the jelly in a glass measuring jug and add water to reach the 250 ml/½-pt level. Cook 2½ to 3 minutes until the jelly begins to dissolve. Stir until the jelly is clear of lumps.
2. Pour the dissolved jelly over the frozen raspberries and stir until the fruit is thawed, the juice well mixed and the jelly beginning to set. Beat vigorously

with a wooden spoon to obtain a whipped appearance.

To serve Leave in refrigerator until quite set.

RICE PUDDING
Serves 2

To use frozen cooked rice for this recipe: cover and thaw by microwave, then add the milk, sugar, butter and vanilla essence, and cook 6 minutes. Finally, add the cream and nutmeg.

100 g/4 oz round-grain rice
250 ml/½ pt creamy milk
50 g/2 oz sugar
25 g/1 oz butter
½ teaspoon vanilla essence

+ + +

4 tablespoons double cream
Grated nutmeg

1. Wash and drain the rice, and put it in a large bowl with 500 ml/1 pt boiling water. Cook 12 minutes. Cover and leave to rest for 5 minutes.
2. Stir in the milk, sugar, butter and vanilla essence, and cook, uncovered, for 6 minutes, stirring occasionally.

To serve without freezing
Stir in the cream, divide between 2 dishes and sprinkle nutmeg over the top.

To freeze Cool and turn into freezer bags in convenient portions. Seal.

To serve from the freezer
Remove from the freezer bags and put rice in a serving dish. To thaw by microwave, cover and switch on for 5 minutes. Stir and continue cooking until

thoroughly reheated. Stir in the cream and sprinkle nutmeg on top.

SAVARIN
Serves 4–6

If the savarin is to be used as a dessert, fill the centre with a macedoine of fruit (a mixture of diced fresh or canned fruit) just before serving.

125 ml/¼ pt milk
15 g/½ oz dried yeast
Castor sugar
100 g/4 oz plain flour
Pinch of salt
75 g/3 oz butter
2 eggs, beaten
Butter for pudding basin
250 ml/½ pt hot Rum syrup
  (page 155)
Apricot glaze (page 153)

+ + +

Flaked almonds

1. Put the milk in a jug and heat to 38°C/100°F, 20 seconds.
2. Whisk in 1 teaspoon castor sugar and the yeast. Leave for 10 minutes until yeast has dissolved and liquid is bubbly.
3. Sift the flour and salt into a mixing bowl. Heat 15 seconds.
4. Rub in the butter.
5. Make a well in the centre and pour in the yeast mixture. Sprinkle a spoonful of the mixture over the yeast liquid and leave for 15 minutes.
6. Add the beaten eggs and 1 tablespoon castor sugar. Beat thoroughly to make a soft batter. Cover and leave in a warm place to rise until the batter is double in size.
7. Butter a large pudding basin and the outside of a 450-g/1-lb jam jar. Stand the jar in the middle of the basin.

8. Pour the batter into the basin and leave for 10 minutes. Then cook 4 minutes.
9. Turn out and baste with hot syrup until thoroughly saturated. Then brush all over with apricot glaze.

To serve without freezing
Sprinkle with flaked almonds and leave to cool before serving.

To freeze
Wrap the savarin in freezer film while still warm. Leave until cold before overwrapping and freezing.

To serve from the freezer
Thaw by microwave, leaving the savarin in its plastic film wrapping. Switch on for 2 minutes. Remove wrapping and serve decorated with flaked almonds.

SHORTCRUST PASTRY

Pastry made with 100 g/4 oz flour is suffcient for a 15-cm/6-inch pastry case. Allow about 1 teaspoon milk to each ounce of flour and add to the mixture all at once.

450 g/1 lb plain flour
½ teaspoon salt
225 g/8 oz soft margarine
6 tablespoons cold milk

1. Sift the flour and salt into a mixing bowl.
2. Add the margarine and mix with the blade of a knife until the mixture resembles breadcrumbs.
3. Stir in the milk and knead gently to form a soft dough. Roll into a ball.
4. Wrap in plastic foil and chill for 30 minutes.

To use without freezing
Roll out quantity required and cook according to instructions below.

To freeze
(a) Divide the dough into the quantities required and put each ball in a freezer bag. Seal. *or*
(b) Roll out the pastry and fit into a suitable dish lined with plastic film. Open-freeze. When the pastry is solid, remove the dish and overwrap the pastry with freezer foil. *or*
(c) Cook and fill as desired, then overwrap with plastic film and freezer foil.

To cook an unfilled pastry case
Lay a piece of absorbent kitchen paper over the pastry and put a small plate on top. This is the equivalent of 'baking blind' and prevents the pastry base from rising during baking. Cook 3 minutes, giving the dish a ¼ turn every minute, then remove the plate and paper, and cook a further ½ minute. Leave to rest for 10 minutes before filling.
To cook a larger case, allow a further minute. However, if the filling requires cooking, the initial baking time should be reduced by 1 minute. The reheating time for pastry in the microwave oven will depend on the amount of filling and the temperature at which the pastry was stored.

SPOTTED DICK
Serves 4

Store suet in its closed packet in a cool place. If it is stored in a warm cupboard, it will soften and form lumps. Stir suet pudding mixtures very lightly to avoid toughening.

100 g/4 oz plain flour
2 teaspoons baking powder
Salt
50 g/2 oz demerara sugar
50 g/2 oz shredded suet
1 large egg
4 tablespoons milk
50 g/2 oz sultanas

+ + +

250 ml/½ pt Cornflour custard (page 154) or thick cream

1. Sift the flour, baking powder and salt into a mixing bowl.
2. Stir in the sugar and suet.
3. Beat the egg and milk together, and lightly stir into the flour mixture together with the sultanas.
4. Grease a ½-litre/1-pt pudding basin and the underside of a tea-plate.
5. Turn the dough into the pudding basin and level it out with the back of a spoon. Rest the plate on top of the basin. Cook 3½ minutes. Leave for 2 minutes, then loosen the sides with the blade of a knife and turn out.

To serve without freezing
Serve immediately and hand warm custard or thick cream separately.

To freeze
Wrap the pudding in freezer film and leave until cold. Overwrap with freezer foil.

To serve from the freezer
Remove wrappings and put the pudding in a serving dish. To thaw by microwave, switch on for 2 or 3 minutes until the pudding is hot. Reheat the custard in a jug in the microwave oven for 1 to 2 minutes, stirring every 15 seconds. Hand the custard or cream separately.

STRAWBERRY MALLOW
Serves 4

A quick and easy dessert that requires no additional sweetening. Served hot, the mallow is like a sauce. When cold, it is slightly stickier but does not become hard.
Use fresh strawberries when in season, but do not use the canned variety, which would make the dish excessively sweet.

250 g/10 oz fresh or frozen strawberries
8 pink marshmallows
10 white marshmallows

1. Cover the base of a wide dish with the frozen strawberries. Cook 2 minutes.
2. Arrange the pink marshmallows in the centre of the dish on top of the strawberries and the white marshmallows round the sides. Cook 2 or 3 minutes, giving the dish a ½ turn after 1½ minutes, until the marshmallows melt.

STRAWBERRY PUDDING
Serves 4

Use raspberries, loganberries, boysenberries or any other soft fruit instead of strawberries to ring the changes. Fresh or frozen berries are equally suitable.

450 g/1 lb frozen strawberries
50 g/2 oz cornflour
2 teaspoons lemon juice
50 g/2 oz castor sugar
2 tablespoons single cream
Cointreau, to taste (optional)

+ + +

Whipped cream

1. Put the strawberries in a bowl and cover lightly with greaseproof paper. Cook 5 minutes.
2. Press the strawberries through a sieve into an ovenproof bowl.
3. Blend the cornflour smoothly with 125 ml/¼ pt water, the lemon juice and 2 tablespoons of the castor sugar.
4. Add to the strawberries, stir well and cook 3 minutes, or until the mixture thickens, stirring occasionally.
5. Stir in the cream and Cointreau if used.
6. Turn into individual dishes and sprinkle with the remaining sugar to prevent a skin forming.

To serve without freezing
Leave the puddings to cool, then decorate each with a rosette of whipped cream.

To freeze Overwrap each with freezer film or foil before cooling. Freeze when cold.

To serve from freezer Remove wrappings. To thaw by microwave, switch on for ½ minute for each dish. Leave at room temperature to thaw fully. Decorate with rosettes of whipped cream.

SWEET CRUMBLE MIX

A versatile topping for fruit puddings. Make up a large quantity for the freezer. The proportions for 4 servings are 150 g/6 oz crumble mix to 300 g/12 oz fruit.

450 g/1 lb plain flour
¼ teaspoon salt
225 g/8 oz butter or soft margarine
150 g/6 oz demerara sugar

1. Sift the flour and salt into a bowl.
2. Rub in the butter or margarine until the mixture resembles fine breadcrumbs.
3. Stir in the sugar.

To serve Turn the required quantity on to the fruit. Flatten with a knife. Cook by microwave, allowing 4 minutes per 150 g/6 oz fresh crumble mix plus 4 to 6 minutes per 450 g/1 lb frozen fruit or 2 minutes for fresh fruit. Leave to rest for 5 minutes, then brown under the grill just before serving.

To freeze Pack loosely in a large freezer bag. Seal.

To serve from the freezer
Remove frozen crumble from bag and scatter over fruit. To cook by microwave, allow 5 minutes per 150 g/6 oz frozen crumble mix plus 4 to 6 minutes per 450 g/1 lb frozen fruit. Leave to rest for 5 minutes, then brown under the grill just before serving.

SYRUP TART
Serves 4

When cooking by microwave, the dish may be lined with plastic film, enabling the tart to be removed after freezing.

150 g/6 oz plain flour
½ teaspoon salt
75 g/3 oz soft margarine
1½–2 tablespoons cold milk
2 wheaten breakfast biscuits (Weetabix)
4–6 tablespoons golden syrup
Squeeze of lemon juice

Sweets, Puddings and Pastries

1. Sift the flour and salt together, and rub in the margarine until the mixture resembles fine breadcrumbs.
2. Add sufficient milk to bind, kneading lightly to make a dough.
3. Roll out and line a round dish 20 cm/8 inches in diameter. Cover with a piece of absorbent paper and stand a 15-cm/6-inch plate on top. Cook 3 minutes, then remove the plate and paper.
4. Crush the biscuits and mix with the syrup and lemon juice. Turn into the pastry case and cook 2 minutes.

To serve without freezing
Leave for 10 minutes, then if the dish has been lined with plastic film, lift out the tart and brown the top lightly under the grill.

To freeze Leave until cold. Overwrap the dish with freezer film and freezer foil.

To serve from the freezer
Remove wrappings. To thaw by microwave, switch on for 4 minutes, giving the dish a ½ turn after 2 minutes.

UPSIDE DOWN PINEAPPLE PUDDING
Serves 4

This is an old favourite which is easy to cook by microwave. Although often described as a cake, it is much better served hot as a pudding.

75 g/3 oz soft brown sugar
75 g/3 oz butter
1 small can (200 g) pineapple rings
3–4 glacé cherries, halved

50 g/2 oz castor sugar
1 egg
50 g/2 oz plain flour
½ teaspoon baking powder

+ + +

Lemon sauce (page 154)
Whipped cream

1. Cream the brown sugar with 25 g/1 oz of the butter and spread evenly over the base and sides of a round glass dish 20 cm/8 inches in diameter.
2. Drain the can of pineapple rings, reserving the syrup. Arrange the pineapple rings and cherries decoratively over the butter mixture, placing the cherries shiny side down.
3. Prepare the cake batter. Cream the remaining 50 g/2 oz butter and sugar together until light and fluffy, then beat in the egg.
4. Sift the flour and baking powder over the mixture and fold in. Thin down with 1 tablespoon reserved pineapple syrup.
5. Spread the cake batter on top of the fruit. Cook 6 minutes, giving the dish a ¼ turn every 1½ minutes.
6. Leave pudding to stand for 1 minute before turning out.

To serve without freezing
Pour over the lemon sauce and hand whipped cream separately.

To freeze Open-freeze in the baking dish to avoid disturbing the topping. Turn out on to a double sheet of freezer foil lined with freezer film. Wrap carefully and freeze, cake side down.

To serve from the freezer
Remove wrappings and put pudding in a serving dish. To thaw by microwave, switch on

for 2 minutes, giving the dish a ¼ turn every ½ minute.
Serve with lemon sauce and whipped cream.

ATHENIAN SLICES
Makes 9–12

A sweet Greek-type pastry. It can be frozen but the crispness is lost in the freezing process.

1 packet (400 g) frozen puff pastry
125 g/5 oz almonds or pecans, chopped
1 teaspoon ground cinnamon
½ teaspoon ground cloves
4–6 tablespoons clear honey
250 ml/½ pt double cream

1. Leave pastry at room temperature until just thawed, 1 hour.
2. Roll out the pastry thinly and cut into strips 10 by 3½ cm/4 by 1½ inches. Prick well on both sides.
3. Cook 4 strips at a time, well spaced out on the oven base, for 4 minutes, or until the pastry stays risen when the oven door is opened. Split each strip in half horizontally and leave to cool on a wire cooling rack.
4. Mix the nuts with the spices.
5. Soften the honey in the microwave oven for ½ minute and mix with the spiced nuts and cream.
6. Fill each pastry with half the mixture and spread the remainder on top.

To freeze Open freeze the slices before wrapping them individually in freezer film.

To serve from the freezer
Thaw at room temperature.

12 Breads, Cakes and Biscuits

Breads, Cakes and Biscuits

Provided you are careful about the recipes you choose, breads, cakes and biscuits can all be cooked successfully in a microwave oven. If you are new to microwave bread- and cake-making, start with Irish Soda Bread (page 136), the Chocolate Cake (page 129), and Peanut Butter Bars (page 135).

BREADS

All kinds of bread can be cooked by microwave, provided there is some fat or oil in the dough, and both yeast and soda breads rise more evenly in the microwave oven than in a conventional one. Wholemeal rolls and loaves are particularly good as, thanks to their natural colour, they do not need to be browned under the grill after cooking.

When baking bread by microwave, better results are obtained if soft (ordinary) plain or self-raising flour is used rather than the strong (high-gluten) flour usually recommended for conventional baking with yeast. The method for making microwave bread dough is the same as for conventional bread. Although the texture of microwave bread is closer than that of a conventionally baked loaf, it keeps better and is never tough or chewy. Milk, or a mixture of milk and water rather than just water, will help to lighten the dough.

Microwave bread dough should be much softer than conventional dough. This has the added advantage of making it unnecessary to knead and pummel the dough, a tedious task for the weak-wristed cook who does not possess an electric dough hook.

The microwave oven will save time and effort at every stage of the bread-making process. The liquid may first be warmed in the measuring jug and the chill taken off the flour by putting them in the oven for a few seconds. Then, to hasten rising and proving, put the dough in the oven for a few seconds occasionally.

When the loaf is ready for baking it may either be cooked completely by microwave, then browned under the grill, or it may be partially cooked by microwave, say for 2 minutes, then completed and browned in a conventional oven heated to 230°C/450°F/Gas 8, although this uses up considerably more fuel.

The microwave oven can, and should, be used in conjunction with the freezer for storing both unbaked bread doughs and baked bread. An unbaked dough can be taken straight from the freezer for thawing and baking by microwave. When freezing bread, do so as soon as possible after baking to ensure maximum freshness on thawing. Cool the bread rapidly and store it wrapped tightly in a freezer bag.

APRICOT GENOESE
Serves 6

This cake may be baked in a deep soufflé dish for 5½ minutes if preferred. To separate the two halves, remove from the dish, leave to cool, then saw round the circumference with a sharp knife to a depth of 2½ cm/1 inch, place the cake on its side and cut it in half.

150 g/6 oz margarine
150 g/6 oz castor sugar
3 large eggs
½ teaspoon vanilla essence
175 g/7 oz plain flour
2 teaspoons baking powder
1–2 tablespoons milk

Apricot topping

8 fresh apricots, peeled, stoned and halved
100 g/4 oz castor sugar
4 tablespoons red wine
2 teaspoons arrowroot
+ + +
125 ml/¼ pt double cream, whipped

1. Cream the margarine and sugar until light and fluffy.
2. Beat the eggs and vanilla essence together, then gradually beat them into the creamed mixture.
3. Sift the flour and baking powder on to mixture gradually and fold it in.
4. Add sufficient milk to form a soft, dropping consistency.
5. Turn the mixture into 2 round, lined sandwich shapes. Cook one at a time for 3 minutes, giving the dish a ¼ turn every 45 seconds.
6. Turn out on to a wire cooling rack.
7. Prepare the apricot topping. Put 2 tablespoons water into a large bowl. Cook ½ minute.

8. Stir in the sugar and leave to dissolve, 10 minutes.

9. Add wine and cook 4 minutes.

10. Add the apricots and cook 2 minutes.

11. Mix arrowroot with 2 to 3 teaspoons cold water and stir in the fruit. Blend well. Cook 1 minute.

To serve without freezing
Sandwich the cake with whipped cream, leaving a little for decoration. Let the apricot topping cool, then arrange on the surface of the cake. Decorate with rosettes of whipped cream.

To freeze Wrap cakes separately in plastic film and overwrap with freezer foil. Freeze the apricot topping in a rigid container.

To serve from the freezer
Remove cake wrappings and thaw cake layers one on top of the other in the microwave oven. Switch on for ½ minute. Leave to rest until completely thawed. Sandwich layers together with cream, reserving a little for decoration. To thaw the apricots, place the block, ice side up, in a dish. Cover and switch on for 3 to 4 minutes, separating the fruit with a knife as soon as the block is partially thawed. Arrange apricot topping on the cake and decorate with rosettes of whipped cream.

Bread and rolls should be thawed on a sheet of absorbent kitchen paper. This will absorb any excess moisture and avoid the danger of finishing up with a soggy loaf. Thaw bread in the microwave oven for 2 or 3 minutes, rolls for about 1 minute, then crisp up under the grill if desired. Large loaves do not usually need this final step, but most bread and rolls are improved by putting them under a hot grill for a few moments before serving.

Fresh yeast should be sweet-smelling and putty-coloured. It will keep, tightly wrapped, in the freezer for about a year, or in the refrigerator, in an open-ended polythene bag away from the freezer element, for about a week. Dried yeast should be stored in a tightly sealed container in a cool place or in the refrigerator. Dried yeast does not keep indefinitely. If it does not froth up when whisked into a little lightly sweetened, lukewarm water and left to stand for about 10 minutes, it has lost its potency and should be discarded. If using dried yeast in a recipe, only half the quantity specified for fresh yeast will be required.

CAKES AND BISCUITS

Generally speaking, a cake batter which is to be cooked by microwave should be wetter than a conventional batter to allow for the 12 per cent moisture loss which occurs while the cake is in the oven. No natural browning will occur, so either the colour must already be present in the raw ingredients, as in the case of chocolate cake, or a little vegetable food colouring should be added to the batter. A fruit cake can be darkened with gravy browning (caramel) or black treacle. The batter should be mixed particularly carefully for if a pocket of unmixed fat remains, the cake will not cook properly at that spot.

There are four conventional methods of cake preparation: rubbing in, creaming, melting and whisking.

Rubbed-in mixtures contain a low proportion of fat to flour. When making scones, rock buns etc. by microwave, increase the fat by a third to prevent them turning out too dry. The slowing down of the cooking process will mean that the cakes remain moist. Nuts, which have a high fat content, also help to keep cakes fresh.

Creamed mixtures are the most rewarding of the microwave cakes, both those prepared traditionally and by the 'all-in-one' method. The former involves much more beating, thus eliminating the need for extra baking powder. The cakes keep well and the beating in of air makes them lighter than cakes made with rubbed-in mixtures.

The melting method is used mainly for ginger cakes and

similar highly spiced mixtures. When making this type of cake in the microwave oven it is wise to cut down the sugar content, otherwise the cake might burn.

The whisking method is not usually recommended for cakes which are to be baked by microwave because there is no fat in the ingredients. A Genoese sponge, which is based on this method but does include a little melted fat, is adequate only if subsequently iced or covered in some way, otherwise it will go dry very quickly.

Dishes suitable for baking cakes in the microwave are not easy to find. On the Continent, Pyrex are now marketing a selection of dishes designed for this purpose under the name Pyrex Patisserie, and this range is now becoming available in the UK and USA. Meanwhile, any suitable dish which resembles the shape of a cake will work, and some ingenuity can be used with existing bowls. For example, a ring mould can be reproduced by placing a jam jar in the middle of a pudding basin. If the jar narrows towards the neck, stand it upside down so that after cooking it can be lifted out without spoiling the shape of the cake.

Flan rings can be made out of the lids of round cardboard cartons. Chocolate, or small tissue boxes, are excellent for square or rectangular cakes. Cardboard boxes lined with plastic film may be used over and over again, but before using them do check that they are not covered with foil and that there is no silver of gold in the decoration.

This ability to cook cake mixtures in cardboard and paper means that unusual shapes can be produced for special occasions without wasting any of the cake, because you will not have to cut the shapes out of a slab.

Glass, china and pottery dishes may be greased and their bases lined with non-stick paper. However, if you decide to use this method, be careful. If too much grease is used it will inhibit baking at that spot. My preferred method is to leave out the greasing altogether and instead just line the dish with plastic film. This should be fitted in loosely and then have any wrinkles smoothed out. When the cake is turned out, the plastic film can be discarded, leaving the dish perfectly clean.

The shape of the container is very important when cooking cakes by microwave. If the box is too long and narrow, there is a danger that the cake will not cook through in the centre. In the microwave oven, the middle of any item which cannot be stirred always cooks more slowly than the outer edges, and further cooking only results in the outer edges being overdone.

Round cakes up to 23 cm/9 inches in diameter cook most evenly, though a wider container with a jam jar in the middle is also suitable and the results are most attractive. The maximum length recommended for both oblong and square con-

BATTENBURG
Each cake serves 8

Battenburg is laborious to make conventionally, but short cuts using the all-in-one-method, cooking by microwave and using commercial marzipan, cut the time by two-thirds. This recipe makes 2 cakes but they are not divided until Step 10.

100 g/4 oz soft margarine
100 g/4 oz castor sugar
125 g/5 oz plain flour, sifted
2 teaspoons baking powder
Pinch of salt
2 large eggs
4 tablespoons milk
2 teaspoons grated lemon rind
Few drops of vanilla essence
Pink food colouring
Apricot jam
450 g/1 lb marzipan
+ + +
Sifted icing sugar
Glacé cherries
Angelica

1. Line a 30- by 15-cm/12- by 6-inch box with plastic film.
2. Cut a piece of card the depth of the box and the measurement of the width plus 5 cm/2 inches. Fold over 2½ cm/1 inch at either end in opposite directions.
3. Fit the card into the box to divide it into two equal sections.
4. Beat together the margarine, sugar, sifted flour, baking powder, salt, eggs and milk in a warm bowl until smooth.
5. Divide the mixture equally in two.
6. Add the lemon rind to one half. Flavour the other half with vanilla essence and colour it pink.
7. Spread the yellow mixture evenly in one half of the box and the pink mixture in the other.
8. Cook 4 minutes, giving the

box a ¼ turn every minute. Leave to cool a little, then turn out on to non-stick paper. If the inner edges of the pieces are undercooked, carefully lift out the cake in its plastic film and turn the pieces of cake round so that the inside edges face outwards. Replace them in the oven on a piece of non-stick paper and switch on for 30 seconds to finish cooking.

9. Cool the cakes and sandwich them together with jam.

10. Cut into 4 strips lengthways. Use two of the strips for each cake. Reverse one piece and join to the other with jam to give a chequered effect.

11. For each Battenburg, roll out 225 g/8 oz marzipan on sifted icing sugar to fit the length and circumference of the cake. Spread with jam.

12. Wrap the cake in marzipan so that the join is underneath. Roll the cake lightly with a rolling pin so that the marzipan adheres. Trim.

13. Pinch up the edges of the top surface.

To serve without freezing
Dust the top of the cake with icing sugar before decorating with glacé cherries and angelica.

To freeze Decorate the cake with glacé cherries and angelica. Wrap the cake in freezer film and overwrap with freezer foil.

To serve from the freezer
Remove wrappings and thaw the cake at room temperature. Dust evenly with sifted icing sugar.

tainers is also 23 cm/9 inches unless the recipe states otherwise. To avoid the cake batter flowing over the sides of the dish as it rises, the dish should be no more than half full at the start. Microwave cakes cook best when the uncooked batter is no more than 5 cm/2 inches deep.

For best results, small cakes should be cooked only four at a time, and larger cakes should be given a ¼ turn four times during cooking. If you find that cakes are rising unevenly, cook them with a sheet of paper over the top of the dish.

Cakes (and biscuits) are ready when the centre is just dry on top. Both continue cooking after the oven has been switched off, so do not be tempted to give them more cooking until they are cold and it is evident that they need it. The microwave oven is remarkably tolerant and failures can usually be put right. In fact, a microwave cake will not come to any harm if it is taken out of the oven for a few minutes before it is fully cooked to make way for a more urgent item. As soon as the cake is put back and the oven is switched on again, cooking resumes. Cakes and biscuits must not be overcooked as the cakes will dry out and the biscuits will scorch. I recommend that you test the power of your oven with a simple cake batter first, and, if necessary, alter the cooking times for other cakes accordingly. This could mean a difference in timing of up to a minute either way.

If a cake cooked in an oblong container has failed to dry out in the middle, turn it out on to a piece of non-stick paper, cut it in half lengthways and replace the two strips in the box with the undercooked parts facing outwards. Cook the strips for 1 or 2 minutes longer, then turn them out and use them as two small cakes or put them together with icing.

As soon as a cake is cooked, it should be turned out on to a wire cooling rack to allow steam to escape and prevent the cake becoming heavy. First turn the cake out on to a sheet of non-stick paper, then reverse it on to the rack. In this way, the danger of the soft top of the cake sticking to the wires will be avoided.

Icing helps to keep cakes moist. It does not have to be a glacé or fudge icing: a thin coating of apricot conserve will do just as well and can be used as a base for chopped nuts, glacé fruit or ratafia biscuits. Alternatively, fondant or marzipan may be rolled out and fixed to the cake with a little egg white. When glacé icing is being used, it will be smoother if spread over warm cake.

The best biscuits to cook by microwave are the cookie type which can be rolled out, cooked in a square or oblong box and then cut into bars. You could also try stuffing a cardboard tube from a kitchen paper roll with biscuit dough. After cooking, leave the roll to cool for 10 minutes, then tear away the cardboard and slice the roll into biscuits. Biscuit mixtures which must be spooned out at well-spaced intervals to allow them to spread are fiddly, for the microwave oven can only cook them a few at a time. Spoonfuls of heavier mixture which will hold their shape are less trouble and give better results.

Cake batters can be made up in large batches, then either frozen in freezer bags in cake-size portions, or divided up, baked one after the other and then frozen. Frozen cake batter should be thawed out at room temperature before baking rather than transferred straight from the freezer to the micro-wave, as this could result in uneven cooking.

Baked sandwich (layer) cakes which are to be thawed by microwave should not be assembled until thawing, as fillings may not thaw satisfactorily in the oven. If, however, the cake is to be thawed at room temperature it may be filled, but avoid using raspberry jam to put together cakes which are to be frozen, as for some unfathomable reason the jam develops a stale taste in the freezer.

Iced cakes, which freeze very well, should be allowed to thaw unwrapped at room temperature. Glacé icing will become very wet at first, but this moisture soon evaporates in a warm atmosphere.

Tea breads and plain cakes can be thawed directly by microwave: small cakes take about $\frac{1}{2}$ minute each, medium-size cakes 2 minutes and large ones 4 minutes.

To freeze uncooked biscuit doughs, roll them in a piece of non-stick paper overwrapped with freezer foil. To cook from frozen, remove the foil and bake the biscuits in the paper roll, cutting them while still soft, or thaw the roll for $\frac{1}{2}$ minute in the microwave oven, then slice and cook.

AMERICAN COFFEE CAKE
Serves 8

Provided it is not too tall to go in the microwave oven, an empty sauce bottle without its lid can be put in the centre of the bowl instead of a jam jar. The diameter of the aperture will then be smaller.

100 g/4 oz butter
100 g/4 oz castor sugar
2 large eggs
$\frac{1}{2}$ teaspoon vanilla essence
175 g/7 oz plain flour
2 teaspoons baking powder
25 g/1 oz cornflour
Pinch of salt
75 g/3 oz icing sugar
About 8 tablespoons milk
1 teaspoon coffee essence
   (Camp)

+ + +

3–4 tablespoons icing sugar
$\frac{1}{2}$ teaspoon coffee essence
   (Camp)

1.   Lightly grease a 3$\frac{1}{2}$-litre/6-pt glass mixing bowl and the outside of a 450-g/1-lb jam jar. Stand the jar in the middle of the bowl.
2.   Cream the butter and sugar together until light and fluffy.
3.   Beat the eggs lightly with the vanilla essence and gradually add to the mixture, beating vigorously between each addition.
4.   Sift the flour, baking powder, cornflour, salt and icing sugar together, and stir in to the mixture.
5.   Beat in sufficient milk to form a thick batter.
6.   Divide the batter in half. Flavour one half with the coffee essence.
7.   Cover the base of the greased bowl with half the coffee batter, then add alternate

layers of plain and coffee mixture.

8. Cook 6 to 8 minutes, giving the bowl a ¼ turn every 1½ or 2 minutes.

9. Leave for 5 minutes before turning out on to a wire cooling rack.

To serve without freezing
Prepare a thin glacé icing with the icing sugar, coffee essence and a teaspoon of water, and spoon over the top of the cake, so that it trickles unevenly down the sides.

To freeze When the cake is cold, put it on a disc of non-stick paper and overwrap with a layer of freezer film and freezer foil.

To serve from the freezer
Remove wrappings and put the cake on a serving dish. To thaw by microwave, switch on for 2 minutes, giving the dish a ¼ turn every ½ minute. Mix the icing sugar, coffee essence and a teaspoon of water to form a thin icing, and spoon on top of the cake so that it trickles unevenly down the sides.

BULGARIAN COFFEE CAKE

This cake should be served as fresh as possible as it becomes stodgy when stale.

150 g/6 oz castor sugar
100 g/4 oz butter
2 eggs
175 g/7 oz plain flour
1 teaspoon baking powder
150 ml/6 fl oz natural yoghurt
½ teaspoon vanilla essence
75 g/3 oz mixed nuts, finely chopped
3 tablespoons demerara sugar
1 teaspoon ground cinnamon

+ + +

1 tablespoon softened butter
1 tablespoon chopped pistachio nuts

1. Cream the castor sugar and butter together.

2. Beat in eggs, one at a time.

3. Sift the flour and baking powder into the mixture, mix well then gently fold in the yoghurt and vanilla essence.

4. Line the base of a round dish with paper and grease the sides of the dish.

5. Mix the nuts, demerara sugar and cinnamon together, and sprinkle a third of the mixture evenly over the base of the dish.

6. Pour in half of the batter and sprinkle with half of the remaining nut mixture.

7. Add the rest of the batter and top with the remaining nut mixture.

8. Cover dish lightly with a piece of paper and cook 6 minutes, giving the dish a ¼ turn every 1½ minutes.

9. Remove the paper and leave the cake to stand for 5 minutes before turning it out on to a cake rack to cool.

To serve without freezing
Spread softened butter over the cake and sprinkle with chopped pistachio nuts.

To freeze Cool cake rapidly. Cover with plastic film and overwrap with freezer foil.

To serve Remove wrappings. Place the cake on a serving dish. To thaw by microwave, switch on for 1 minute, then leave at room temperature for 10 minutes. Repeat if necessary. Spread softened butter over the top of the cake and sprinkle with chopped pistachio nuts.

CHOCOLATE CAKE

An old favourite which never goes wrong. You could also ice it with lemon or chocolate butter icing or leave unadorned.

50 g/2 oz butter
50 g/2 oz castor sugar
1 large egg, beaten
50 g/2 oz plain flour
½ teaspoon baking powder
25 g/1 oz cocoa
25 g/1 oz ground almonds
2 tablespoons milk
50 g/2 oz golden syrup
½ recipe Fudge icing (page 153)
Walnuts
Glacé cherries

1. Beat the butter and sugar until light and fluffy.

2. Beat in the egg with 1 tablespoon of the flour.

3. Sift the remaining dry ingredients on to the mixture. Fold them in, adding the milk, a tablespoon at a time.

4. Stir in the golden syrup.

5. Turn the batter into a 15-cm/6-inch glass soufflé dish. Cook 4 minutes, giving the dish a ¼ turn every minute.

6. Leave to rest for 2 or 3 minutes, then turn out on to a wire cooling rack.

7. Coat with fudge icing and decorate with walnuts and glacé cherries.

To serve without freezing
Lift carefully on to a dish when completely cold.

To freeze Open-freeze the cake until the icing is firm, then wrap loosely in freezer foil.

To serve from the freezer
Remove the wrappings and leave the cake to thaw at room temperature. The icing will tend

to become wet at first, but will dry again after about an hour.

CHOCOLATE COFFEE TORTE
Serves 6

Apricot preserve concealed beneath the chocolate icing lends a Continental touch to this recipe. The cake should be coated with jam while still hot.

75 g/3 oz cooking chocolate
2 tablespoons strong coffee
3 large eggs
100 g/4 oz castor sugar
75 g/3 oz plain flour
½ teaspoon baking powder
**4–6 tablespoons apricot
  conserve**

Chocolate glaze

100 g/4 oz cooking chocolate
1 tablespoon strong coffee
1 teaspoon butter

1. Put the chocolate and the coffee in a small bowl and cook until melted, 1 minute. Leave to cool.
2. Beat the eggs with the sugar until very thick, when a spoonful of the mixture dropped on to the top momentarily rests on the surface before sinking in.
3. Fold in the chocolate mixture.
4. Sift the flour and baking powder on top and fold in lightly.
5. Pour batter into a prepared rectangular dish 11 by 23 cm/ 4½ by 9 inches. Cook 6 minutes, giving the dish a ¼ turn every 1½ minutes. Leave to cool a little.
6. Turn cake out on to a cooling rack over a tray and coat with apricot conserve.
7. When the cake is cold, make

the chocolate glaze. Put chocolate and coffee in a small bowl. Cook until melted, 1 minute.
8. Stir in the butter and beat until smoothly blended.
9. Spread chocolate glaze over the top and sides of the cake, using a palette knife that has been dipped in very hot water.

To serve without freezing
When the icing is set, lift the cake on to a serving platter.

To freeze Open-freeze the iced cake on the wire rack and tray. When the chocolate is hard and set, lift the cake from the rack and wrap in freezer film. Overwrap with freezer foil.

To serve from the freezer
Remove wrappings and thaw the cake at room temperature. It may be sliced as soon as the icing is soft enough.

CINNAMON BISCUITS
Makes 40

Overcooking these biscuits will produce burnt spots. Bear in mind that they will continue cooking after the oven is switched off.

3 egg whites
200 g/8 oz castor sugar
150 g/6 oz ground almonds
1 tablespoon ground cinnamon
Icing sugar

1. Beat the egg whites until stiff but not dry.
2. Fold in the sugar, almonds and cinnamon.
3. Roll into small balls, coating your hands with a little icing sugar to prevent sticking.
4. Place 6 balls at a time, well

spaced out, on a sheet of non-stick paper and flatten slightly. Cook 3 minutes.

To serve without freezing
Leave the biscuits to cool, then dust liberally with sifted icing sugar.

To freeze Leave to cool and pack into freezer bags. Seal.

To serve from the freezer
Pile on to a serving plate and thaw by microwave. Switch on for 1 minute, then leave to complete thawing at room temperature. Dust with sifted icing sugar.

COCONUT PYRAMIDS
Makes 20

Coconut Pyramids may appear underdone on the outside and yet be burnt inside. *It is important not to overcook them.*

225 g/9 oz desiccated coconut
150 g/6 oz castor sugar
2 eggs, beaten
+ + +

Glacé cherries, quartered
Apricot jam

1. Put the coconut in a dish. Cook 2 or 3 minutes, stirring frequently, until the coconut is golden.
2. Mix the coconut with the sugar and bind with the eggs.
3. Form into pyramids and place 4 at a time, well spaced out, on a piece of non-stick paper. Cook 1 minute.

To serve without freezing
Decorate each pyramid with a piece of cherry, fixed to the apex with apricot jam.

To freeze When the pyramids are cold, layer them in a freezer container, separated with freezer film. Seal.

To serve from the freezer Thaw pyramids at room temperature. Stick a piece of glacé cherry to the apex of each one with apricot jam.

DOUGHNUTS
Makes 8

This recipe can *only* be cooked with a browning skillet.

1 packet doughnut mix prepared according to the directions on the packet
or

125 g/5 oz plain flour
2 teaspoons baking powder
75 g/3 oz castor sugar
Pinch of salt
15 g/½ oz butter, softened
1 egg
4 tablespoons milk
½ teaspoon vanilla essence

+ + +

6 tablespoons cooking oil

+ + +

Granulated sugar

1. Sift the flour, baking powder, sugar and salt into a mixing bowl.
2. Rub in the butter.
3. Beat the egg, milk and vanilla essence together, and stir into the mixture.
4. Turn out home-made or prepared mix on to a floured board and shape into a sausage. Leave to rest for 5 minutes.
5. Preheat the browning skillet for 5 minutes, then add the oil and cook 2 minutes longer.
6. Meanwhile, cut the roll of dough into 8 equal pieces and shape each into a ring.

7. Cook the doughnuts in the browning skillet 4 at a time for 1 minute, then flip them over with a fish slice and cook for a further minute on the other side.
8. Preheat the skillet for 1 minute before cooking the remaining 4 doughnuts.

To serve without freezing Toss the hot doughnuts in granulated sugar spread on a piece of greaseproof paper.

To freeze Drain the doughnuts on absorbent kitchen paper. Freeze in a sealed container, separating the layers with greaseproof paper.

To serve from the freezer Remove the doughnuts from the freezer container and place them 4 at a time on a piece of absorbent kitchen paper. To thaw by microwave, switch on for 1½ minutes, or until hot. Toss the doughnuts in granulated sugar and serve immediately.

LEMON MADEIRA CAKE
Serves 8

To vary the flavour, substitute a few drops of almond essence for the lemon rind and mix with milk, or substitute orange juice to make an Orange Madeira Cake.

100 g/4 oz butter or soft margarine
100 g/4 oz castor sugar
100 g/4 oz plain flour
25 g/1 oz cornflour
1 teaspoon baking powder
2 large eggs
2 teaspoons grated lemon rind
½ teaspoon vanilla essence
1 tablespoon lemon juice
Yellow food colouring

1 tablespoon apricot jam
2 tablespoons mixed chopped peel

1. Grease a 15-cm/6-inch soufflé dish and line the base with a disc of non-stick paper.
2. Beat the butter and sugar until light and fluffy.
3. Sift the flour, cornflour and baking powder together.
4. Beat the eggs with the lemon rind and vanilla essence.
5. Stir 1 tablespoon of the flour mixture into the creamed mixture, then add the beaten eggs. Mix well.
6. Fold in the remaining flour and mix to a soft dropping consistency with the lemon juice. Mix in a few drops of yellow food colouring if necessary.
7. Turn batter into the prepared dish, smooth the top evenly and cook 4 minutes.
8. Leave to rest for a few minutes. Loosen the sides of the cake with a greased knife and turn it out on to a sheet of foil.
9. Warm the apricot jam in the microwave oven for 15 seconds.
10. Spread the jam over the top and sides of the cake, and press the chopped peel on top.

To serve without freezing Leave the cake until quite cold then transfer it to a cake dish.

To freeze Cover the top of the cake with plastic film, then draw up the sides of the foil to cover. When frozen, overwrap with another piece of foil.

To serve from the freezer Remove wrappings. Thaw by microwave for ½ minute, then leave to thaw out completely at room temperature.

GLAZED GINGERBREAD

Serves 6–8

Do not overbeat the batter, as the bicarbonate of soda will cause the cake to rise unevenly and toughen the mixture.

50 g/2 oz soft margarine
50 g/2 oz demerara sugar
50 g/2 oz golden syrup
50 g/2 oz black treacle
1 large egg
3–4 tablespoons milk
100 g/4 oz plain flour
25 g/1 oz cornflour
Pinch of salt
$\frac{1}{2}$ teaspoon bicarbonate of soda
3 teaspoons ground ginger
25 g/1 oz preserved ginger, chopped

+ + +

Apricot glaze (page 153)
2 teaspoons Stock syrup (page 156)
1 teaspoon water
4–6 tablespoons icing sugar
25 g/1 oz preserved ginger, sliced

1. Put the margarine, sugar, syrup and treacle into a large glass bowl. Cook 1 minute. Stir thoroughly.
2. Beat the egg and milk together, and stir into the sugar mixture.
3. Sift the flour, cornflour, salt, bicarbonate of soda and ground ginger into the mixture, and beat until smooth. Add a little more milk if necessary to form a loose batter.
4. Stir in the chopped ginger.
5. Turn the batter into a box 20 by 18 cm/8 by 7 inches and 8 cm/3 inches deep, lined with plastic film. Cook 6 minutes, giving the box a $\frac{1}{4}$ turn every $1\frac{1}{2}$ minutes.

To serve without freezing
Leave for a few minutes, turn out on to a wire cooling rack, then reverse on to a sheet of non-stick paper. Brush the surface of the cake with Apricot glaze. Mix the stock syrup, water and icing sugar in a small bowl. Heat in the microwave oven for $\frac{1}{2}$ minute, then beat thoroughly. Pour over the cake. Decorate the top with slices of ginger before the icing sets.

To freeze Leave the cake to cool in the box. Remove the box and overwrap the cake with freezer film and freezer foil.

To serve from the freezer
Remove wrappings and put the cake on a piece of non-stick paper. To thaw by microwave, switch on for 3 minutes. Brush the cake with apricot glaze. Mix the stock syrup, water and icing sugar in a small bowl. Heat in the microwave oven for $\frac{1}{2}$ minute, then beat thoroughly. Pour over the cake. Decorate the top with slices of ginger before the icing sets.

FUDGE SHORTCAKE

Serves 6

150 g/6 oz plain flour
50 g/2 oz demerara sugar
100 g/4 oz butter
200 g/8 oz vanilla fudge
2 tablespoons milk

1. Sift the flour into a mixing bowl and stir in the sugar.
2. Cut in the butter with two knives or a pastry blender until the mixture resembles large crumbs.
3. Lay a piece of non-stick paper on an ovenproof plate.

Stand a suitable flan ring on top. Turn the mixture into the centre, pressing it well down and paying attention to the edges.
4. Cook 3 minutes, giving the plate a $\frac{1}{4}$ turn every 45 seconds. Remove from the oven.
5. Put the fudge and milk in a bowl. Cook until melted, $1\frac{1}{2}$ minutes. Stir.
6. Remove the flan ring from the shortcake and pour the melted fudge on top, tipping the cake to avoid the fudge running over the edges.
7. Leave to cool.

To serve without freezing
Cut into 6 or 8 wedges when the fudge has set.

To freeze Open-freeze the cake until firm, then wrap in freezer foil.

To serve from the freezer
Remove wrappings. To thaw by microwave, switch on for 1 minute, then leave the cake at room temperature for a few minutes to complete thawing.

LEMON SPONGE BIRTHDAY CAKE BASE

Serves 8

This batter is ideal for a child's birthday cake, so it can be cooked in any shape you like. Bake it in a large, oval casserole, then coat with chocolate butter icing and stick with toasted flaked almonds to resemble a hedgehog. A pudding basin is a good shape to choose to make an igloo. Cover in white icing, use chocolate buttons to form a door and arrange pieces of chocolate flake around the base of the cake to simulate logs.

100 g/4 oz butter
100 g/4 oz castor sugar
2 large eggs
¼ teaspoon vanilla essence
2 teaspoons lemon juice
2 teaspoons grated lemon rind
175 g/7 oz plain flour
25 g/1 oz cornflour
2 teaspoons baking powder
Pinch of salt
75 g/3 oz icing sugar
7 tablespoons milk

+ + +

200 g/8 oz icing sugar
2–2½ tablespoons lemon juice
Yellow food colouring
Orange and lemon jelly
   decorations

1. Grease a loaf shape or deep, round dish 18 cm/7 inches in diameter, and line the base with non-stick paper.
2. Cream the butter and castor sugar together.
3. Beat the eggs, vanilla essence, lemon juice and rind together, and gradually add to the mixture, beating vigorously.
4. Sift the flour, cornflour, baking powder, salt and 75 g/3 oz icing sugar together, and blend into the mixture.
5. Beat in sufficient milk to form a thick batter.
6. Turn batter into the prepared shape, so that the batter reaches halfway up the dish. Cook 7 to 8 minutes (depending on the shape of the cake), giving the dish a ¼ turn every 1½ minutes.
7. Leave cake to cool in the dish for a few minutes before turning it out on to a wire cooling rack.
8. Mix the icing sugar and lemon juice with a few drops of yellow food colouring, and spread over the cake.
9. Decorate with orange and lemon slices.

To serve without freezing
Lift the cake on to a serving dish with 2 fish slices.

To freeze Open-freeze the cake on a baking sheet, then wrap in freezer film and overwrap with foil.

To serve from the freezer
Remove wrappings. Place the cake on a serving dish and leave to thaw at room temperature.

LIGHT FRUIT CAKE
Serves 6–8

Do not overcook cakes. When done, they should be just dry on top. Overcooking will make fruit cake puddingy. If preferred, the mixture can be cooked in a 12½-cm/5-inch soufflé dish for 4 minutes. The dish will not then need to be relined for the second cake.

75 g/3 oz butter
75 g/3 oz soft brown sugar
2 large eggs, beaten
100 g/4 oz plain flour
50 g/2 oz raisins
50 g/2 oz sultanas
50 g/2 oz chopped mixed peel
5 glacé cherries, chopped
25 g/1 oz ground almonds
2 teaspoons baking powder
1 teaspoon mixed spice
1 teaspoon caramel or gravy
   browning
3–4 tablespoons milk

+ + +

2 tablespoons sieved apricot
   jam
4 tablespoons toasted flaked
   almonds

1. Cream the butter and sugar until light and fluffy.
2. Add the beaten eggs

gradually with 1 tablespoon of the flour.
3. Stir in the raisins, sultanas, peel, cherries and ground almonds.
4. Sift remaining flour, baking powder and spice into the mixture, add gravy browning and enough milk to give batter a soft, dropping consistency.
5. Turn into a lined 23- by 11½-cm/9- by 4½-inch dish.
6. Smooth out the mixture and cook 6 minutes, giving the dish a ¼ turn every 1½ minutes.

To serve without freezing
Leave for 2 or 3 minutes before turning cake out on to a wire cooling rack. Transfer cake to a serving dish. Spread the jam over the top of the cake and cover with toasted almonds.

To freeze Leave cake to cool for 2 to 3 minutes before turning out on to a wire cooling rack. When cold, wrap in freezer film and overwrap with freezer foil.

To serve from the freezer
Remove wrappings and place cake on a dish. To thaw by microwave, switch on for ½ minute. Give the dish a ½ turn, then continue cooking for ½ minute. Leave to thaw out completely at room temperature. Using a palette knife dipped in boiling water, spread the jam over the top of the cake and cover with toasted almonds.

LOW CHOLESTEROL RAISIN CAKE

This is an eggless cake made with polyunsaturated oil instead of butter, which is high in cholesterol.

200 g/8 oz plain flour
3 teaspoons baking powder
½ teaspoon bicarbonate of soda
Pinch of salt
1 teaspoon ground cinnamon
Pinch of ground cloves
5½ tablespoons safflower oil
150 g/6 oz soft brown sugar
100 g/4 oz seedless raisins
5 tablespoons sweet red wine
2 tablespoons Grand Marnier

+ + +

1 tablespoon icing sugar

1. Sift the flour, baking powder, soda, salt and spices into a mixing bowl.
2. Rub in the oil, then add the sugar and raisins.
3. Mix in the wine, Grand Marnier and 3 tablespoons water. Leave to rest for 10 minutes.
4. Line a box measuring 20 by 18 cm /8 by 7 inches and 8 cm/3 inches deep with plastic film.
5. Pour in the batter and smooth out. Cook 6 minutes, giving the box a ¼ turn every 1½ minutes.
6. Leave to cool for 2 minutes before turning out on to a wire cooling rack and marking into fingers.

To serve without freezing
Sift the icing sugar over the top of the cake before serving.

To freeze Allow cake to cool completely before wrapping it in freezer film. Overwrap with freezer foil.

To serve from the freezer
Remove wrappings. To thaw by microwave, switch on for 1 minute, then leave to thaw out completely at room temperature. Dust with icing sugar.

OATMEAL GINGER CAKE
Serves 6

This cake may be cooked in a 15-cm/6-inch soufflé dish or a 23- by 12½-cm/9- by 5-inch loaf dish. It may be eaten plain or sliced and buttered. To prevent the cake from sticking to the plate, transfer it on to a piece of non-stick paper the size of the base of the cake soon after turning it out.

75 g/3 oz rolled porridge oats
75 g/3 oz plain flour
1 teaspoon bicarbonate of soda
Pinch of salt
1 teaspoon ground ginger
50 g/2 oz soft brown sugar
25 g/1 oz butter
2 tablespoons black treacle
125 ml/¼ pt milk
4 tablespoons natural yoghurt
1 egg, beaten

1. Mix the oats, flour, bicarbonate of soda, salt, ginger and sugar together.
2. Rub in the butter and add the treacle.
3. Combine the milk and yoghurt in a wide-mouthed jug. Heat for 1 minute in the microwave oven.
4. Add the egg and beat lightly.
5. Pour into the cake mixture and mix well until ingredients are thoroughly blended.
6. Turn the batter into a dish lined with plastic film. Cook 5 minutes, giving the dish a ½ turn halfway through cooking. Leave for a few minutes before turning out on to a sheet of non-stick paper.

To serve without freezing
Transfer the cake to a serving platter.

To freeze Leave the cake to cool, then cover with freezer film and overwrap with freezer foil. Freeze on a flat surface.

To serve from the freezer
Remove wrappings and put cake on a serving dish. To thaw by microwave, switch on for 2 minutes. Leave to rest for 5 minutes.

ICED FANCIES
Makes 20

125 g/5 oz plain flour
2 teaspoons baking powder
Pinch of salt
100 g/4 oz soft margarine
100 g/4 oz castor sugar
2 large eggs
3 tablespoons orange juice
450 g/1 lb icing sugar
Yellow, orange and pink food
  colouring

+ + +

Orange and lemon slices
Crystallised rose petals or
  violets
Smarties, angelica or glacé
  cherries

1. Sift the flour, baking powder and salt into a mixing bowl.
2. Add the margarine, sugar, eggs and orange juice all at once, and beat until smooth.
3. Turn the batter into a straight-sided box 23 cm/9 inches square lined with plastic film. The mixture should not reach more than halfway up the box.
4. Cook 4 minutes, giving the box a ¼ turn every minute.
5. Remove box from the oven and leave to cool for 2 to 3 minutes, then turn out on to a board and cut into 5-cm/2-inch

squares with a sharp knife dipped in hot water and wiped dry. Lift the squares carefully on to a wire cooling rack.

6. Sift the icing sugar and beat in hot water, a teaspoonful at a time, until the icing has a smooth coating consistency. Divide between 3 bowls and colour each batch with a few drops of different colouring.

7. Arrange a few cakes at a time on the cooling rack. Rest the rack over a bowl and pour the icing over the cakes. Spoon the icing over the cakes another time if necessary until they are completely coated.

8. Coat the rest of the cakes with the other icings in the same way.

9. Put a decoration on the top of each cake just before the icing sets.

To serve without freezing
Leave the cakes until cold, then remove surplus icing around the bottoms. Arrange the cakes on a platter lined with paper doily.

To freeze Open-freeze. Cut away surplus icing around the bottoms of the cakes, then pack into a freezer container, making sure that they are separated. Overwrap. Seal.

To serve from the freezer
Remove the cakes from the container and thaw at room temperature. The icing will first become damp and then dry out.

PEANUT BUTTER BARS
Makes 12–16

25 g/1 oz soft margarine
25 g/1 oz demerara sugar
25 g/1 oz granulated sugar
75 g/3 oz crunchy peanut butter
50 g/2 oz plain flour
⅛ teaspoon bicarbonate of soda
Pinch of salt
1 large egg, beaten
Few drops of vanilla essence

1. Beat the margarine, demerara and granulated sugars and peanut butter together until well mixed.

2. Stir in half the flour sifted with the bicarbonate of soda and salt.

3. Stir the beaten egg, vanilla essence and the remaining flour into the mixture to form a soft dough.

4. Press into a 23- by 15-cm/9- by 6-inch box lined with plastic film. Cook 4 minutes, giving the box a ¼ turn every minute.

5. Turn out on to a flat surface, leave to cool a little, then cut into bars.

To serve without freezing
Leave until cold, then pack into an airtight tin.

To freeze Leave until cold. Pack flat in freezer foil and seal tightly.

To serve from the freezer
Remove wrappings. Spread the biscuits out, 8 at a time, on a piece of paper on the microwave oven base. Switch on for ½ minute, then leave to complete thawing at room temperature.

ORANGE SULTANA TEA BREAD

It is not necessary for this bread to look brown when it comes out of the oven, since it is meant to be eaten sliced and toasted.

Grated rind and juice of 1 large orange
1 teaspoon bicarbonate of soda
25 g/1 oz butter
½ teaspoon vanilla essence
75 g/3 oz sultanas
75 g/3 oz soft brown sugar
1 large egg
150 g/6 oz plain flour
1 teaspoon baking powder
½ teaspoon salt
75 g/3 oz chopped mixed nuts

1. Measure the orange juice and make up to 125 ml/¼ pt with boiling water. Pour into a mixing bowl.

2. Stir in the bicarbonate of soda and butter.

3. Add the grated orange rind, vanilla essence, sultanas and brown sugar.

4. Beat in the egg.

5. Sift the flour, baking powder and salt together, and beat into the mixture.

6. Stir in the nuts.

7. Turn the batter into a loaf-shaped dish 23 by 11½ cm/9 by 4½ inches lined with plastic film. Smooth out the top and cook 8 minutes, giving the dish a ¼ turn every 2 minutes.

8. Turn out on to a wire cooling rack.

To serve without freezing
Leave until cold, then slice with a sharp knife and toast. Serve with plenty of unsalted butter and jam.

To freeze Allow to cool completely, then wrap in non-stick paper and overwrap with freezer foil.

To serve from the freezer
Remove wrappings. To thaw by microwave, switch on for ½ minute. Slice while still partially frozen and toast on both sides. Serve with butter and jam.

Breads, Cakes and Biscuits

PRUNE AND WALNUT TEA BREAD

200 g/8 oz pitted prunes
100 g/4 oz butter
150 g/6 oz castor sugar
2 eggs
50 g/2 oz walnuts, chopped
175 g/7 oz self-raising flour
1 teaspoon baking powder
4–6 tablespoons milk

1. Cover prunes with water in a bowl. Cook in the microwave oven 3 to 4 minutes until the water boils, then cook for a further minute.
2. Drain off the surplus water and mash the prunes. Leave to cool.
3. Beat the butter and sugar until fluffy.
4. Add the eggs one at a time, beating continuously.
5. Stir in the chopped walnuts and the mashed prunes.
6. Sift the flour and baking powder together, and fold half into the mixture.
7. Mix in enough milk to form a very soft batter.
8. Stir in the remaining flour.
9. Turn the batter into a lined 23- by 11½-cm/9- by 4½-inch dish.
10. Cook 6 minutes, giving the dish a ¼ turn every 1½ minutes.
11. Leave to cool in the dish for 5 minutes, then turn out on to a wire cooling rack.

To serve without freezing
Leave until cold, then slice thinly and serve with butter and jam or honey.

To freeze Leave until quite cold, then wrap in non-stick paper and overwrap with freezer foil.

To serve from the freezer
Remove the wrappings and put cake on a dish. To thaw by microwave, switch on for 1 minute. Slice and butter, or toast lightly and serve buttered with jam or honey.

BREAD MADE FROM FROZEN DOUGH

Use this method for cooking commercial frozen bread dough. The rising process takes from 30 to 45 minutes, occupying only 4 minutes oven time. The dough should never feel hot to the touch. If the conventional oven is on, cook the bread for 3 minutes by microwave at Step 3, then bake it for 8 minutes in the oven at 230°C/450°F/Gas 8.

1. Put the loaf on a sheet of non-stick paper in the microwave oven. Switch on for 15 seconds. Then cover with a greased polythene sheet.
2. Rest for 3 minutes, then continue thawing by microwave and resting until the dough is double its original size.
3. Cook, uncovered, for 5 minutes until the dough rises and retains its shape. This will be double the proved size.
4. Brown on the top and bottom under the grill.

GARLIC BREAD

Prepare four loaves at a time and defrost as required. Make sure that the stick of bread is not too long to fit into the oven.

4 French loaves
225 g/8 oz salted butter
2 garlic cloves, crushed

1. Cut the bread three-quarters through into 2½-cm/1-inch slices.

2. Put the butter in a bowl with the garlic. Cook until melted, 2 minutes. Leave to rest 10 minutes.
3. Strain the butter and spoon between the slices.

To serve without freezing
Place a loaf on absorbent paper and heat in the microwave oven for ½ minute. Crisp under the grill.

To freeze Wrap the loaves separately in a double thickness of freezer foil to prevent the odour from escaping.

To serve from the freezer
Remove wrappings. Place loaf on a piece of absorbent paper. To thaw by microwave, switch on for 1 minute. Crisp in a hot oven or under the grill, turning over once.

IRISH SODA BREAD

200 g/8 oz wholewheat flour
300 ml/generous ½ pt milk
25 g/1 oz soft margarine
2 tablespoons black treacle
175 g/7 oz plain white flour
1 teaspoon salt
6 teaspoons baking powder

1. Put the wholewheat flour in a large bowl and heat in the microwave oven for 30 seconds. Stir in the milk.
2. Leave to stand for 20 minutes. Heat ½ minute.
3. Stir in the margarine and treacle.
4. Sift the white flour, salt and baking powder together, and mix with the wholemeal mixture.
5. Knead lightly to make a soft dough.

6. Form the dough into a ball and put it on a sheet of absorbent kitchen paper. Flatten it gently and mark with a deep cross.

7. Cook 7 minutes, leave to rest for 2 minutes, then remove the paper. Brown both the top and bottom lightly under the grill.

To serve without freezing
Break off a quarter of the loaf and slice as required.

To freeze When cold, put the bread into a freezer bag. Seal.

To serve from the freezer
Remove from the bag. To thaw by microwave, place the bread on a piece of absorbent paper on the oven base and switch on for 2 minutes. Crisp under the grill on both sides if desired.

MILK LOAF
Makes 1 large or 2 small loaves

Self-raising flour is never used when making bread conventionally, because the gluten is not strong enough to hold it in shape during cooking. Microwave bread is an exception to prove the rule. If small loaves are preferred, divide the dough in two and bake separately for 2½ to 3 minutes. Microwave bread can be browned under the grill before or after freezing.

250 ml/½ pt milk
15 g/½ oz dried yeast
2 teaspoons sugar
450 g/1 lb self-raising flour
2 teaspoons salt
1 tablespoon vegetable oil

1. Put the milk in a jug and heat to 38°C/100°F (blood heat), 45 seconds.

2. Stir in the yeast and sugar. Leave for 15 minutes or until frothy, stirring occasionally.

3. Sift the flour and salt into a large bowl. Heat ½ minute.

4. Stir the yeast mixture and oil into the flour. If the mixture is too dry, add a little more warm milk to form a soft dough. Knead gently.

5. Cover with plastic film and leave in a warm place to rise until doubled in size.

6. Knead the dough lightly and press into a greased loaf dish. Leave to rise for 10 minutes.

7. Cook 4 to 4½ minutes. The bread is ready when the top is soft but resilient to the touch.

8. Leave for a few minutes before turning on to a wire cooling rack.

To serve without freezing
Brown on the four long sides under the grill or in a 220°C/425°F/Gas 7 conventional oven for 5 minutes.

To freeze Leave the loaf until completely cold. Pack into a freezer bag. Seal.

To serve from the freezer
Remove the bag. To thaw by microwave, switch on for 2 minutes, then brown top and bottom under the grill.

WHOLEMEAL ROLLS
Makes 16

To hasten rising, the dough may be heated in the microwave oven for 5 seconds after 10 minutes, and a futher 5 seconds after 20 minutes.

250 ml/½ pt milk
15 g/½ oz dried yeast
2 teaspoons sugar
450 g/1 lb wholewheat flour
2 teaspoons salt
2 teaspoons malt extract
1 tablespoon vegetable oil

1. Put the milk in a jug and heat to 38°C/100°F (blood heat), 45 seconds.

2. Stir in the yeast and sugar. Leave for 15 minutes until frothy, stirring occasionally.

3. Sift the flour and salt into a large bowl. Heat ½ minute.

4. Stir the yeast mixture, malt extract and oil into the flour. If the mixture is too dry, add a little more milk. Knead until the mixture loses its stickiness. Cover with plastic film and leave in a warm place until doubled in size.

5. Knead dough lightly, then divide it into 16 pieces and shape into rolls without further kneading. Cover and leave to rise for 20 to 30 minutes.

6. Arrange 8 rolls spaced out in a circle on the oven base. Cook 3 minutes, turning rolls over once during cooking.
Do not overcook.

7. Cook the remaining rolls.

To serve without freezing
Cool rolls on a wire rack, then serve them as they are or crisp them under the grill.

To freeze Leave until quite cold. Pack into a freezer bag. Seal.

To serve from the freezer
To thaw the rolls by microwave, place four rolls at a time, well spaced out, on a piece of absorbent paper in the microwave oven. Switch on for 1 minute. Crisp under the grill if desired.

13 Savoury Sauces, Chutneys and Stuffings

Savoury Sauces, Chutneys and Stuffings

SAVOURY SAUCES

There are two kinds of savoury sauce based on a *roux* (a mixture of fat and flour). For white sauce, the fat and flour are blended and cooked together briefly so that the flour does not change colour. To make a brown sauce, they are cooked until brown and nutty. The latter has a richer flavour and is the base for Brown (Espagnole) sauce which, in turn, is the foundation for many others. The flavour can be varied by frying vegetables in the fat before adding the flour and by adding different kinds of wine. All these sauces can be cooked by microwave and stored in the freezer.

When making a *roux*-based sauce by microwave, use a large bowl and stir frequently. The fat should be melted in the oven before the flour is blended in. After the mixture has cooked for 1 minute, it will resemble uncooked pastry and the liquid can be stirred in. It is quite in order to use half of the liquid specified to make the sauce. Then, when it has thickened, blend in the remainder and reheat.

Freezer experts disagree on the best form of starch to use for a sauce which is to be frozen. Some feel that it is best to thicken with cornflour, in which case you need only half the usual quantity of starch to fat. Others recommend using flour, then beating the thawed sauce thoroughly while it is reheating. All have their pros and cons. Cornflour sauce will not separate but it can go lumpy. Flour does not do this but it can separate. Potato starch is perfectly textured but it can sour a frozen sauce. In the recipes which follow I have chosen the form of starch I believe to be most suitable for that particular sauce. Whichever kind of starch you choose, it is a good idea to stir the cold sauce gently but thoroughly before freezing it to eliminate any air bubbles, which could cause it to curdle.

To prevent a sauce separating during freezing, a little flour blended with water is stirred in just before freezing. This helps to 'hold' the sauce below freezing point, but the sauce must then be reheated very thoroughly after thawing to make sure that the raw flour is cooked.

When seasoning a sauce which is to be frozen, use a light touch. The freezer tends to intensify flavours and seasonings can always be adjusted when reheating if necessary.

Not all savoury sauces are thickened with starch. Fruit sauces to enhance the flavour of savoury dishes are simple to prepare by microwave either in the same way as for stewing fruit or for making jam.

Emulsion sauces such as mayonnaise, Hollandaise and Béarnaise, involve combining egg yolks with fat or oil, which is tricky to ensure chemically, but it can be obtained by gently heating the ingredients in the microwave oven and then

BASIC WHITE (BÉCHAMEL) SAUCE
Makes 1 litre/1¾ pt

A classic sauce of coating consistency used as a basis for infinite variations. For a sauce of pouring consistency, halve the quantities of butter and flour.

1 litre/1¾ pt Herbed milk (page 142)
100 g/4 oz butter
100 g/4 oz flour

+ + +

1 tablespoon flour

1. Put the butter in a large bowl. Cook until melted, 1 minute.
2. Blend in the flour. Cook 1 minute.
3. Strain the milk into the flour gradually, beating all the time.
4. Cook 5 to 6 minutes, stirring every minute.

To serve without freezing
Mix the quantity required with flavouring ingredients (below). Pour the remaining white sauce into a glass jar and place a dampened disc of greaseproof paper, wet side down, on the surface of the sauce to prevent a skin forming. Store in the refrigerator for up to 24 hours.

To freeze Cool sauce rapidly, stirring frequently. Blend 1 tablespoon flour with 3 tablespoons cold water. Stir into the sauce. Pour convenient quantities of the sauce into freezer bags resting in bowls. Remove bowls when the sauce is frozen. Seal.

To serve from the freezer
Turn the block of sauce out into a bowl. To thaw by microwave,

cover and switch on for 4 minutes. Break up the lumps with a fork. Leave to rest for 5 minutes. Beat, then continue cooking until thoroughly reheated. Beat vigorously once more. Thin down with milk or stock as required.

Variations based on 250 ml/½ pt White sauce include:

1. Anchovy sauce
Use fish stock in place of milk. Add 2 teaspoons anchovy essence.

2. Caper sauce
Add 2 tablespoons chopped capers and 1 teaspoon vinegar.

3. Cheese sauce
(Sauce Mornay) Add 4 tablespoons grated cheese and ¼ teaspoon dry mustard.

4. Mushroom sauce
Add 50 g/2 oz sautéed mushrooms and 1 teaspoon lemon juice.

5. Onion sauce
(Sauce Soubise) Add 1 chopped, cooked onion and 1 tablespoon cream.

6. Shrimp sauce
Add 50 g/2 oz chopped cooked shrimps, 1 teaspoon anchovy essence and 1 teaspoon lemon juice.

7. Tomato sauce
(Sauce Aurore) Add 4 tablespoons tomato purée and a pinch of dried basil, or 2 tablespoons of finely chopped fresh basil.

vigorously beating them together at room temperature. However, as soon as the sauce is frozen the ingredients will separate again. Thawing must be carried out slowly and the mixture must then be beaten thoroughly to reunify the ingredients.

CHUTNEYS AND PICKLES

Chutneys are easy to prepare in the microwave and will not scorch at the bottom of the bowl, which can happen if you are not careful when making chutney conventionally. Four or 5 jars are the most that can be made in the oven at one time. The vinegar in chutneys and pickles acts as a preservative, but lemon juice may be substituted if preferred. Chutney improves with keeping and should be allowed to mature for at least 3 months before unsealing.

There is no need to freeze chutney, but if you wish to store jars in the freezer, be sure to leave a 2½-cm/1-inch headspace to allow for expansion, otherwise the glass may break.

The microwave oven can be used at all the various stages in the preparation of pickles (see page 146). Vegetables may be pickled raw or cooked. The spiced vinegar in which they are preserved should be made and set aside for 1 week before straining.

STUFFINGS AND DUMPLINGS

A clever cook can use stuffings and dumplings to make a dish go further and taste more exciting. All kinds of stuffing can be stored in the freezer, packed in the quantities required. If the stuffing is to be served separately, shape it into balls and open freeze on a tray before packing in freezer bags. They can then be thawed and cooked by microwave as needed.

If you wish to stuff poultry with frozen stuffing, it is advisable to thaw them both first. However, rolled pieces of meat or fish may be frozen ready stuffed. Cooking times will then be the same as if the weight were all meat or fish.

HERBED MILK
Makes 1 litre/1¾ pt

Herbed milk improves the flavour of all savoury white sauces. Dieters may substitute skimmed milk to halve the calories. If herbed milk is to be frozen, use skimmed or homogenised milk as pasteurised milk does not freeze satisfactorily.

1 litre/1¾ pt milk
1 onion, quartered
2 cloves
1 bay leaf
6 black peppercorns
3 blades mace
1 sprig fresh thyme or ¼
    teaspoon dried thyme
Salt, white pepper
2 sprigs fresh parsley or ½
    teaspoon dried parsley

1.   Combine all the ingredients in a large jug. Heat until the milk steams, 4 minutes.
2.   Cover and set aside until cold. Strain.

To serve without freezing
Use the quantity required and freeze the remainder.

To freeze   Strain convenient quantities of the milk into freezer bags resting in bowls. When frozen, remove the bowls. Seal.

To serve from the freezer
Remove wrappings. Return the block to the bowl. To thaw by microwave, cover and switch on for 5 minutes. Stir. Continue cooking until completely thawed. Use as required.

PARSLEY SAUCE
Makes 1 litre/1¾ pt

Parsley contains Vitamin C and a useful quantity of iron. This sauce is normally served with egg and fish dishes.

1 litre/1¾ pt milk
2 onions, sliced
4 bay leaves, crumbled
6 black peppercorns, bruised
50 g/2 oz butter
25 g/1 oz cornflour
8 tablespoons finely chopped
    parsley
1 teaspoon grated nutmeg
Salt, pepper

1.   Combine the milk, onions, bay leaves and peppercorns in a large jug. Cook 4½ to 5 minutes until boiling point is reached. Cover and leave to infuse for 30 minutes.
2.   Put the butter in a large bowl. Cook until melted, 1 minute.
3.   Blend in the cornflour and cook ½ minute.
4.   Strain the milk and gradually stir 500 ml/1 pt into the cornflour. Cook until the sauce thickens, 4 minutes, stirring frequently.
5.   Stir in the remaining milk and cook a further 2 minutes, stirring occasionally.
6.   Beat in the parsley and nutmeg, and season with salt and pepper.

To serve without freezing
Pour the required amount of sauce into a heated sauceboat. Place a disc of dampened greaseproof paper, wet side down, on surface of remaining sauce and store in the refrigerator for up to 24 hours.

To freeze   Cool the sauce and pour quantities required into freezer bags resting in bowls. Remove from the bowls when the sauce is frozen. Seal.

To serve from the freezer
Remove wrappings and place block of sauce in a bowl. To thaw by microwave, cover and switch on for 2 minutes. Break up the lumps with a fork. Leave to rest for 4 minutes. Stir, then continue cooking until thoroughly reheated, stirring frequently.

CREAM SAUCE
Makes 500 ml/1 pt

A delicate, smooth sauce to serve with white fish or poultry. The sauce must be mixed quickly while the water is still boiling.

3 egg yolks
4 tablespoons double cream
75 g/3 oz unsalted butter
25 g/1 oz flour
1 tablespoon fresh lemon juice
Salt

1.   Blend the egg yolks with the cream.
2.   Put 25 g/1 oz butter in a bowl and cook until melted, 1 minute.
3.   Blend in the flour, then gradually whisk in 500 ml/1 pt *boiling* water.
4.   Quickly beat in the cream mixture and flavour with lemon juice and salt to taste.
5.   Dice the remaining butter. Add it to the sauce and stir until melted.
6.   Reheat in the microwave oven for 20 seconds.

To serve   Serve hot.
Do not freeze.

ASPARAGUS SAUCE
Makes 375 ml/$\frac{3}{4}$ pt

Not just a sauce, but rather a superior creamy coating to be served with delicately flavoured fish fillets, poached eggs or thinly sliced breast of chicken.

25 g/1 oz butter
25 g/1 oz flour
1 can (298 g) asparagus spears
About 125 ml/$\frac{1}{4}$ pt milk
1 teaspoon lemon juice
Salt, white pepper
+ + +
1 tablespoon double cream
+ + +
1 teaspoon flour

1. Put the butter in a large bowl. Cook until melted, 1 minute.
2. Blend in the flour and cook $\frac{1}{2}$ minute.
3. Drain the asparagus into a measuring jug and make up the liquid to 250 ml/$\frac{1}{2}$ pt with milk.
4. Gradually add the liquid to the butter and flour mixture, stirring until the mixture is smooth again. Cook 4 minutes, beating every minute.
5. Chop the asparagus spears roughly and stir them into the sauce. Add lemon juice and season with salt and pepper.

To serve without freezing
Reheat sauce in the microwave oven for 2 minutes, adding a little water if it is too thick. Stir in the cream before serving.

To freeze Blend 1 teaspoon flour with 2 tablespoons cold water and stir into the sauce. Pour the sauce into a freezer bag resting in a bowl. Remove the bag when the sauce is frozen and seal the bag.

To serve from the freezer
Turn block of sauce out into a bowl. To thaw by microwave, cover and switch on for 4 minutes. Break up the lumps with a fork. Leave to rest for 5 minutes. Stir thoroughly, then continue cooking until the sauce is thoroughly reheated and starting to boil. Thin down with milk or water and stir in the cream just before serving.

BASIC BROWN (ESPAGNOLE) SAUCE
Makes 500 ml/1 pt

Canned consommé is excellent in this recipe, but home-made brown stock may be used if preferred.

25 g/1 oz butter
1 rasher streaky bacon, rinded and chopped
1 onion, finely chopped
1 carrot, scraped and finely chopped
1 celery stalk, thinly sliced
500 ml/1 pt beef consommé
1 tablespoon tomato purée
Salt, pepper
25 g/1 oz cornflour

1. Preheat the browning skillet for 5 minutes.
2. Quickly add the butter, followed by the bacon, onion, carrot and celery, and stir rapidly to brown slightly. Cook 4 minutes, stirring once during cooking.
3. Add the consommé and tomato purée, and season with salt and pepper. Cover and cook 5 minutes. Leave to rest for 30 minutes.
4. Blend the cornflour with a little cold water. Stir into the sauce. Cook 3$\frac{1}{2}$ to 4 minutes until the mixture boils.

5. Strain the sauce through a sieve.

To serve without freezing
Pour required amount into a heated sauceboat. Store the remainder in jam jars in the refrigerator for up to 3 days with a dampened disc of greaseproof paper, wet side down, on the surface of the sauce.

To freeze Cool the sauce. Pour in the quantities required into freezer bags resting in a bowl. When the sauce is frozen, remove bowls. Seal.

To serve from the freezer
Remove wrappings and place block of soup in a bowl. To thaw by microwave, switch on for 2 minutes. Break up the sauce with a fork. Leave to rest for 4 minutes. Continue cooking for 4 minutes, or until thoroughly reheated.

Variations based on 250 ml/$\frac{1}{2}$ pt Basic Brown (Espagnole) sauce include:

1. **Bordelaise sauce**
Add 125 ml/$\frac{1}{4}$ pt red wine and 2 tablespoons finely chopped shallots. Cook until reduced by a third, about 5 minutes.

2. **Chasseur sauce**
Add 50 g/2 oz chopped sautéed mushrooms, 4 tablespoons Tomato Concassé (page 144) and 4 tablespoons dry white wine. Cook until reduced by half, about 7 minutes.

3. **Sauce Diable**
Add 1 small chopped onion, 1 tablespoon white wine, and 1 tablespoon vinegar. Cook until reduced by a third, about 5 minutes.

4. Sauce Italienne

Cook 50 g/2 oz mushrooms and 1 small chopped shallot for 2 minutes in 15 g/½ oz butter. Add 25 g/1 oz chopped ham and 4 tablespoons Tomato Concassé (this page), and add to sauce. Cook 3 to 4 minutes.

5. Madeira sauce

Add 2 tablespoons Madeira wine and 25 g/1 oz butter.

6. Reform sauce

Add 2 tablespoons redcurrant jelly, 1 teaspoon vinegar, 125 ml/¼ pt red wine and 25 g/1 oz butter. Cook until reduced by a third, about 5 minutes.

7. Sauce Robert

Cook 1 chopped onion in 15 g/½ oz butter for 3 minutes, stirring occasionally. Add to sauce with 2 tablespoons lemon juice, 1 teaspoon anchovy essence, 1 teaspoon French mustard and salt and pepper. Cover and cook 3 minutes, stirring occasionally.

TOMATO SAUCE

Makes 250 ml/½ pt

Serve this sauce with pasta and meat dishes.

15 g/½ oz butter
½ rasher bacon, rinded and chopped
1 small onion, chopped
1 small carrot, chopped
200 g/8 oz tomatoes, peeled and sliced
1 tablespoon tomato purée
125 ml/¼ pt chicken stock
Salt, pepper
Pinch of sugar
1 teaspoon cornflour

1. Put the butter in a bowl with the bacon, onion and carrot. Cook 3 minutes, stirring occasionally.
2. Add tomatoes, tomato purée, stock, salt, pepper and sugar. Cook 3 minutes to bring to the boil. Stir.
3. Skim the sauce if necessary. Cook a further 2 minutes.
4. Purée the sauce in a liquidiser and correct seasoning, then press through a nylon sieve to remove the tomato pips.
5. Blend the cornflour smoothly with 1 tablespoon cold water, add to the sauce and cook until it thickens, about 3 minutes, stirring every minute.

To serve without freezing
Pour the required amount into a heated sauceboat and freeze the remainder.

To freeze Cool the sauce and pour it into a freezer bag resting in a bowl. When the sauce is frozen, remove from the bowl. Seal.

To serve from the freezer
Remove wrappings and place block of sauce in a bowl and cover. To thaw by microwave, switch on for 5 minutes, breaking up the block with a fork occasionally. Continue cooking for about 6 minutes until the sauce is thoroughly reheated, stirring occasionally.

TOMATO CONCASSÉ

If you are likely to use tomato concassé frequently, make a double batch and freeze it in small quantities. It is very useful for sauces, as a garnish, as a filling in savoury dishes such as stuffed aubergine, and as a topping for pizza, risotto and pasta.

450 g/1 lb tomatoes, peeled, seeded and roughly chopped
1 small onion, finely chopped
25 g/1 oz butter
Salt, pepper

1. Put the onion and butter in a bowl and cook 3 minutes, stirring occasionally.
2. Add the tomatoes. Season with salt and pepper and cook 10 minutes, stirring occasionally, until all the excess liquid has evaporated and the sauce is thick.

To serve without freezing
Use the quantity required and refrigerate or freeze the remainder.

To freeze Cool. Turn into small freezer containers or freezer bags resting in bowls. Seal.

To serve from the freezer
Remove wrappings and place frozen block in a bowl. To thaw by microwave, cover and switch on for 5 minutes. Stir, then continue cooking until thoroughly reheated, 2 to 6 minutes, depending on the quantity.

BARBECUE SAUCE

Makes 500 ml/1 pt

Serve this sauce with spare ribs, pork chops, sausages or hamburgers.

250 ml/½ pt tomato ketchup
2 tablespoons olive oil
2 tablespoons water
2 tablespoons brown sugar

2 tablespoons Worcestershire
  sauce
50 g/2 oz butter
½ garlic clove, crushed
4 tablespoons malt vinegar
Juice of 1 lemon
1 teaspoon paprika
2 teaspoons soy sauce

1.   Mix all ingredients together
in a bowl. Cook until the butter
has melted, 3½ minutes. Stir
well.

To serve without freezing
Reheat quantity required in a
jam jar or sauceboat, allowing 1½
to 2 minutes for 125 ml/¼ pt
sauce when heating from cold.

To freeze   Cool the sauce and
pour into 2 jam jars, leaving
2½ cm/1 inch headspace. Cover
with freezer film and overwrap
with freezer foil.

To serve from the freezer
Remove the foil. To thaw by
microwave, switch on for 4
minutes for 1 jar and 6½ minutes
for 2 jars, stirring after 2
minutes.

CRANBERRY SAUCE
Makes 500 ml/1 pt

Serve with poultry or game.
Redcurrant or blueberry sauce
can be prepared in the same
way.

200 g/8 oz cranberries, fresh or
  frozen
225 g/9 oz soft brown sugar
1 tablespoon lemon juice

1.   Remove the stems and put
the cranberries in a large bowl
with the sugar, lemon juice and
250 ml/½ pt water.
2.   Cover and cook 6 minutes,

stirring occasionally, until the
mixture is mushy.

To serve without freezing
Pour the required amount into a
sauceboat. Cover sauceboat
loosely with a piece of plastic
film and reheat in the
microwave oven for ½ to 1
minute until the film bubbles
up.

To freeze   Leave to cool for 10
minutes. Stir to distribute
berries evenly. Fill 2 jam jars to
within 2½ cm/1 inch of the top.
Cover with plastic film and cook
until the film bubbles up. Leave
to cool. Freeze.

To serve from the freezer
To thaw by microwave, switch
on for 1 to 2 minutes for each jar.

MAYONNAISE
Makes 125 ml/¼ pt

If the mayonnaise is too thick,
stir in 1 teaspoon each boiling
water and vinegar. If it is not
thick enough, up to
25 ml/1 fl oz more oil may be
beaten in.

1 tablespoon vinegar
¼ teaspoon salt
Pepper
¼ teaspoon dry mustard
125 ml/¼ pt olive oil
1 egg yolk

1.   Mix vinegar, salt, pepper
and mustard together in a small
bowl. Cook 20 seconds.
2.   Pour oil into a jug with a
good pouring lip. Cook 30
seconds.
3.   Place egg yolk in a mixing
bowl. Add vinegar mixture and
beat for 1 minute, using a rotary
beater or a hand whisk.

4.   Add oil in a thin stream,
beating vigorously. Serve
immediately.

Should the mayonnaise curdle,
which is highly unlikely, place 1
teaspoon made mustard and 1
teaspoon curdled mayonnaise in
a warm bowl, heat for no more
than 5 seconds, beat them
together, then beat in the
remaining curdled mayonnaise,
a spoon at a time.

HOLLANDAISE SAUCE
Serves 3–4

A light, frothy sauce, delicious
served with fish, asparagus,
cauliflower or eggs. Should the
sauce start to curdle, briskly stir
in 1 tablespoon boiling water.

125 g/5 oz unsalted butter
2 egg yolks, at room
  temperature
125 ml/¼ pt double cream
½ teaspoon salt
¼ teaspoon white pepper
2 tablespoons lemon juice
1 teaspoon butter, to finish
  sauce.

1.   Put the butter in a large
bowl. Cook until melted, 1
minute.
2.   Beat the egg yolks with
cream. Add the salt, pepper and
lemon juice, and stir into the
melted butter. Cook until
thickened, 1 minute, stirring
every 15 seconds.
3.   Remove the bowl from the
oven and whisk the sauce until
frothy. Beat in the remaining
teaspoon of butter.

To serve without freezing
Transfer sauce to a heated
sauceboat and use immediately.
Alternatively, leave to cool and

serve cold, or reheat in the microwave oven for 1 minute, stirring every 15 seconds.

To freeze Pour the sauce into a freezer container. Cool and seal.

To serve from the freezer Transfer frozen sauce to a bowl. To thaw by microwave, switch on for 1 minute, then leave to thaw at room temperature. Reheat by microwave. Switch on for 15 seconds, then repeat 3 times at 15-second intervals, stirring each time. Beat until light and foamy.

SPICED VINEGAR

Makes 1 litre/1¾ pt

To be used for all vinegar pickles.

1 litre/1¾ pt brown malt vinegar
2 teaspoons ground mace
2 teaspoons ground cinnamon
2 teaspoons ground ginger
10 cloves
1 tablespoon allspice berries
1 tablespoon black peppercorns

1. Place all the ingredients in a large bowl and bring to boiling point in the microwave oven, 6 minutes.
2. Pour into heated bottles, cover each with a piece of plastic film and set aside for at least 1 week.

To use Strain and use according to the recipe.

VINEGAR PICKLES

Makes 3 large jars or 6 jam jars

Green beans, beetroot, cabbage, cauliflower, cucumber, onions and tomatoes are all suitable for pickling. Beetroot should be precooked by microwave and will not require salting.

1½ kg/2¾ lb prepared vegetables, cut into small pieces
300 g/10 oz salt
500 ml/1 pt Spiced Vinegar (above)

1. Spread out the vegetables on a plastic tray, cover with a thick layer of salt and leave for 2 days.
2. Rinse vegetables thoroughly in cold water. Drain well.
3. Three-quarters fill clean jars with the vegetables and top up with spiced vinegar to within 2½ cm/1 inch of the top.
4. Cover each jar loosely with plastic film and put in the microwave oven for 1 minute, or until the film bubbles up.

To serve Store for 3 months in a larder before using, then serve with bread and cheese, or meat or poultry.

TOMATO PICKLE

Makes 6 450-g/1-lb jam jars

Use ripe, firm, undamaged tomatoes for pickling.

1¾ kg/4 lb ripe tomatoes
50 g/2 oz salt
500 ml/1 pt Spiced Vinegar (see above)
450 g/1 lb soft dark brown sugar

1. Slice the tomatoes thickly, spread them on a tray and cover with a thick layer of salt. Leave for 24 hours.
2. Rinse tomato slices in cold water and drain thoroughly.
3. Pour spiced vinegar into a large bowl. Stir in the sugar and

leave for 1 hour, or until the sugar has dissolved.
4. Bring vinegar mixture to the boil in the microwave oven, 6 to 8 minutes, stirring occasionally. Continue boiling 2 minutes, or until the thermometer registers 108°C/218°F.
5. Add the tomato slices and bring back to the boil (about 2 minutes), then cook a further minute.
6. Pack tomatoes and vinegar into hot jars to within 2½ cm/1 inch of the top. Cover each jar with a piece of plastic film and return to microwave oven to continue cooking for ½ minute, or until the plastic bubbles up.

To serve Leave until cold, then store in a cool, dark place for 2 months before using.

BANANA AND DATE CHUTNEY

Makes 6 450-g/1-lb jam jars

Like pickles, chutneys do not need to be frozen, since the vinegar acts as a preservative.

2 dessert apples, peeled, cored and chopped
200 g/8 oz onions, finely chopped
500 ml/1 pt malt vinegar
4 tablespoons brown sugar
3 bananas, peeled and mashed
450 g/1 lb dates (stoned weight), finely chopped
1 small garlic clove, crushed
2 teaspoons salt
2 teaspoons ground ginger
1 teaspoon mustard powder
½ teaspoon cayenne pepper

1. Mix the apples, onions and vinegar in a large bowl. Cover and cook 5 minutes, stirring occasionally.

2. Add the remaining ingredients. Cook 8 minutes, or until thick, stirring occasionally.

3. Pot in hot jars, leaving 2½ cm/1 inch headspace.

4. Cover the top of each jar with a piece of plastic film.

5. Replace jars in the microwave oven and cook for ½ to 1 minute until the film bubbles up.

To serve without freezing
Leave in a larder for at least 3 weeks for the flavour to develop.

To freeze Leave until cold. Freeze in the jars.

To serve from the freezer
To thaw by microwave, switch on for 1 minute for 1 jar.

BASIC FORCEMEAT STUFFING
Serves 4

Stuffing should be slightly sticky but firm enough to shape. Make up a large quantity when you have stale bread to use up and freeze in convenient portions.

100 g/4 oz stale white breadcrumbs
50 g/2 oz shredded suet
2 tablespoons finely chopped parsley
½ teaspoon dried mixed herbs
Salt, pepper
4 tablespoons milk
½-1 egg, lightly beaten

1. Mix the breadcrumbs, suet, parsley and mixed herbs together and season with salt and pepper.

2. Add the milk and enough of

the egg to bind the mixture. Adjust the seasoning.

To use without freezing
Use as required.

To freeze Pack into a freezer bag. Seal.

To use from the freezer
Remove stuffing from the bag and put it in a dish. To thaw by microwave, switch on for ½ minute, leave to rest for ½ minute, then cook for another ½ minute. Use as required.

CHESTNUT STUFFING
Enough to stuff a 2¾ kg/6 lb or half a 7¼ kg/14 lb oven-ready turkey

A rich stuffing for turkey or veal. For a large bird, stuff one end with Chestnut stuffing and the other with Forcemeat or sausage meat stuffing.

450 g/1 lb chestnuts
Salt
250 ml/½ pt chicken stock
25 g/1 oz butter
½ teaspoon yeast extract
2 teaspoons chopped parsley
Pinch of nutmeg
¼ teaspoon sugar
Pepper

1. Slit the chestnuts with a sharp knife.

2. Put them in a large bowl with a pinch of salt and 125 ml/¼ pt water. Cover and cook 5 minutes, stirring occasionally.

3. Drain the chestnuts and wrap them in a hot towel. Peel and skin as quickly as possible.

4. Put the chestnuts back in the bowl. Add the stock and cook 10 minutes.

5. Drain chestnuts, reserving the stock.

6. Press the chestnuts through a sieve.

7. Mix in the butter and all the other ingredients, adding salt and pepper to taste, and moisten with enough reserved stock to bind.

To serve without freezing
Stuff the poultry or meat just before roasting.

To freeze Cool. Pack into a freezer bag. Seal.

To use from the freezer
Transfer stuffing to a dish. To thaw by microwave, cover and switch on for 2 minutes. Leave to rest for 5 minutes, then use as required.

BROWN RICE AND APPLE STUFFING
Serves 4–6

Suitable for rich poultry or meat, such as duck, goose or pork. Frozen cooked rice and apples may be used. Combine 150 g/6 oz thawed rice and 350 g/12 oz stewed frozen apple slices, and cook as instructed in Steps 3 and 4.

50 g/2 oz brown long-grain rice
¼ teaspoon salt
375 g/14 oz cooking apples
1 tablespoon sugar
25 g/1 oz butter
Grated nutmeg
1 egg, beaten

1. Put the rice in a large casserole. Add 250 ml/½ pt boiling water and the salt. Cover and cook 5 minutes. Leave to rest for 5 minutes, then drain.

2. Peel, core and quarter the

apples and cut into thin slices.

3. Put the apple slices in a loaf-shaped dish. Sprinkle with the sugar, cover and cook 4 minutes.

4. Mash the apples and add the butter and a pinch of nutmeg.

5. Combine apple purée with the rice and the beaten egg. Cook 4 minutes, giving the dish a ¼ turn every minute.

To serve without freezing
Serve hot separately, or leave to cool before stuffing the bird.

To freeze Cool. Turn out on to a sheet of freezer film and overwrap with freezer foil. Seal.

To serve from the freezer
Remove wrappings and place block in a dish. To thaw by microwave, cover and switch on for 5 minutes. Leave to rest for 5 minutes, then continue cooking for 5 more minutes, or until thoroughly reheated, giving the dish a ¼ turn every minute.

DUMPLINGS
Makes 16

Dumplings may be served with stews, goulash or clear soups. Incorporate your favourite herbs into the dough. Dumplings are cooked when a sharp knife inserted in the middle comes out clean.

200 g/8 oz plain flour
2 teaspoons baking powder
1 teaspoon salt
75 g/3 oz shredded suet

1. Sift the flour, baking powder and salt together.

2. Stir in the suet and add

enough water to form a soft dough.

3. Using floured hands, shape the dough into dumplings.

To serve without freezing
Drop a few dumplings at a time into boiling soup or stew and cook for 5 minutes in the microwave oven.

To freeze Uncooked dumplings should be frozen as soon as they are made. Open-freeze, then pack into a freezer bag. Seal.

To serve from the freezer
Remove dumplings from bag and put a few at a time on a dish in the microwave oven. Partially thaw by microwave. Switch on for 15 seconds, rest for 2 minutes, then repeat twice. Leave to stand at room temperature until completely thawed. Bring the stew or soup to the boil in the microwave oven. Drop in the dumplings and switch on for 5 minutes. Cover and leave to rest for 5 minutes.

14 Sweet Sauces, Jams and Sweetmeats

Sweet Sauces, Jams and Sweetmeats

SWEET SAUCES

A variety of sweet sauces thickened with starch or egg yolks can be prepared by microwave. Custard sauces can be served with desserts instead of cream or ice cream. A jam sauce will add sweetness and moisture to more substantial puddings.

A simple jam sauce can be made by stirring a little cornflour blended with cold water into the jam, bringing it to the boil and straining it. Use 15 g/½ oz cornflour and 7 tablespoons water to 225 g/8 oz jam. Arrowroot, which is the most refined of the starches, can be substituted for cornflour in similar quantities and produces a much clearer sauce. Arrowroot is also suitable for glazing fruit tarts.

Cornflour custard sauces are easy to make in the microwave (see page 154). Sauces thickened with cornflour freeze well. However, since jam sauces are so quick and simple to make, there is no point in preparing them for the freezer.

Custard sauces based on egg yolks are cooked in a water bath to slow the speed of cooking and ensure an even set. They should be frozen uncooked, then thawed at room temperature and cooked by microwave (see page 154).

JAMS

Whether a jam is cooked conventionally or in the microwave oven, success will depend on the proportion of sugar to fruit, the ripeness of the fruit (it should, if anything, be slightly under-ripe and not mushy), and the amount of pectin and acid it contains.

A jam's setting potential depends largely on the natural pectin content of the fruit. Pectin is a cellulose substance which is extracted from fruit by slow cooking before sugar is added. Acid also helps to draw out the pectin. In microwave jam-making, always leave the fruit to rest after initial softening (before adding sugar) to assist this process. Fruits high in natural pectin and acid are apples, plums, blackcurrants, redcurrants and gooseberries. Those low in pectin include strawberries, blackberries, cherries, pears and peaches. When making jam with fruit which is low in natural pectin, add bottled pectin, commercially prepared from sour apples.

Test for pectin after the fruit has softened. Pour 3 teaspoons methylated spirit on to a teaspoon of the fruit juice. If the juice turns into a firm clot, the pectin is good and sugar should now be added. If it is poor, add commercial pectin and bring to boiling point again before adding the sugar: 450 g/1 lb fruit rich in pectin will need 450 g/1 lb sugar, 450 g/1 lb fruit poor in pectin will take 325 g/¾ lb sugar. The fruit should boil until it reaches a temperature of 110°C/220°F. If you do not have a

GOOSEBERRY CONSERVE

Makes 4 450-g/1-lb jars

Only the microwave oven can produce this conserve, retaining the gooseberries whole. Fresh gooseberries should be topped and tailed and cooked for 3 minutes only at Step 1.

900 g/2 lb frozen gooseberries
1 kg/2½ lb sugar

1. Put the gooseberries into a large glass bowl. Cook 2 minutes. Stir. Cook for a further 6 minutes, or until the fruit begins to soften, stirring occasionally.
2. Pierce some of the fruit with the point of a sharp knife so that the juice will come out more readily.
3. Add 12 tablespoons boiling water, stir in the sugar and leave at room temperature until it has dissolved. The process can be hastened by frequent stirring and occasional warming for 1 or 2 minutes in the microwave oven.
4. Cover bowl with greaseproof paper to prevent spattering and cook, stirring every 5 minutes, until the conserve reaches setting point. It will take 20 to 25 minutes before boiling point is reached and about another 20 minutes to reach setting point. Test with a cooking thermometer, which should register 105°C/220°F, or dip a wooden spoon into the conserve and allow the syrup to drip off. The jam is ready when a single drop hangs from the side of the spoon.
5. Leave the conserve until just warm, then stir and spoon into sterilised heated jam jars, filling them to within 2½ cm/1 inch of the rim.

6. Cover each jar loosely with a piece of plastic film reaching 5 cm/2 inches down the sides.

7. Place the jars one at a time in the microwave oven and cook 1 minute until the jam boils and the plastic film bubbles up.

8. Remove from the microwave oven, using oven gloves, and leave until cold.

To use Store in the refrigerator or a cool larder.

STRAWBERRY JAM

Makes 5 450-g/1-lb jars

1 kg/2¼ lb frozen strawberries
1¼ kg/2¾ lb sugar
3 tablespoons lemon juice
1 teaspoon margarine
125 ml/¼ pt liquid commercial pectin (Certo)

1. Stir the fruit, sugar and lemon juice together in a large heatproof glass bowl, and leave in a warm place for about 2 hours until the sugar has dissolved, stirring occasionally.

2. Add the margarine to the fruit. Cook 6 to 8 minutes until the mixture comes to a full rolling boil. Continue cooking 5 minutes, stirring occasionally.

3. Stir in the pectin.

4. Leave to cool for ½ hour, stir, then pot in sterilised jars, leaving 2½ cm/1 inch headspace.

5. Cover each pot loosely with plastic film. Return to the microwave oven and cook one at a time for approximately 1 minute until the plastic film bubbles up.

6. Remove from oven with oven gloves and leave until cold.

To freeze Jam may be stored in the freezer, or in a cool, dark larder.

thermometer, use the flake test. Dip a wooden spoon into the jam, then twist the handle until a single drop of liquid hangs from the lip of the spoon. If this cannot be done, cook the jam for a little while longer.

Jam should be stirred during cooking to equalise the temperature. Use a large bowl when making jam in the microwave oven to avoid the risk of spillage, and a wooden spoon. The spoon may be left in the bowl for short periods while the jam is cooking, but remember that the handle will become hot.

Marmalade made from citrus fruits is less successful when cooked by microwave. The peel can be softened by soaking it overnight, but most of the pectin lies in the pith and the pips, and these require long cooking at simmering point to form a satisfactory gel. Only microwave ovens with low settings can achieve this.

Jam should be potted in hot, sterilised jars. To sterilise jars, wash them thoroughly and rinse but do not dry. Put the jars in the microwave oven and switch on for 1 to 2 minutes, until the water has evaporated. Remove the jars using oven gloves and set them on a dry heatproof surface. Instructions for sealing jam pots by microwave are given in the recipes. However, only full pots can be sealed in this way as the plastic film must actually touch the surface of the jam. With a pot which is half-full, the build-up of hot air inside the jar would cause the plastic film to burst.

There is no reason to freeze jam, except that no special jampot covers will be needed. Jam will also thicken during storage in the freezer. Lemon curd will keep much longer in the freezer than in a refrigerator, 3 months as opposed to a recommended maximum of 3 weeks.

SWEETMEATS

Sweetmeats and candies prepared by microwave are less likely to burn than sugar syrups boiled conventionally. They will burn only if overcooked and this is indicated by an overall darkening of the mixture.

Timing is critical and frequent tests must be made. *Do not forget to remove the thermometer before the bowl is put back in the oven* if one is being used to test the mixture. Sugar should always be dissolved completely before fast boiling is allowed to take place.

Sweetmeats are not usually frozen but storage time will be greatly increased by so doing. Admittedly, dishes such as this with a high sugar content will not freeze completely but if they are stored in the freezer, deterioration will not take place.

Microwave makes it possible and easy to produce *marrons glacés*, praline and crystallised fruits.

Sweet Sauces, Jams and Sweetmeats

PLUM OR GREENGAGE JAM
Makes 3 450-g/1-lb jars

When making this jam by microwave, remove the stones from the fruit after cooking.

900 g/2 lb ripe plums
900 g/2 lb sugar

1. Put the plums in a large heatproof glass bowl with 8 tablespoons water. Cover with greaseproof paper and cook 15 minutes, stirring occasionally.
2. Add the sugar and leave for about ½ hour until dissolved, stirring occasionally.
3. Cook, stirring from time to time, until the mixture begins to boil (about 20 minutes). Continue boiling and stirring occasionally until setting point is reached (about another 20 minutes), when a globule of jam should hang from the side of a wooden spoon without dropping off.
4. Cool jam and remove as many stones as possible.
5. Pot the jam when cool, filling each heated jar to within 2½ cm/1 inch of the rim.
6. Cover the jars loosely with plastic film and place each jar individually in the microwave oven until the jam boils and the plastic film bubbles up.
7. Remove the jars from the oven with oven gloves and leave until cold.

To use Store in the refrigerator or a cool larder.

BLACKCURRANT JAM
Makes 3 450-g/1-lb jars

Blackcurrants are rich in pectin, which is usually extracted by slow cooking in water. In microwave cookery, however, the water is omitted and instead a rest period is recommended after the fruit has softened. Add 3 tablespoons water when using fresh blackcurrants and cook 5 minutes at Step 1.

450 g/1 lb frozen blackcurrants
450 g/1 lb sugar
2 tablespoons lemon juice

1. Put the blackcurrants in a large, ovenproof glass bowl and cook 7 minutes, stirring once halfway through cooking. Leave to rest for 10 minutes.
2. Stir in the sugar and lemon juice, cover the bowl loosely with greaseproof paper and cook 5 minutes.
3. Stir. Cook 10 minutes longer and test for setting (page 150). Leave until just warm.
4. Stir. Fill jam jars to within 2½ cm/1 inch of the rim. Cover each jar loosely with a piece of plastic film reaching 5 cm/2 inches down the sides.
5. Place each jar in the microwave oven and cook 1 minute, or until the jam boils.
6. Remove the jar carefully, using oven gloves, and leave until cold.

To serve Store in the refrigerator or a larder.

LEMON CURD
Makes 1½ 450-g/1-lb jars

Lemon curd will keep for 3 weeks in the refrigerator and 3 months in the freezer. The rind is included in this preserve, but if preferred, the syrup may be mixed with the egg yolks before straining.

200 g/8 oz granulated sugar
Juice and grated rind of 3 lemons
100 g/4 oz unsalted butter
4 egg yolks, beaten

1. Stir the sugar, lemon rind and juice together in a large heatproof bowl. Cook until melted, 2 minutes.
2. Add the butter and cook 2 minutes. Stir.
3. Leave to cool for 2 minutes, then strain in the beaten egg yolks. Mix well. Cook 3 to 4 minutes, until the mixture is boiling rapidly.
4. Remove from the oven and beat thoroughly.
5. Fill a hot jar with curd, leaving 2½ cm/1 inch headspace. Cover loosely with a piece of plastic film.
6. Place in the microwave oven and reheat ½ minute until the film bubbles up. Remove from the oven with oven gloves and leave until cold. The remaining curd may be refrigerated for immediate use.

To freeze Overwrap the top of the jar with freezer foil.

To serve from the freezer Remove the foil outer wrapping but leave the plastic film intact on the jar. To thaw by microwave, switch on for ½ minute, then allow to thaw completely at room temperature.

BUTTER ICING

Enough for 1 layer of icing for a
15-cm/6-inch cake

Use as a filling for sandwich
cakes or as a coating, spreading
evenly with a warmed palette
knife. Butter icing may also be
piped decoratively through a
forcing bag fitted with a star
nozzle.

50 g/2 oz butter
75–100 g/3–4 oz icing sugar,
**   sifted**
Flavouring and colouring:
   Lemon – add 2 teaspoons
   grated lemon rind and 2
   teaspoons lemon juice
   Chocolate – add 1 tablespoon
   powdered drinking chocolate
   and ½ teaspoon vanilla essence
   Coffee – slowly add 1 teaspoon
   instant coffee powder
   dissolved in 2 teaspoons water

1.   Put the butter in a large
bowl and soften in the
microwave oven for 15 seconds
only. Beat thoroughly until soft
and creamy.
2.   Gradually beat in the icing
sugar and continue to beat until
the mixture is white and fluffy.
3.   Beat in flavouring and
colouring.

To serve without freezing
Use as required.

To freeze   Turn into a freezer
container. Seal.

To serve from the freezer
Transfer block to a bowl. To
thaw by microwave, switch on
for 15 seconds, then stir. Repeat
as necessary, but do not
overheat, or icing will become
oily.

FUDGE ICING

There are two types of fudge
icing. The easy-to-prepare,
uncooked kind freezes well, but
its more sophisticated cooked
cousin should be used as soon as
it has cooled.

Uncooked Fudge Icing

2 tablespoons milk
50 g/2 oz unsalted butter
Flavouring (few drops of
**   vanilla, almond or rum**
**   essence, or 1 tablespoon**
**   cocoa)**
175 g/7 oz icing sugar, sifted
Colouring

1.   Put the milk, butter and
flavouring in a bowl, and cook to
melt butter, 1½ minutes.
2.   Stir in the icing sugar and
beat until smooth.
3.   Add colouring.

To serve without freezing
Use immediately or cover with a
damp disc of greaseproof paper,
wet side down, and store in the
refrigerator until required.

To freeze   Pour into a freezer
bag. Seal.

To serve from the freezer
Turn out block of icing into a
bowl. To thaw by microwave,
switch on for 1 minute, beat
thoroughly, then continue
cooking until the icing is soft.

Cooked Fudge Icing

200 g/8 oz granulated sugar
25 g/1 oz butter
175 ml/7½ fl oz full-cream
**   evaporated milk**
Flavouring (½ teaspoon vanilla,
**   almond or rum essence or**
**   15 g/½ oz cocoa or instant**
**   coffee)**

1.   Put the sugar and butter in a
large glass bowl. Add 3
tablespoons boiling water and
mix well.
2.   Mix in the evaporated milk
and flavourings. Cook, stirring
occasionally, for about 10
minutes or until a teaspoonful
dropped into a glass of cold
water forms a soft ball.
3.   Remove from the oven and
beat mixture until it cools and
thickens.

To serve   This quantity is
enough either to pour over the
top and sides of a 15-cm/6-inch
cake, or to use as a filling and
top covering only.

APRICOT GLAZE

Apricot glaze is frequently
required in cake-making. It will
keep for several weeks if it is
brought to a full boil before
storing.

8 tablespoons apricot jam
8 tablespoons water

1.   Stir the jam and water
together in an ovenproof glass
bowl. Cover and cook 4
minutes.
2.   Rub through a sieve, then
replace in the microwave oven
and bring to the boil, 2 to 3
minutes.
3.   Leave to cool. Store in a
covered jar in the refrigerator.

To serve   Reheat the quantity
required in a jug in the
microwave oven.

CORNFLOUR CUSTARD
Makes 500 ml/1 pt

The proportions given are for a thick pouring custard. Add more milk for a thinner sauce or cut down the liquid if using the custard in trifle.

2 tablespoons custard powder or
   2 tablespoons cornflour and 1
   teaspoon vanilla essence
1–2 tablespoons sugar (to taste)
500 ml/1 pt milk
1 teaspoon butter

1. Put the custard powder or cornflour in a large bowl with the sugar.
2. Gradually stir in the milk and the vanilla essence if used, blending thoroughly.
3. Cook in the microwave oven 5½ minutes, beating occasionally.
4. Add the butter.

To serve without freezing
Pour into a heated sauceboat and serve at once, or cover with a disc of damp greaseproof paper, wet side down, leave to cool and use as required.

To freeze Turn into a freezer bag or bags in the quantities required. Seal. Leave to cool before freezing.

To serve from the freezer
Turn the block of custard into a bowl. To thaw by microwave, switch on for 5 minutes, breaking up the lumps with a fork as soon as defrosting begins. Continue cooking until the custard is thawed or reheated. Beat thoroughly before serving.

EGG CUSTARD SAUCE
Makes 500 ml/1 pt

Stir the custard frequently during cooking and do not overcook it or it will curdle. However, curdling is less likely to occur when the custard is cooked by microwave.

4 egg yolks
50 g/2 oz sugar
Pinch of salt
375 ml/¾ pt milk
125 ml/¼ pt single cream
Few drops of vanilla essence

1. Beat the egg yolks, sugar and salt together in a large bowl.
2. Stir in the milk, cream and vanilla essence.

To serve without freezing
Cook in the microwave oven 2½ minutes, stirring every ½ minute. Serve warm or chilled.

To freeze Pour into a freezer container. Seal.

To serve from the freezer
Leave to thaw at room temperature. Pour into a large bowl and cook in the microwave oven for 2½ to 3 minutes, stirring every ½ minute. Serve warm or cold.

HOT CHOCOLATE SAUCE
Makes 200 ml/8 fl oz

The perfect sauce to serve with profiteroles, which cannot be cooked in a microwave oven but can be thawed by microwave. Hot chocolate sauce is also suitable for puddings and is particularly good served with microwave bananas.

50 g/2 oz castor sugar
50 g/2 oz cooking chocolate,
   broken into pieces
½ teaspoon instant coffee
1 teaspoon cornflour
2 tablespoons milk
½ teaspoon vanilla essence

1. Stir the sugar into 125 ml/¼ pt water. Cook 1½ minutes until boiling point is reached.
2. Stir, bring to boiling point again and cook 2 minutes.
3. Mix in the chocolate and the coffee. Stir until smooth.
4. Blend the cornflour smoothly with the milk and add the vanilla essence. Mix into the sauce. Cook 1 minute or until the sauce boils.
5. Beat thoroughly.

To serve without freezing
Pour into a heated jug and cover with plastic film until ready to serve.

To freeze Leave to cool. Pour the sauce into a freezer bag resting in a bowl. Remove the bag from the bowl when sauce is frozen and seal.

To serve from the freezer
Remove block of sauce from the bag and put in a bowl. To thaw by microwave, switch on for 1 minute. Stir. Leave to rest for 2 minutes, then continue cooking for 1 or 2 minutes until warm.

LEMON SAUCE
Makes 250 ml/½ pt

Lemon sauce will enhance the flavour of most hot puddings. If preferred, you can substitute the syrup from canned pineapple, pears, peaches or apricots for the diluted fruit juice. Adjust the quantity of sugar to taste.

50 g/2 oz sugar
1 tablespoon cornflour
250 ml/½ pt equal quantities of
    fruit juice and water, mixed
25 g/1 oz butter
Grated rind and juice of ½ lemon

1. In a large jug, blend the
sugar, cornflour, juice and water
to a smooth paste. Cook 2
minutes, stirring occasionally.
2. Blend in the butter, lemon
rind and juice. Cook ½ minute.

To serve without freezing
Pour into a heated jug.

To freeze Pour the sauce into a
clean jam jar, leaving at least
2½ cm/1 inch headspace. Cover
with freezer film and leave until
cold before putting jar in the
freezer.

To serve from freezer
Place jar in the oven. To thaw by
microwave, switch on for 2
minutes. Stir, then reheat for a
further 1 or 2 minutes. Add a
little water if necessary to thin
the sauce down.

ORANGE VELVET SAUCE
Makes 250 ml/½ pt

A thin sauce to pour over
puddings, pancakes or waffles.
Frozen concentrated orange
juice is excellent, provided it is
reconstituted according to the
instructions on the carton.

125 g/4 oz demerara sugar
125 ml/¼ pt fresh orange juice
25 g/1 oz unsalted butter
1 tablespoon Grand Marnier

1. Stir the sugar into the
orange juice in a large bowl and
leave for 10 minutes.
2. Cook until syrup reaches
105°C/215°F, 2 minutes. Stir.

3. Stir in the butter until
melted. Cook 3 minutes.
4. Add the Grand Marnier.

To serve without freezing
Pour into a heated jug.

To freeze Cover the sauce with
plastic film and leave to cool.
Pour into a glass jar, leaving
2½ cm/1 inch headspace, and
cover the top with freezer foil.

To serve from the freezer
Remove the foil and place jar in
the oven. To thaw by
microwave, switch on for 1
minute. Stir. Continue cooking
until the sauce is warm and the
butter has melted, about 3½
minutes. Stir.

RUM SYRUP
Makes 250 ml/½ pt

Use with thawed fruit or to
impregnate savarins and
sponge-type cakes.

200 g/8 oz granulated sugar
Juice of ½ lemon
1 tablespoon rum

1. Stir the sugar into
125 ml/¼ pt water in a large jar.
Cook 2½ minutes.
2. Stir and cook ½ to 1 minute
longer until the syrup boils.
Continue cooking 2 minutes.
3. Leave to cool for a few
minutes, then add the lemon
juice and rum.

To serve Store in a screwtop
jar in the refrigerator and use as
required.

SABAYON SAUCE
Makes 750 ml/1½ pt

Sabayon sauce may be served
warm or cold. It is normal for it
to separate before freezing. The
mixture does not freeze solid.

3 large egg yolks, threads
    removed
50 g/2 oz castor sugar
125 ml/¼ pt Marsala

+ + +

1 tablespoon single cream

1. Blend the egg yolks with the
sugar. Whisk for 2 minutes.
2. Pour the Marsala in a bowl
and bring to the boil in the
microwave oven, 2 minutes.
3. Quickly whisk in the egg
yolks and continue beating until
the sauce thickens.

To serve without freezing
Beat in the cream and serve
immediately with sponge finger
biscuits.

To freeze Pour immediately
into a freezer container. Seal.

To serve from the freezer
Scrape the sauce into a bowl.
Heat in the microwave oven for
10 seconds. Beat thoroughly.
Switch the oven on for 10
seconds and beat again. Cook
for a further 10 seconds, then
whisk until the mixture is pale
and forms a trail on the surface
when the beaters are lifted. Stir
in the cream.

Sweet Sauces, Jams and Sweetmeats

STOCK SYRUP
Makes 250 ml/½ pt

Used to sweeten frozen or freshly cooked fruits, stock syrup will keep for several weeks in a screwtop jar in the refrigerator.

200 g/8 oz granulated sugar
125 ml/¼ pt water

1. Stir the sugar into the water in a large jar. Cook 2½ minutes.
2. Stir. Cook ½ to 1 minute until the syrup boils, then continue cooking for 2 minutes.

To serve Store in a screwtop jar in the refrigerator and use as required.

VANILLA FUDGE
Makes 36 pieces

Glucose is obtainable from chemists and is often used in sweet-making, because it prevents crystallisation.

200 g/8 oz granulated sugar
100 g/4 oz powdered glucose
150 ml/6 fl oz condensed full-cream milk
50 g/2 oz butter
½ teaspoon vanilla essence
2 teaspoons sifted icing sugar

1. In a large bowl, mix the sugar, glucose and condensed milk with 1 tablespoon water. Stir thoroughly.
2. Add the butter and vanilla essence, and mix well. Cook 8 to 10 minutes to soft ball stage (see Orange Candy), stirring twice during cooking.
3. As soon as the mixture stops bubbling, stir in the icing sugar.

4. Pour into a 15-cm/6-inch square tin lined with non-stick paper.
5. Leave to cool, then mark into squares with a greased knife.

To serve without freezing
Break into squares and store in an airtight tin.

To freeze Leave the block of fudge on the non-stick paper. When cold, wrap in plastic film and overwrap with foil.

To serve from the freezer
Remove the wrappings. Put the fudge on the non-stick paper in the microwave oven. Switch on for ½ minute, then leave to thaw at room temperature, cutting the fudge into squares as it softens.

ORANGE CANDY
Makes 50–60 pieces

Soft ball stage is registered at 120°C/235°F on a cooking thermometer. It can be tested by dropping a little mixture into a glass of cold water, when it should form a soft ball. If the mixture is stirred with a wooden spoon, this may be left in the bowl during cooking.

450 g/1 lb castor sugar
125 ml/¼ pt evaporated milk
50 g/2 oz butter
2 tablespoons orange juice
1 tablespoon grated orange rind
2 teaspoons icing sugar, sifted

1. Mix the castor sugar and milk together in a large bowl. Leave for 30 minutes until the sugar has dissolved, stirring occasionally. Cook 2 minutes.
2. Stir in the butter, orange juice and grated orange rind.

Cook 8 minutes to soft ball stage (see above), stirring occasionally. The boiling candy should just be starting to darken.
3. Stir in the icing sugar and pour into a 20-cm/8-inch square tin lined with non-stick paper.
4. Cool candy slightly before marking into squares with a knife.

To serve without freezing
Break into squares and store in an airtight tin.

To freeze Leave until cold. Separate the squares. Open-freeze, then turn into a freezer bag. Seal.

To serve from the freezer
Spread out candies on a piece of non-stick paper in the microwave oven. Switch on for ½ minute, then leave to thaw at room temperature.

Index

Index